The Art of Leadership

Unless otherwise stated, Scripture quotations are taken from the King James Version of the Bible.

Scripture quotations marked (NLT) are taken from the Holy Bible, New Living Translation, copyright © 1996. Used by permission of Tyndale House Publishers, Inc., Wheaton, Illinois 60189. All rights reserved.

Scripture quotations marked (NASB) are taken from the New American Standard Bible ®, Copyright © 1960, 1962, 1963, 1968, 1971, 1973, 1975, 1977, 1995 by The Lockman Foundation. Used by permission.

Excerpts in Chapter 10 from John Foxe (1516-1587), Foxe's Book of Martyrs, Public Domain.

Book design and production for the publisher by BCS, P.O. Box 827, BN21 3YJ, England.

First published by Parchment House 2003

2nd Printing 2006

ISBN: 9988-596-40-5

Copyright © Parchment House 2003

Second Edition 2006

All rights reserved under international copyright law. Written permission must be secured from the publisher to use or reproduce any part of this book, except for brief quotations in critical reviews or articles.

The
Art of Leadership

Dag Heward-Mills

PARCHMENT HOUSE

Dedication

I dedicate this book to the memory of my father,
Nathaniel Nii Lanquaye Heward-Mills
Thank you for making things possible for us.
I am grateful to have had
a father like you.

Contents

Foreword 13

1. Decide to Become One of the Few Good Leaders in This World 15

2. Interact with the Great and Small 21

3. Maintain Personal Integrity 26

4. Give People Hope 27

5. Never Use Power without Wisdom or Wisdom without Power! 30

6. Do Not Be a Lifeless Leader. Have a Conviction! 32

7. Wait for Your Season 34

8. Use the Secret of Concentration 36

9. Help the People around You to Accomplish Great Things with Their Lives .39

10. Make People Obey You Gladly 43

11. Contemplate, Reflect, Be Thoughtful and Consider the Things You See around You 53

12. Strive for Excellence 57

13. Everything Depends on the Leadership 59

14. Rally People around You .64

15. Choose Hard and Difficult Things Instead of Nice and Easy Things 70

16. Readily Embrace New Ideas 73

17. Value People 76

18. Spend Any Amount of Money and Time to Get a Book 79

19. See Ahead! Prepare for the Future! 83

20. Always Learn New Things 86

21. Know Your Strengths and Flow in Them! 88

22. Be Ready for a Long Fight! 90

23. Count Your Pennies! 92

24. Tell the Truth 94

25. Don't Lose Your Focus 96

26. Recognize the Small Beginnings of a Great Career 99

27. Treat People as Equals but Make the Differences Clear 102

28. Predict the Future in a General Way 107

29. Do Not Allow Yourself to Be Poisoned by Bitterness 109

30. Change People's Minds 112
31. Know a Little about Everything That Goes on ..117
32. Be a Leader with Emotion 119
33. Take Your Privileges at the Right Time and for the Right Reason 123
34. Relate with Individuals and Relate with the Crowd 128
35. Overcome the Disadvantages of Youthfulness and Inexperience by Studying History 131
36. Take Responsibility and Give Account 135
37. Don't Give up Your Source of Power! 137
38. Be Decisive! It Is the Greatest Attribute of a Leader 140
39. Know about the Power of Habits and Develop Good Habits 151
40. Know Where You Are! Know Where You Are Not! And You Will Know Where to Go! 158
41. Become Self-Motivated. Do Not Expect Direction or Encouragement from Outside 160
42. Be Flexible, Rigidity Is Costly! 164
43. Command Your Troops! 166
44. Balance Your Priorities 168
45. Live by the Logical Laws of Teamwork 170
46. Get Angry Sometimes 173
47. Control the People You Lead by the Power of Teaching 175

48. Be a Great leader, Go the Extra Mile 177
49. What Have You Survived? 179
50. Acknowledge the Gifts of Others 189
51. Be a Creative Leader 191
52. Respect Principles and You Will Build a Great Organization 194
53. Don't Think of How Much Money You Can Get from the People You Lead. Think of How Much You Can Help Them. 199
54. Grow in Your Influence 201
55. Develop Personal Proverbs and Dark Sayings ..206
56. Negotiate with Authorities on Behalf of Your Followers 208
57. Convince People to Make Great Sacrifices 211
58. Take Everyone to the Top with You 214
59. Build Something if You Are a Leader! 218
60. Be Constantly Aware of Your Life's Vision 220
61. Always Stay One Step Ahead 222
62. Avoid Distraction 224
63. Make People Obey You When You Are Not Present 228
64. Hide and Flourish Like a Snake 231
65. Overcome the Effect of Rumours, Questions and Controversies about Your Person 235

66. Take That Decision! Most Decisions Will Involve Choosing between Two Bad Options Anyway! . . .239

67. Don't Destroy Your Ministry by Saying the Wrong Things in Public 244

68. Avoid Becoming an Artificial Leader. Develop Natural Leadership Skills 247

69. Do Not Allow Tiredness to Be an Excuse 250

70. Gain Control over Your Domestic Life 252

71. Be Sincere, Not a Hypocrite 254

72. Know Your Limitations .256

73. Be Courageous 258

74. Get People to Follow You Somewhere 260

75. Mix Truth with Grace to Gain More Followers 262

76. The Eight Greatest Decisions of a Leader 268

77. Carefully Choose Your Mentors 271

78. Inspire People 275

79. Find Solutions and Solve Problems 277

80. Be a Thinker 281

81. Reproduce Yourself in Others 286

82. Be a Can-Do Leader 289

83. Accept the Reality of Loneliness 295

84. Don't Forget Those Who Helped You.. 300

85. Translate Your Vision into Reality 303

86. Go in First and People Will Follow
    You Anywhere 304

87. Make Your Followers Love You. Make Sure They
    Don't Resent You 306

88. Watch out for Discontentment and Deal With it
    Decisively 309

89. Waste No Time on Critical People 315

90. Familiarity Is a Leadership Emergency.
    Deal with it Urgently 320

91. Fight Only Battles You Can Win 327

92. Use Symptoms and Signs to Guide You 330

93. Be a Loyal Leader 333

94. Overcome Hatred and Opposition 337

95. Relate with All Kinds of People Including People
    Who Are Not Your "Type" 341

96. Don't Be Surprised by Ingratitude 344

97. Allow People to Know You So They Can
    Trust You and Follow You 346

98. Influence People by Example 348

99. Recognize Your Desire As a Symptom
    of Your Call to Leadership 350

100. Do Not Rush around from One Emergency to
     Another 354

101. Always Remember: "Nobody Wins
     until We All Win!" 359

102. Know the Names of Many People 362

103. Invest in Yourself 364

104. Value Time and Manage Time 367

105. Great Achievements Require Great Discipline ..370

106. Have a Vision 372

107. Value Every Moment in the Presence of a Great Leader 374

108. Take Charge! 377

109. Master the Art of Raising Money 379

110. Be Merciful 382

111. Have Genuine Friends 384

112. Work Harder Than All Those around You 386

113. Start Humble and End Humble 388

114. Convince People to Believe in You 392

115. Say a Lot or Say Nothing, Depending on Who You Are Talking to 396

116. Accept the Principle of Ranking 401

117. Turn the People around You into Better Human Beings 404

118. Move into High Gear by Moving to the Right Geographical Location 407

119. Control Your Carnal Instincts 412

120. Understand the Difference between the Ideal and the Real 414

121. Identify the Different Types of Employees in Your Organization 417

122. Develop the Art of Keeping People Together . . .420
123. Constantly Think about the Day of
     Accountability 425
Notes 427
Bibliography 455

Foreword

I would like to introduce Dr. Dag Heward-Mills' new book entitled, *The Art of Leadership* with tremendous enthusiasm as I highly recommend this book to you.

Dag Heward-Mills is a brilliant man of God, and he is an example of what he is teaching in this great book. He has lived up to its standards, and he can lead countless others to this high road of excellence in leadership. We cannot lead others where we have not gone ourselves, and so this book depicts the path of all great leaders in the history of the Church.

It reveals the prerequisites for leadership, and the goals for every potential leader. This book is biblically-based, and it embraces the challenges found only in the Word of God.

Dr. Heward-Mills has learned so many great truths throughout his many years of service. He has led other leaders, and he has pioneered many Lighthouse Chapels throughout the world. He is a prolific author, and he is a very sought after conference speaker.

He has been a true inspiration to all of us in the Church Growth International ministry, and he is one of our honoured Board Members.

His wisdom, insight and his experience can inspire you, as you follow him as he follows Christ. Dr. Heward-Mills is interested in making disciples of Jesus Christ who will become the future leaders in the church.

The Art of Leadership will show you the way, and it will provide a guide into the secrets of a true leader. It is an art and as such, it must be learned. This book will teach you everything that you need or desire to learn about the important art of leadership in the church today and the church of the new millennium.

November 2, 2001

> Dr. David Yonggi Cho
> Senior Pastor
> Yoido Full Gospel Church
> Seoul, South Korea

Chapter 1

Decide to Become One of the Few Good Leaders in This World

If you believe that you are called to the ministry, then you are called to leadership. That is why this book is very important for your life. So that you will be a good leader for the Lord Jesus Christ. Paul wrote to Timothy and told him to do certain things to make him a good leader. There are good ministers and bad ministers. Decide to be a good minister!

…thou shalt be a good minister of Jesus Christ…

1 Timothy 4:6

If you are going to be effective in the ministry, you must study leadership. Whenever I go into a bookshop, I find myself gravitating towards the leadership section. I have read countless books on leadership. I have studied this all-important subject. I want to be a good leader. Good things do not drop on you like ripe mangoes from a tree. You have to study and discover all that there is to learn.

It is obvious that there are not many good leaders around. If there were, you and I would be able to point them out without much difficulty! I believe that there are many reasons why there are few outstanding leaders, but let us start by looking at why people do not want to be leaders in the first place!

Five Reasons Why People Avoid Leadership Responsibilities

1. Many people do not know that they are leaders.

They do not know because no one has told them so! They don't even know that they have the ability to lead. Some people think that only a few people are born to lead. I do not believe that few people are born to lead. I believe that many people are born with the ability to lead but they are not prepared to pay the price to become leaders.

So the last shall be first, and the first last: for many be called, but few chosen.

Matthew 20:16

For many are called, but few are chosen.

Matthew 22:14

The Bible teaches us that many are called to service. Anyone who yields himself to the ministry of the Lord Jesus Christ becomes an automatic leader. *A minister of the gospel has to demonstrate leadership qualities and abilities all the time.*

If you are called to His service, then you are called to be a leader. You cannot avoid it!

2.   People fear that they will be accused and hated.

Leaders are often accused of being ambitious. They are often accused of having bad motives. I was very surprised when I heard some people accuse me of being in the ministry for money. But God spoke to me and told me that it is inevitable that I should be accused. Every good leader has many enemies. The nature of good leadership is that it charts out a course and maintains the direction. This means that you may cross over and hurt certain people.

And whosoever doth not bear his cross, and come after me, cannot be my disciple.

Luke 14:27

Many years ago, I told a brother that I did not want to be a leader in a certain fellowship. I told him that I was a quiet person and that I enjoyed my privacy. I told him that I did not want to preach or to lead. But God had another plan for me and today I am a leader in God's house. Becoming a leader will cost you your valued life. I have very little private life left. Most people know a lot of things about me. I am discussed in people's homes and cars. Like all leaders, I am praised by some and criticized by others. This is the lot of a leader. This is why some people shun leadership. But Jesus said that you should take up the cross and follow him. Christianity involves sacrifice. It is worth becoming a leader within the church.

3.   People do not want to end up disgraced and hated as many prominent leaders have been.

There are many leaders who have ended up in disgrace after taking up the mantle of leadership. Others have experienced terrible hurts and had bitter experiences. Some have been crucified by the people they led.

I have personally watched how leaders have been rewarded with evil after many years of service. I have seen several (and I mean several) churches throw out their pastor after he has led them for many years. I have seen pastors ridiculed and humiliated by members they have ministered to for years and at great expense. I have watched pastors being rejected over issues like cars and houses. How sad! We all know how Jesus was crucified after three and a half years of ministry. That was his reward for being a shining light to His people.

In my country, I have seen several Heads of State come to unnatural deaths after ruling the nation for some years. We have seen judges being murdered in cold blood after delivering judgments they thought were right. Who then would like to be a leader in such an environment? When you study the fate of the leaders around, it is only natural that people shun leadership and choose a quiet life of peace and anonymity. I can understand why somebody would stay away from the world of lying politicians and corrupt leadership.

In this book, I am urging you to take up the mantle of Christian leadership. I am urging you to take up the call to leadership in the church. It is worth it! The challenges are very similar to secular leadership. The accusations are often the same. But it is worth it!

Secular leaders work for human rewards like money and fame. But these are perishable rewards. When you work for Jesus you receive an everlasting reward.

> **…Now they do it to obtain a corruptible crown; but we an incorruptible.**
>
> **1 Corinthians 9:25**

There are many times that I have experienced the pains of being in leadership. But when I think of the rewards that await those who faithfully do the will of God, I become encouraged. I know that one day I will be glad about everything.

Looking unto Jesus the author and finisher of our faith; who for the joy that was set before him endured the cross, despising the shame, and is set down at the right hand of the throne of God. For consider him that endured such contradiction of sinners against himself, lest ye be wearied and faint in your minds.

Hebrews 12:2,3

4.   People think that they are not good enough to be leaders.

Some people think they are not morally up to the standard of leadership. Others think that they have no leadership qualities. Others feel that they have too many personal problems to become leaders. They cannot imagine being saddled with other people's problems.[1]

I have good news for you today! *God does not work with perfect people. He works with willing people.* He looks at the heart and he understands your human weakness. If Jesus had looked for perfection, I can assure you that none of the disciples would have qualified for leadership positions in the church. Take Peter for example; he betrayed the Lord Jesus three times just a few weeks before he was ordained. He swore and cursed as though he had received no training. Yet, the Lord used him. Take the other disciples, who argued over their positions in Heaven. "Who would be the greatest?" they asked.

And there was also a strife among them, which of them should be accounted the greatest.

Luke 22:24

After arguing over who would be the greatest, they all deserted Christ when he needed them most. Would you trust such people? Would you use such people? Yet the Lord did!

You do not have to be perfect to become a leader. If that were the case, then there would be no leaders in the world or in the church. This does not mean that there are no standards. God expects the highest standards of character and morality. And yet, he works with imperfect people.

God looks at the heart. Make sure that your heart is right and God will be able to use you.

...for the Lord seeth not as man seeth; for man looketh on the outward appearance, but the Lord looketh on the heart.

1 Samuel 16:7

5.   Most people are too selfish to be leaders.

Such people care only about themselves. They are happy to have salvation. They are happy to have the Holy Spirit. They are happy to have prosperity. But they couldn't care less about anybody else. "Once I am okay," they think, "Everything is okay." That is a spirit of selfishness.

A selfish person cannot be bothered to go through any training or sacrifice to become a leader. He will not expend any energy to help another soul. If Christ had decided to stay in the comfort of Heaven, where would you be today? He rose out of the grave and you cannot even get out of bed. I rebuke that spirit of laziness and selfishness! Thank God for missionaries. Thank God for people who traveled away from their homes into foreign cultures just because they wanted to help somebody.

Chapter 2

Interact with the Great and Small

A good leader will interact with two main groups of people: the great (humanly speaking) and the small (humanly speaking). The great people are the nobles, the rich, the influential and powerful people of society. There are not many of such people in the church.

For ye see your calling, brethren, how that not many wise men after the flesh, not many mighty, not many noble, are called:

1 Corinthians 1:26

The "small" speaks of the poor, the down-and-out, and the people of little material substance.[1]

Four Reasons Why it Is Important to Relate with the Great

1. Jesus interacted with great people.

Jesus interacted with Nicodemus privately. Jesus honoured several invitations to dine with influential and powerful people. These interactions were so important that they were recorded in the Bible.

There was a man of the Pharisees, named Nicodemus, a ruler of the Jews: The same came to Jesus by night...

John 3:1,2

When the even was come, there came a rich man of Arimathaea, named Joseph, who also himself was Jesus' disciple:

Matthew 27:57

2. Great people have their role to play in the church.

Some of them will play vital roles for the church such as Joseph of Arimathaea, who helped to bury the body of Jesus. This was an important fulfilment of Scripture.

When the even was come, there came a rich man of Arimathaea, named Joseph... And when Joseph had taken the body [of Jesus], he wrapped it in a clean linen cloth, And laid it in his own new tomb, which he had hewn out in the rock:...

Matthew 27:57,59,60

3. Great people are used by God to finance the gospel.

If you think that everyone will contribute the same amount of money to the work of God, then you are ignorant and inexperienced. God raises up certain people so that the income of some churches is far more than others. This creates a necessary balance so that the work of God can go on among both the poor and the rich.

As it is written, He that had gathered much had nothing over; and he that had gathered little had no lack.

2 Corinthians 8:15

4. The contribution of one influential person can result in the salvation of an entire nation.

Esther's strategic relationship with the king was the one factor that saved the entire nation of Israel from being wiped out by Haman. Her uncle reminded her that she had been strategically placed for the salvation of an entire nation.

…who knoweth whether thou art come to the kingdom for such a time as this?

Esther 4:14

A Christian billionaire once told me of how he had used his relationship with the president of a country to obtain permission to hold open-air crusades that had hitherto been banned in that country.

Three Reasons Why it Is Important to Relate with the Poor

1. The principal calling of Christ was to the poor.

When Jesus spoke of the anointing on his life, he was specific about whom his anointing would affect. He specifically said that he had been anointed to preach the gospel to poor people. We are Christ's body and that same anointing is upon us.

> **The Spirit of the Lord is upon me, because he hath anointed me to preach the gospel to the poor; he hath sent me to heal the brokenhearted, to preach deliverance to the captives, and recovering of sight to the blind, to set at liberty them that are bruised, To preach the acceptable year of the Lord.**
>
> **Luke 4:18,19**

2.   Most people in the world are poor, therefore our ministries must reach the poor.

If we are to bear much fruit, a lot of the fruit will be among the poor people.

3.   The sign of a higher anointing is that we are ministering to the poor.

Today, most ministers are excited if they are able to visit with the president of a country. They gladly take pictures with presidents and publish them in their monthly magazines. There is nothing wrong with this. However, when Jesus was asked whether the great messianic ministry had arrived on earth, he replied that *poor people have the gospel preached to them.* It takes a higher anointing to minister to poor people.

> **And said unto him, Art thou he that should come, or do we look for another? Jesus answered and said unto them, Go and show John again those things which ye do hear and see: The blind receive their sight, and the lame walk, the lepers are cleansed, and the deaf hear, the dead are raised up, and THE POOR HAVE THE GOSPEL PREACHED TO THEM.**
>
> **Matthew 11:3-5**

Three Reasons Why it Is Difficult to Minister to the Poor

1. The poor cannot pay for the gospel.

Almost every ministry to poor people must be pre-financed. Books must be paid for, crusades must be paid for, salaries must be paid by others, etc.

2. The poor do not understand the gospel.

Poor people have many problems. Their reasoning is affected by the many problems that surround them. Poor people are often frustrated and desperate. They cannot understand why God will give Heaven to us when things are so bad on Earth. Can he not first make some changes on Earth? How can there be a solution to my problems through Bible study?

3. The poor sometimes see you as the cause of their problems.

In my dealings with poor people I have learnt that many of them actually see their help as the source of their problems. Many poor people are also too proud to receive help.

Five Types of People You Cannot Help

1. People who do not accept the biblical solution to their problems.
2. People who do not think that they have problems.
3. People who feel too proud to receive help.
4. People who think that you are their problem.
5. People who think that you are the cause of their problems.

Chapter 3

Maintain Personal Integrity

Integrity is wholeness. It means being totally or completely sound. To have personal integrity means you are upright, sincere, loyal and pure. You need personal integrity to be a good leader.[1]

Your integrity is shattered by lies and deception. The reason why very few of us believe in politicians is because their integrity has been greatly compromised by the deceptions of past political leaders.

Are you sound? Are you whole?[2]

Chapter 4

Give People Hope

Do you wonder why nobody stays in your company or church for very long? Perhaps there is not much hope for the future. Perhaps they cannot see good things in store for them in the future.

Six Ways to Give People Hope

1.   Make promises and keep them.

Every time you break a promise, you erode people's trust in you. It is very difficult to make people trust you. When people do not trust you, they will not follow you. The whole of Jesus' ministry was centred around a promise for the future.

> ...I go to prepare a place for you. And if I go and prepare a place for you, I will come again, and receive you unto myself; that where I am, there ye may be also.
>
> **John 14:2,3**

Jesus' disciples were made to believe that there were good things in store for them in the future. They knew that Jesus would keep his promise so they had hope.

2. Preach the Word of God.

The Word of God is full of hope. Anyone who preaches the Word of God will not minister discouragement, disappointment and disillusionment.[1]

3. Speak more about rewards than punishment.

The disciples had hope. They had hope in the glory and the rewards of Heaven. This was a great source of motivation to them. You must understand that Jesus' disciples were so highly motivated that they had left their secular jobs for the ministry. They eventually died for their beliefs.[2]

4. Show positive examples that inspire hope.

In your business or church, you must accept the fact that people need to be motivated. The key to having motivated people is "hope for the future". That is why Jesus often spoke of Heaven and the rewards that await his faithful servants. If you want to inspire pilots for instance, show them how many pilots have successfully flown for years and eventually retired. That is the sort of example that will give hope. If you want to inspire pastors, show them examples of ministers who have made it in ministry.[3]

5. **Avoid speaking about examples that bring about discouragement and depression.**

If people see how badly others have fared, they will be discouraged. They will say to themselves, "This is how I will end up one day." If you are an airline pilot, there is no point in discussing all the terrifying air crashes in aviation history.

6. **Build permanent structures.**

People have more hope in permanent things. It is natural to gravitate towards something that is more permanent. Every pastor who puts up a building, inspires hope in his congregation.

Chapter 5

Never Use Power without Wisdom or Wisdom without Power!

A leader is someone who employs wisdom as an essential tool of life. Christian leaders have the task of combining the Spirit of God and the wisdom of God. That is the will of God. Every Christian leader must learn to achieve a balance between the power and the wisdom.

But unto them which are called, both Jews and Greeks, Christ the power of God, and the wisdom of God.

1 Corinthians 1:24

I have highlighted the words *"Power"* and *"Wisdom"*. That is what I want you to get as you read this book. Christ Jesus is not only power to us. He is *power* and *wisdom*.

When you are able to effectively combine the power and the wisdom of God, you will begin to experience success as a leader. Remember, one without the other is not enough.

If you are a pastor, do not rely solely on spiritual direction; remember that pastors are supposed to use their minds as well. If you use your mind, God will lift you up in ministry.

I once noticed a church that was meeting in somebody's house in an exclusive and quiet residential neighbourhood. Although I was about one hundred meters away, I could hear everything that was being said in the service. The prayer, the worship and the praise were so loud and offensive that no one on the entire street could concentrate as long as they were shouting through their microphones. The pastor was anointed and he had the power of God at work for him. Unfortunately, he had left out wisdom.

Although there were just a few people there, they were using a public address system meant for large halls and hundreds of people. Even Jesus spoke to five thousand people without a microphone. I thought to myself, "Very soon this church will be shut down by the neighbours or the police." I knew that church was soon going to come face to face with a very big enemy it would be unable to handle. Never use power without wisdom and never use wisdom without power!

Chapter 6

Do Not Be a Lifeless Leader. Have a Conviction!

The Apostle Paul was a man of conviction. He was a man with a strong belief in God and he was ready to die for it. At one point he said openly, "I am ready to die."

For I am now ready to be offered...

2 Timothy 4:6

If you really consider yourself a leader, you must have a conviction about something! A leader without a conviction is a lifeless personality. People who have convictions rule the world. Suicide bombers who attack innocent citizens have the conviction that they are doing something right. They also believe that they will go to Heaven for that act of brutality. Men of conviction are difficult to contain. You cannot put them in a box. You cannot tie them down. You cannot keep them still. You cannot de-motivate them.

I firmly believe that it is conviction that many lifeless leaders lack. Why do I do the things I do? Because I have a conviction. I believe in Heaven and Hell. I have a conviction that one day Christ will reward me for all my labour on this earth. I believe that Jesus is the Son of God and that he rose from the dead. I believe that Jesus is the only way to Heaven. I do not just give mental assent to these facts. I believe them with all my heart. That is the driving force that made me abandon my medical career.

A leader without a conviction is a lifeless, speech-reading and emotionless puppet. Nobody takes any notice of him. Nobody believes his words. Nobody follows him. Do you sometimes wonder why people are not following you? It may be because you are not a man of conviction. A man of conviction is prepared to sacrifice many things for his conviction. When I see people who claim to be called by God, but are not prepared to sacrifice anything for their calling, I wonder if they are really called. A calling is a conviction to work for the Lord.

In the political world, the masses will follow someone who seems to have a conviction. They will follow someone who speaks from his heart. They will follow someone who is prepared to die for his beliefs.

Are you a real leader? Decide to be a man of conviction. Conviction, of what you may ask? Have conviction about the things God has called you to do. Have a conviction about the things you are supposed to accomplish in your lifetime. Have a conviction about the things that God has told you. Live by these convictions! Be prepared to give up anything so that you can fulfil your conviction.

Chapter 7

Wait for Your Season

And he shall be like a tree planted by the rivers of water, that bringeth forth his fruit in his season; his leaf also shall not wither; and whatsoever he doeth shall prosper.

Psalm 1:3

All of God's blessings have their season. Church growth has a season. Promotion has a season. Personal prosperity has a season.

A leader knows that the blessings he desires will not come overnight. He is prepared to stay at it until the breakthrough and promotion arrive. If you cannot wait for your God-given promotion, you are not a leader. I have had to wait many years for many things.[1]

If you cannot wait for the mangoes on your tree to ripen, you are never going to enjoy them. You will always pluck them off before they arrive. Mind you, unripe mangoes are very different from ripe ones.

I know of a pastor who bought a very expensive car. For several months, he had to use the entire income of the church to pay off the debt. This caused ripples in the church. Funds were raised in a desperate attempt to pay for this expensive car. In the end a blessing turned into a controversy.

To every thing there is a season, and a time to every purpose under the heaven: He hath made every thing beautiful in his time: also he hath set the world in their heart, so that no man can find out the work that God maketh from the beginning to the end.

Ecclesiastes 3:1,11

In his time, God makes all things beautiful. Are you a leader? Then never forget that a leader is someone who is prepared to wait for his season.[2]

Chapter 8

Use the Secret of Concentration

…but this one thing I do…

Philippians 3:13

Sixteen Things Every Leader Should Know about Concentration

1. Every great human achievement is the result of concentration.[1]

2. Every great military battle is won by bringing all forces to concentrate on a single objective.

3. Every great ministry accomplishes things for God by concentrating on a single vision.

When I was in university, I had the opportunity to join several Christian groups. I decided to stay with a particular ministry. I realized that I could not divide my time amongst the many Christian ministries on campus. Because I concentrated on one thing I was able to establish a ministry which is still there today.[2]

4. **Concentration makes people work faster.**

5. **The faster you work the more energy and interest you will have.**

6. **The slower you work the more tired and uninterested you become.**

7. **The more suspensions and delays to projects, the more discouraged everyone becomes.**

Hope deferred maketh the heart sick.

Hope deferred maketh the heart sick: but when the desire cometh, it is a tree of life.

Proverbs 13:12

8. **Concentration depends solely on the ability to distinguish between the relevant and the irrelevant.**

Anyone who cannot decide on what is important will never use the power of concentration. Do not be deceived by the pressure of urgent calls, requests, invitations, emergencies and crises. Urgent things are not usually important in the total picture, and important things are seldom urgent.

9. **The greatest thief of concentration is the telephone.**

When I start praying, I switch off all phones. This helps me to concentrate on the Lord.

10. Another thief of concentration is useless socializing and the television.

11. Inject urgency into all your projects.

This will make people concentrate on the task.

12. Concentration keeps everyone from backbiting, envy, jealousy and strife.

13. Few people can juggle with many projects at the same time.

Finish one thing at a time.

14. Unfinished projects break concentration.

The last uncompleted aspects of projects are often the cause of a future loss of concentration. They distract you and pull you into the past. People who concentrate on their God-given tasks are usually accused of being unsociable, proud, unfriendly, unpatriotic and inward-looking. But wisdom is justified of her children.

15. In the name of good works and being socially acceptable, the church has divided its attention into four main areas: health, education, relief services and Christian teaching.

It is no wonder that other religions are growing at a very fast rate. If only the Church were to once again concentrate on her God-given goal!

16. Concentration makes everything grow.

Chapter 9

Help the People around You to Accomplish Great Things with Their Lives

And he goeth up into a mountain, and calleth unto him whom he would: and they came unto him. And he ordained twelve, that they should be with him, and that he might send them forth to preach, And to have power to heal sicknesses, and to cast out devils: And Simon he surnamed Peter; And James the son of Zebedee, and John the brother of James; and he surnamed them Boanerges, which is, The sons of thunder: And Andrew, and Philip, and Bartholomew, and Matthew, and Thomas, and James the son of Alphaeus, and Thaddaeus, and Simon the Canannite, And Judas Iscariot, which also betrayed him: and they went into an house.

Mark 3:13-19

Notice this list of men who were going nowhere until they met Jesus. Jesus led these people to accomplish great feats. He led them until they were anointed and became preachers.

Through the influence of Jesus, they laid the foundations of the Christian Church with their very lives. Most of them died in the process of laying the foundation of the Church. The leadership of Jesus had turned nonentities into great achievers.

If God has called you to lead, do not see it as just YOU accomplishing great things. See it as you helping others to accomplish great things for God and for themselves. That is a true leader's heart. Leadership stems from the heart. The Bible teaches us that the heart is the footing for all the things that men do.[1]

Keep thy heart with all diligence; for out of it are the issues of life.

Proverbs 4:23

No one can really train you to be a leader. It comes from your heart! It comes by having the right heart! When you have the right heart, you do the right things. Until you see the heart of a leader, you will not be a true leader. *If you are the head of a church or organization and you try to suppress the achievements of others, I assure you that you do not have a true leader's heart.* Jesus wanted his disciples to do greater things than he himself had done (John 14:12).[2]

I often pray for the junior pastors around me that they would achieve great things for God. I keep encouraging them and praying for them that they would rise up mightily in ministry. I see some people with gifts that I do not have. I want my interaction with these people to help them accomplish great things for God. Every leader should have goals for the people around him. If you do not have these goals I seriously doubt if you are a leader.[3]

Four Goals a Leader Should Have for His Followers

1.   Aim for them to do well spiritually.

Your desire should be for the people you lead to prosper spiritually.[4]

I have no greater joy than to hear that my children walk in truth.

3 John 4

2.   Aim for your followers to do well financially.

I have a strong desire for the people who follow me to do well financially. It is my vision that everyone who works in my organization should have his own house, more cars than they need and enough money. This vision is steadily coming to pass. A leader is someone who thinks about others. If you just think about yourself, you are not a leader. Jesus thought about the financial state of his followers. He wanted them to have houses, lands and enough money. Many people don't know that Jesus actually promised that his followers would have these things.[5]

And Jesus answered and said, Verily I say unto you, There is no man that hath left house, or brethren, or sisters, or father, or mother, or wife, or children, or lands, for my sake, and the gospel's, But he shall receive an hundredfold now in this time, houses, and brethren, and sisters, and mothers, and children, and lands, with persecutions; and in the world to come eternal life.

Mark 10:29,30

3. Aim for your followers to be physically, socially and maritally healthy.

Beloved, I wish above all things that thou mayest prosper and be in health, even as thy soul prospereth.

3 John 2

And in that day ye shall ask me nothing. Verily, verily, I say unto you, Whatsoever ye shall ask the Father in my name, he will give it you. Hitherto have ye asked nothing in my name: ask, and ye shall receive, that your joy may be full.

John 16:23,24

Why did Jesus want the joy of his followers to be full? Because a good leader wants his followers to be happy in every aspect of their lives.

4. Aim for your followers to fulfil their ministry.

My greatest passion is to see the ones I have raised up fulfilling their ministries. Every father wants his sons and daughters to fulfil their ministry. If you are a leader, your vision and passion is not for yourself but for the ones you lead.

But watch thou in all things, endure afflictions, do the work of an evangelist, make full proof of thy ministry.

2 Timothy 4:5

Chapter 10

Make People Obey You Gladly

So when they had dined, Jesus saith to Simon Peter, Simon, son of Jonas, lovest thou me more than these? He saith unto him, Yea, Lord; thou knowest that I love thee. He saith unto him, Feed my lambs.

John 21:15

Jesus was able to make people follow his instructions. He told Peter to feed the flock of God and that is exactly what he did. If you call yourself a leader, ask yourself, "Do people carry out my instructions?" Why are some people obeyed and some others ignored? Develop the art of making people obey your instructions. There are several things you can do.[1]

Nine Ways to Make People Obey You Gladly

1. **Do not give unreasonable instructions.**

People rebel against wicked and unreasonable men.

2. **Teach your followers why certain things have to be done.**

Make people see that your instructions are for their own good. When people understand why they are doing something, they often do it better! That is why for example I preach on: "Fifty Reasons Why Christians Should Be Soul Winners". I want people to understand the last instruction of Jesus.[2]

3. **Explain instructions in detail so that everyone understands the instructions.**

Sometimes people do not obey simply because they did not understand what you said.[3]

4. **Show people that you are not partial or partisan.**

5. **Let the people see that you obey instructions yourself.**

Many rebellious people do not realize that they are teaching their followers to be rebellious by their very actions. The Centurion who sent for Jesus illustrated this principle beautifully.[4]

> **For I also am a man set under authority, having under me soldiers, and I say unto one, Go, and he goeth; and to another, Come, and he cometh; and to my servant, Do this, and he doeth it.**
>
> Luke 7:8

This man was enumerating the instructions which he had given and which were being obeyed. But he was careful to let us know that *he also was under authority*. In other words, he himself was obeying instructions. The army officer often has to lead people to their deaths. How does he make young men sacrifice their lives on the frightening fields of war? By leading the charge himself when he's told to do so. If you cannot make people gladly do things they naturally do not like doing, then you are not a leader. Develop this art of making people obey you gladly and people will always wonder about the team who work with you and who love to sacrifice and to serve.[5]

6. Get rid of complaining and murmuring individuals.

Such people poison the atmosphere and make everyone feel that they are into a bad thing. It is very important to maintain a cheerful spirit in the workplace. Systematically eradicate complainers and murmurers from your system.

7. Correct wrong attitudes even when they are not fully developed into full-blown disobedience or rebellion.[6]

8. Punish people who disobey.

Your organization cannot be established unless people believe that judgment will fall when the wrong thing is done. Punishment is a good thing because it establishes the land. Many disorganized offices are the way they are because no one is ever dismissed. Warnings are issued but no one ever dares to carry out the threat. Let everyone see that when you break the rules, the rules will break you! When you are fair, people will believe in the laws and obey you gladly. If they feel that one rule applies to some people and another rule to other special people, they will rebel against your instructions.[7]

The king by judgment establisheth the land: but he that receiveth gifts overthroweth it.

Proverbs 29:4

9. Reward people accordingly.

Even Jesus expected his reward.

For consider him that endured such contradiction of sinners against himself, lest ye be wearied and faint in your minds.

Hebrews 12:3

Jesus was motivated by the thought of his reward. Rewards are some of the highest form of motivation in existence. Why do you think an athlete runs around for hours everyday? Why do you think boxers subject themselves to severe, dangerous and life-threatening knocks on the head? It is because of the joy of a million dollars or more that will come after the knocking is over.

The joy that is set before people will make them do almost anything. Rewards can make people do almost anything! People who have died for the cause of Christ, died willingly, thinking of the reward that lay ahead.

When Jesus spoke to Peter, he told him about his death. He predicted that Peter would die in a way that he might not like.

Verily, verily, I say unto thee, When thou wast young, thou girdest thyself, and walkedst whither thou wouldest: but when thou shalt be old, thou shalt stretch forth thy hands, and another shall gird thee, and carry thee whither thou wouldest not. This spake he, signifying by what death he should glorify God. And when he had spoken this, he saith unto him, Follow me.

John 21:18,19

He told Peter to follow him even to that end. Peter was willing and obedient. Perhaps, the key that made Peter willing to die was the fact that Jesus himself had set the example. Jesus had shown that there was a great reward in following. You see, leadership is all about setting examples. When a leader leads the way personally, his words become more powerful. Do you want your words to be respected? Do you want to be such a powerful leader that people would be prepared to die for your cause? I believe you do! It's time to set the example and lead the way.

Master John Hooper, Bishop of Worcester and Gloucester, was a student and graduate of Oxford University. He found the Lord and was stirred with a strong desire and love for the Scriptures. In 1555, Master Hooper was urged to return to the unity of the Catholic Church and to acknowledge the Pope's holiness to be head of the Church. He was promised that he would receive the Pope's blessing and the Queen's mercy if he would condescend to the Pope's holiness.

Mr. Hooper answered that the Pope taught doctrine contrary to the doctrine of Christ. And that he was not worthy to be the head of the Church. Wherefore he would in no wise condescend to any such jurisdiction. Mr. Hooper made it clear that he did not consider the Catholic Church of which the Pope was the head, to be the real Church.

He explained that the Church only followed the voice of Christ and run away from strangers. However, he said if he had said anything to offend the Queen he would ask for mercy. But he added, "Mercy must be had with safety of conscience and without the displeasure of God."

An old friend, Anthony Kingston, spoke to him.

Kingston: *'But I am sorry to see you in this case; for as I understand you be come hither to die. But, alas, consider that life is sweet, and death is bitter. Therefore, seeing life may be had, desire to live; for life hereafter may do good.'*

Hooper: *'Indeed it is true, Master Kingston, I am come hither to end this life, and to suffer death here, because I will not gainsay the former truth that I have heretofore taught amongst you in this diocese, and elsewhere; and I thank you for your friendly counsel, although it be not so friendly as I could have wished it. True it is, Master Kingston, that death is bitter, and life is sweet: but, alas, consider that the death to come is more bitter, and the life to come is more sweet. Therefore, for the desire and love I have to the one, and the terror and fear of the other; I do not so much regard this death, nor esteem this life, but have settled myself, through the strength of God's Holy Spirit, patiently to pass through the torments and extremities of the fire now prepared for me, rather than to deny the truth of His Word; desiring you, and others, in the meantime, to commend me to God's mercy in your prayers.'*

Kingston: *'Well, my lord, then I perceive there is no remedy, and therefore I will take my leave of you: and I thank God that ever I knew you; for God did appoint you to call me, being a lost child.'*

Hooper: *I do highly praise God for it: and I pray God you may continually live in His fear.'*[8]

His final speech to the mayor was even more revealing about his willingness to obey God and to stand for the truth.

'Master mayor, I give most hearty thanks to you, and to the rest of your brethren, that you have vouchsafed to take me, a prisoner and a condemned man, by the hand; whereby to my rejoicing it is some deal apparent that your old love and friendship towards me is not altogether extinguished; and I trust also that all the things I have taught you in times past are not utterly forgotten, when I was here, by the godly King that dead is, appointed to be your bishop and pastor. For the which most true and sincere doctrine, because I will not now account it falsehood and heresy, as many other men do, I am sent hither (as I am sure you know) by the Queen's commandment to die; and am come where I taught it, to confirm it with my blood. And now, master sheriffs, I understand by these good men, and my very friends' (meaning the guard), 'at whose hands I have found so much favour and gentleness, by the way hitherward, as a prisoner could reasonably require (for the which also I most heartily thank them), that I am committed to your custody, as unto them that must see me brought to-morrow to the place of execution. My request therefore to you shall be only, that there may be a quick fire, shortly to make an end; and in the meantime I will be as obedient unto you, as yourselves would wish. If you think I do amiss in any thing, hold up your finger, and I have done: for I am not come hither as one enforced or compelled to die (for it is well known, I might have had my life with worldly gain); but as one willing to offer and give my life for the truth, rather than consent to the wicked papistical religion of the Bishop of Rome, received and set forth by the magistrates in England, to God's high displeasure and dishonour; and I trust, by God's grace, to-morrow to die a faithful servant of God, and a true obedient subject to the Queen.'[9]

The description of his death in the fire, which lasted about an hour, is revealing.

When he came to the place appointed where he should die, smilingly he beheld the stake and preparation made for him, which was near unto the great elm-tree, over against the college of priests, where he was wont to preach. The place round about the houses, and the boughs of the tree, were replenished with people; and in the chamber over the college-gate stood the wolvish blood-suckers and turnelings, the priests of the college. Then kneeled he down, forasmuch as he could not be suffered to speak unto the people. After he was somewhat entered into his prayer, a box was brought and laid before him upon a stool, with his pardon (or at least-wise it was feigned to be his pardon) from the Queen, if he would turn. At the sight whereof he cried, 'If you love my soul, away with it! if you love my soul, away with it!'

Prayer being done, he prepared himself to the stake, and put off his host's gown, and delivered it to the sheriffs, requiring them to see it restored unto the owner, and put off the rest of his gear, unto his doublet and hose, wherein he would have burned. But the sheriffs would not permit that, such was their greediness; unto whose pleasures, good man, he very obediently submitted himself; and his doublet, hose, and petticoat were taken off. Then, being in his shirt, he took a point from his hose himself, and trussed his shirt between his legs, where had a pound of gunpowder in a bladder, and under each arm the like quantity, delivered him by the guard.

So desiring the people to say the Lord's prayer with him, and to pray for him (who performed it with tears, during the time of his pains), he went up to the stake. The hoop of iron prepared for his middle was brought, but when they offered to have bound his neck and legs with the other two hoops of iron, he utterly refused them.

Thus being ready, he looked upon all the people, of whom he might be well seen (for he was both tall, and stood also on a high stool), and in every corner there was nothing to be seen but weeping and sorrowful people. Then, lifting up his eyes and hands unto heaven, he prayed to himself. By and by, he that was appointed to make the fire, came to him, and did ask him forgiveness. Of whom he asked why he should forgive him, saying, that he knew never any offence he had committed against him. 'O sir!' said the man, 'I am appointed to make the fire.' 'Therein,' said Master Hooper, 'thou dost nothing offend me; God forgive thee thy sins, and do thine office, I pray thee.'

Then the needs were cast up, and he received two bundles of them in his own hands, embraced them, kissed them, and put under either arm one of them, and showed with his hand how the rest should be bestowed, and pointed to the place where any did lack.

Another commandment was given that the fire should be set to. But because there were put to no fewer green faggots than two horses could carry upon their backs, it kindled not by and by, and was a pretty while also before it took the reeds upon the faggots. At length it burned about him, but the wind having full strength in that place (it was a lowering and cold morning), it blew the flame from him, so that he was in a manner nothing but touched by the fire.

Within a space after, a few dry faggots were brought, and a new fire kindled with faggots (for there were no more reeds), and that burned at the nether parts, but had small power above, because of the wind, saving that it did burn his hair, and swell his skin a little. In the time of which fire even as at the first flame, he prayed, saying mildly and not very loud (but as one without pains), 'O Jesus, the Son of David, have mercy upon me, and receive my soul!' After the second was spent, he did wipe both his eyes with his hands, and beholding the people, he said with an indifferent loud voice, 'For God's love, good people, let me have more fire!' And all this while his nether parts did burn: for the faggots were so few, that the flame did not burn strongly at his upper parts.

The third fire was kindled within a while after, which was more extreme than the other two: and then the bladders of gunpowder brake, which did him small good, they were so placed, and the wind had such power. In the which fire he prayed with somewhat a loud voice, 'Lord Jesus, have mercy upon me: Lord Jesus receive my spirit.' And these were the last words he was heard to utter. But when he was black in the mouth, and his tongue swollen, that he could not speak, yet his lips went till they were shrunk to the gums: and he knocked his breast with his hands, until one of his arms fell off and then knocked still with the other, what time the fat, water, and blood, dropped out at his fingers' ends, until by renewing of the fire his strength was gone, and his hand did cleave fast, in knocking, to the iron upon his breast. So immediately, bowing forwards, he yielded up his spirit.

Thus was he three quarters of an hour or more in the fire. Even as a lamb, patiently he abode the extremity thereof, neither moving forwards, backwards, nor to any side: but he died as quietly as a child in his bed. And he now reigneth, I doubt not, as a blessed martyr in the joys of heaven, prepared for the faithful in Christ before the foundations of the world; for whose constancy all Christians are bound to praise God.[10]

Chapter 11

Contemplate, Reflect, Be Thoughtful and Consider the Things You See around You

So I returned, and considered all the oppressions that are done under the sun: and behold the tears of such as were oppressed, and they had no comforter; and on the side of their oppressors there was power; but they had no comforter. Wherefore I praised the dead which are already dead more than the living which are yet alive. Yea, better is he than both they, which hath not yet been, who hath not seen the evil work that is done under the sun. Again, I considered all travail, and every right work, that for this a man is envied of his neighbour. This is also vanity and vexation of spirit. The fool foldeth his hands together, and eateth his own flesh. Better is an handful with quietness, than both the hands full with travail and vexation of spirit. Then I returned, and I saw vanity under the sun. There is one alone, and there is not a second; yea, he hath neither child nor brother: yet is there no end of all his labour; neither is his eye satisfied with riches; neither saith he, For whom do I labour, and bereave my soul of good? This is also vanity, yea, it is a sore travail.

Ecclesiastes 4:1-8

When I applied mine heart to know wisdom, and to see the business that is done upon the earth: (for also there is that neither day nor night seeth sleep with his eyes:) Then I beheld all the work of God, that a man cannot find out the work that is done under the sun: because though a man labour to seek it out, yet he shall not find it; yea farther; though a wise man think to know it, yet shall he not be able to find it.

Ecclesiastes 8:16,17

For all this I considered in my heart even to declare all this, that the righteous, and the wise, and their works, are in the hand of God: no man knoweth either love or hatred by all that is before them.

Ecclesiastes 9:1

King Solomon, a political leader of his day, wrote these Scriptures. You will notice the phrase *"and I considered"*. You will also notice the phrase *"I applied my heart to wisdom"*. Do you consider yourself to be a real leader? It is time to start turning things over in your mind. Be a deep thinker.

Consider the happenings around you. As you consider, you will receive wisdom. That wisdom will help you to be a better leader. Consider why some people are successful. Analyse why some people fail.[1]

Think about what makes others victorious. A true leader is a deep thinker. I reflected on why certain people became disloyal. That is what gave rise to my book on *Loyalty and Disloyalty*. As I ponder over many issues, I receive revelation that becomes the basis for my teachings.

The Brain Seller

I remember the story of a man who went into a store to buy some brains. There were four different brains on sale. The salesperson was on hand to help the customer.

The customer said, "I would like to buy the best brains you have."

The salesperson showed the customer what he had in store.

He said, "These are the brains from a nation that invented airplanes, rockets, and satellites."

He continued, "These next ones are from a nation that invented televisions, videos, telephones, radios and stereo systems."

He went on, "This third set of brains comes from a nation that has developed beautiful cities, roads, bridges, trains, airports, tunnels, etc."

He then showed the fourth set of brains. He continued, "This last set of brains are from a nation which has invented nothing and built nothing for itself. This nation even has foreigners coming from outside to build roads and toilets.

"I see," he said, "How much are they anyway?"

The salesman replied, "The first three brains are affordable, but the fourth set of brains is very expensive."

"Why is that? Why should they be so expensive when they have not been used to accomplish anything?"

"Oh, that is simple," the salesman replied, "Those brains are fresh, unused and full of potential. Because they have not been used for anything, all the potential is still within."

This unfortunate story tells us how important it is to use the brains God has given us. No matter how spiritual you are, God still expects us to use our brains. A great leader is someone who contemplates, reflects, ponders and deliberates over issues. Thinking is not a non-spiritual activity. It is a God-given privilege to have the large brains we have. Did you know that human beings have the largest and most developed brains of all creation? Think about the size of a bird's head. How small their brains must be. Are you not glad that God has given you something bigger? Every great leader uses this gift——his brains!

Chapter 12

Strive for Excellence

Excellence is the attainment of the highest level of quality and perfection. Being excellent means becoming a person of distinction. A true leader is someone who wants to distinguish himself in his field. The blessings of the Lord are to make you the head and not the tail.

And the Lord shall make thee the head, and not the tail; and thou shalt be above only, and thou shalt not be beneath; if that thou hearken unto the commandments of the Lord thy God, which I command thee this day, to observe and to do them:

Deuteronomy 28:13

God had plans for his people to attain the highest levels of excellence. That is why he said you would be above only. Excellence is not an accident. It is something you must strive for. If you want to work for eight hours a day, you are not likely to achieve distinction in this life. *People who distinguish themselves in this life often work for more than sixty hours a week.* Excellence demands hard work. Excellence in ministry, government or business does not come by osmosis. It comes by diligence.

To become excellent you must emulate excellent people. *Life is too short to discover everything yourself. Life is too short not to learn from your fathers and seniors.* Excellence in the practice of medicine has been achieved by constantly building upon what our predecessors have learnt. That is why today, we are able to transplant hearts. If the heart surgeon used his time to discover which direction the blood flowed, he would be taking us back to the eighteenth century.

Be humble and depend upon the discoveries of others. God does not want you to be mediocre. Insist on the highest standards. You can be an excellent businessman. You can have a high yielding factory. Your church can be the best in the city. Decide today for excellence. Read the books that excellent people have written. Read the books. Listen to the tapes. Excellence is yours for the taking!

Chapter 13

Everything Depends on the Leadership

For, behold, the Lord, the Lord of hosts, doth take away from Jerusalem and from Judah the stay and the staff, the whole stay of bread, and the whole stay of water, The mighty man, and the man of war, the judge, and the prophet, and the prudent, and the ancient, The captain of the fifty, and the honourable man, and the counsellor, and the cunning artificer, and the eloquent orator. And I will give children to be their princes, and babes shall rule over them. And the people shall be oppressed, every one by another, and every one by his neighbour: the child shall behave himself proudly against the ancient, and the base against the honourable. When a man shall take hold of his brother of the house of his father, saying, Thou hast clothing, be thou our ruler, and let this ruin be under thy hand: In that day shall he swear,

saying, I will not be an healer; for in my house is neither bread nor clothing: make me not a ruler of the people. As for my people, children are their oppressors, and women rule over them. O my people, they which lead thee cause thee to err, and to destroy the way of thy paths.

Isaiah 3:1-7,12

In this Scripture, God predicts a mighty judgement on Jerusalem and on Judah. God had determined to punish and destroy those nations. How was he going to do it? The Scriptures make it very clear. God was going to take away all kinds of leaders from the community. The community was going to be left leaderless. Almighty God knows this principle very well: No leader, no progress! No leader, no development! No leader, no blessing! No leader, no deliverance! God knew that the community would fall into judgement if he removed leaders from their midst. This is because everything rises and falls on leadership.[1]

Almighty God was unleashing one of the most terrible punishments anyone, nation or group of people could ever have. That is to have no leaders. If you look closely at this Scripture, you will see that God was predicting the removal of every type of leader from the community.

…the Lord doth take away… the mighty man, the man of war, the judge, the prophet, the prudent, the ancient, the captain of fifty, the honourable man, the eloquent orator…

If you study this list closely, you will come to the frightening realization that the community is left without anyone who can lead the people in any aspect. Pastors were taken away. Politicians were taken away. Senior citizens were taken away. Wise people were taken away. They were all taken away from the community. This is what I call a headless society. A body without a head is no body. A church without a true leader is truly pathetic! A nation without a real leader is cursed! Truly every nation rises and falls based on its leaders.

This was probably one of the most severe judgments that God could give to his people—the removal of all kinds of leaders. As you know, nature abhors a vacuum. And in place of real leaders, Jehovah predicted the rise of bogus leadership.

And I will give children to be their princes, and babes shall rule over them...

These children and babies represent incapable and useless leaders. It is obvious that a baby cannot rule his own bowels, how much more rule a nation. Some years ago I asked a friend whom he would vote for in an upcoming election. He hesitated, so I asked a more direct question. I asked, "Will you vote for President X?"

At that point he responded and said, "If I had to choose between your four-year-old son, David, and President X, I would certainly prefer to vote for your four-year-old son."

He continued and said, "I would rather vote for a goat to be our President than for that person."

It is obvious that neither my son nor a goat would be able to help our nation very much. To have the leadership of children or babies, or as this person said, a goat, is certainly a curse.

What would be the result of having such inappropriate and flunkey leaders? The Bible has the answers.

The people shall be oppressed, everyone by another and everyone by his neighbour; and the child shall behave himself proudly against the ancient.

Have you not seen this picture somewhere—oppression, injustice, intimidation and the proliferation of all sorts of evil? What gives rise to rebels in Africa, and to thousands of young people in a drug culture in Europe and America?

Almost every bad situation within the church can be attributed to the lack of a good leader. Church splits and scandals are often the result of a lack of strong leadership. The Scripture we read above tells us how God was going to curse the land by taking away leaders. Churches rise and fall on leadership. With a good strong leader, a church will grow into a megachurch. With bad leadership, churches don't go anywhere even if the pastor is very anointed. You sometimes see an anointed minister who has bad leadership qualities. His ministry usually falls into chaos because of bad leadership qualities.

Leadership is an art. It is a secular subject which is necessary for ministers of the gospel to understand. The ability to write and read is not a spiritual thing; it is a secular skill which needs to be learned. Without that ability you are going nowhere in this world. Same thing for leadership! Without the knowledge and skills of leadership your ministry is going nowhere.

Africa without Leaders

A debate I often get into with friends is about the state of the African continent. I often marvel at the lack of development and the level of poverty in Africa. I ask myself, "What is it? Can we not build our own roads? Why do we need a foreign company to build roads and toilets for us?" It would be very unusual to go to a European country and find foreign companies engaged in building roads or toilets in that country. Why is there so much suffering and sickness in developing countries?

There are many theories that have attempted to explain the condition of poor and unstable nations. Some people say that there is a curse on the black man. Others claim that it is the lack of democracy. And some even think that there is a curse on the African continent. I believe that the principal reason for the poor state of affairs is the lack of good leaders.

Whenever there is a good leader, you will notice a great deal of development and you will notice prosperity. The absence of leaders can be seen clearly in two worlds. You will notice the absence of leaders in the natural or secular world. You can also notice the absence of leaders in the spiritual or church world. When there is a lack of leadership in the Church world, you will notice the same signs of a lack of development of ministry, poverty, lack of teaching and a lack of knowledge, and the proliferation of sin.

Churches without Leaders

In a nation where there is little or no good leadership, you will notice the rise of false leaders, rebels and pirates. In the Church, the lack of true leadership gives rise to the proliferation of sin and evil doers as well as false church leaders. The lack of real leaders in a church causes many people to lose their souls, die and go to Hell. How can this be?[2]

A real leader in the church will lead the congregation to win souls and do missionary work. Whenever the church's leadership stopped concerning itself with the lost and dying souls, false religions and alternative faiths crept in and took over.

This is why I am writing this book. There is a need for leaders in every sphere of life. There is a need for genuine leaders in the secular world. There is a genuine need for leaders in the church world. It is my prayer that God will raise you and many others up to be true leaders for your generation! Truly, everything depends on the leadership!

Chapter 14

Rally People around You

>...Rezon, the son of Eliadah... And he gathered men unto him, and became captain over a band...
>
>   1 Kings 11:23,24

This man Rezon became a leader in his time. The Bible tells us that he gathered people unto himself. Every true leader is able to rally a team of people around himself. Jesus gathered a team of twelve people around himself. He lived with them and fellowshipped with them for three and a half years. Decide to be a gathering point for people. Whatever is offensive in your personality and whatever scatters people must be dealt with if you take leadership seriously. Learn how to speak without offending and scattering people.

22 Steps to Rally People around You

1.   **Make people feel that you really want them around you.**

2.   **Appreciate the people around you.**

   Rejoice with the people around you over their little successes and breakthroughs. Their joy will increase when they feel there is another person rejoicing with them.

3.   **Genuinely admire people's cars, houses, furniture and clothes.**

   Cars, houses and clothes represent people's choices and achievements. If you admire and respect people's choices and achievements, you are admiring them personally! They will naturally warm up to you!

4.   **Show people that you respect them, no matter who they are or what they have.**

   People will warm up to you once they know you respect them. In this world, many people are not respected. Generally speaking, black people are often not respected by white people. In my opinion, Europeans and Americans do not respect Africans. Some tribes are also despised and hated. People are looking for someone who genuinely respects them in spite of where they come from, who they are or how much money they have. Anyone who has this ability to respect people, no matter who they are, will have people rallying around him.

5.   **Be conscious of people who have inferiority complexes and treat them carefully.**

6. Never tease someone who does not like being teased.

There are some people who hate being teased. Often this is because of a complex they had from childhood.

7. Call people by their names soon after you have met them.

No one likes to feel that he is a mere number. People will warm up to you when they realize that you know them by name. They will be even more touched if you call them by their pet names.

8. Show interest in people's personal lives.

Ask about their homes, jobs and schools. People need to feel that the leader has a genuine interest in their lives.[1]

9. Show an interest in people's aspirations, visions and goals.

When you are only interested in *your vision* and goal, people will silently withdraw from you. When they sense that you have an interest in making them successful they will rally around you.

10. Offer food and drinks to visitors whenever you can.

When I was in the university I visited many people on campus. I always remember a particular lady called Adelaide Baiden. Whenever we would go to her room she would offer us something to eat. Many times she and her roommate shared their supper with us. This made her room a natural rallying point! If you want to be a natural rallying point, learn to offer food and drinks to visitors anytime you can!

11.   Listen to people's problems.

Learn the art of listening rather than talking. When you allow people to talk about themselves they psychologically feel that they are closer to you. This makes them rally around you.[2]

12.   Let the conversation centre around others and what they are doing rather than yourself and what you are.

It is vain to have self-centred conversations. If your conversations are all about yourself, your achievements, your vision, people will soon be tired of listening to you and move away.

13.   Be an encourager.

Always notice when somebody has made an effort to achieve something. Perhaps they sang a song or did a new hairstyle. Even if you didn't like it, appreciate the effort that was made. There is no need to say that you didn't like what they did. All you need to do is to notice the effort and appreciate it.[3]

14.   Say thank you for everything.

It is better for people to think that you are saying thank you too often than for them to feel that you are ungrateful.

15.   Smile.

People gravitate around smiling and friendly people. We know that we are not perfect and so we do not need a stern, frowning person to remind us of our failings. People need someone to encourage them that in spite of their failings, they are accepted.

16. Do not be partial.

One of the first things that people notice about leaders is when they are partial. The Bible says in the Book of James, Chapter 3 and verse 17, that it is not wise to be partial:

> **But the wisdom that is from above is... without partiality...**

Even little children notice when their parents are partial toward one child. No one wants to follow someone who is biased and partisan without cause. What about if you fall into his bad books without knowing it? It is difficult to live in a country where the head of state begins to dislike you because of unsubstantiated tales. It is difficult to work in an organization where the boss can begin to dislike you based on a new feeling he has.

17. Whenever there is an opportunity, give a gift.

A gift makes room for a man. "A man's gift maketh room for him, and bringeth him before great men" (Proverbs 18:16). This means that space is created within the person's heart for you. You will be accepted and the person will rally around you.

18. Mourn with people who are mourning.

Times of sorrow are some of the most remembered times in people's lives. If you remember them during that period they will never forget you. I have had people joining my church simply because I was by their side when their parents died.[4]

Gift Aid declaration

giftaid it

Name of charity or CASC _____

Please treat the enclosed gift of £ _____ as a Gift Aid donation.

You must pay an amount of income tax and/or capital gains tax in this tax year at least equal to the tax that the charity or Community Amateur Sports Club (CASC) will claim from HM Revenue & Customs on your Gift Aid donation.

Donor's details

Title _____ Initial(s) _____ Surname _____

Home address _____

_____

_____

Postcode _____ Date _____

Signature _____

Please notify the charity or CASC if you:

1. Want to cancel this declaration.
2. Change your name or home address.
3. No longer pay sufficient tax on your income and/or capital gains.

Tax claimed by the charity or CASC

- The charity or CASC will reclaim 25p of tax on every £1 you give.
- The Government will pay to the charity or CASC an additional 3p on every £1 you give between 6 April 2008 and 5 April 2011. This transitional relief for the charity or CASC does not affect your personal tax position.

If you pay income tax at the higher rate, you must include all your Gift Aid donations on your Self Assessment tax return if you want to receive the additional tax relief due to you.

19. Go the extra mile to help someone.

Whenever you help someone in need he remembers you. People see when you make the extra effort and it touches their hearts. When you ask them to rally around you for a cause, they will be there because they remember how you helped them. I assure you of this one thing: if you do not sow a seed of help in someone's life, no one will help you in the future.[5]

20. Be friendly, greet people in a pleasant way.

Be easygoing, be sociable: shake hands, hug people, give a pat on the back, be affable and pleasant. Warmth is attractive. A cold and crisp person is not a natural rallying point.

21. Be concerned when listening to people's problems.

When listening to people's problems, your facial expression must show deep concern and interest. Try to pick up the details and show that you are following the story.

22. Notice when people are absent.

People are offended when they find out that you did not even notice when they were away. How can they be important to you if you do not even notice their absence?

These twenty-two steps will make you a natural rallying point and a natural leader.[6]

Chapter 15

Choose Hard and Difficult Things Instead of Nice and Easy Things

Now is my soul troubled; and what shall I say? Father, save me from this hour: but for this cause came I unto this hour.

John 12:27

By choosing hard and difficult things instead of nice and easy things you will make yourself a natural leader. Most people choose nice and easy things. That is why most people are on the broad and easy way that leads to Hell.

If you choose things that are hard and difficult instead of things that are nice and easy, you will move forward very rapidly in life. A leader needs to move forward so that he can be one step ahead. It is only when you are a step-ahead that you are truly a leader.[1]

Many of the things that will take you forward in life are hard and difficult to do. Yet, these are the most important things for you. Prayer is one of these things. Bible study is one of the important things you need to do. Fasting is an important habit that every Christian should cultivate. Yet these are things we all do not like doing. A true leader can make people do these very things. I often lead my people into fasting and prayer. It is difficult for me, and it is difficult for them. Yet we do it! How am I able to make hundreds of people fast and pray for several gruelling hours? By doing it myself and letting them see me do it!

Seven Hard and Difficult Things You Must Do to Stay Ahead

1. Have a daily quiet time.
2. Read the Bible everyday.
3. Pray for hours everyday.
4. Fast regularly.
5. Learn things that are new to you.

In the ministry, I have had to learn new things that I was not naturally inclined to. It is doing some of these difficult things that have taken me forward. For instance, going into the healing ministry was probably one of the most difficult things I have ever done. It was hard and difficult! But I am forever grateful I took those hard and difficult steps. The healing ministry has given me a level of visibility I would not have had without it. I see my ministry becoming more and more Christ-like because I took that hard and difficult step. Anytime I share about doing hard and difficult things, I always remember the healing ministry. It is not easy to pray for the sick, even after years of doing it.

6.　　Educate yourself constantly by reading books.

7.　　Obey whatever God tells you to do.

Obeying God is one of the most vital keys to moving forward. I cannot explain the power that is released when you obey God. Jesus Christ achieved his purpose by obeying God. It was hard and difficult, but he did it! It would have been nice and easy to stay in Heaven where he belonged. Jesus grimaced at the thought of obeying his instructions. Yet he composed himself. Notice the words of Jesus as he pondered on the cross that lay before him.

> **Now is my soul troubled; and what shall I say? Father, save me from this hour: but for this cause came I unto this hour.**
>
> **John 12:27**

Jesus steeled himself and resolved to go through with it. Decide to be like Jesus – choose what is hard and difficult rather than what is nice and easy and you will find yourself in a good place.

Chapter 16

Readily Embrace New Ideas

Your leadership will be stunted if you are not prepared to embrace new ideas. The world is constantly changing. Old systems and approaches no longer work. Computers have refashioned the way we do things. Seasons change. Needs change. And people change. That is why God constantly introduces fresh and new things.

I am very open to new ideas. I do not mind changing things I have been doing in a particular way for a long time. I find that God is a God of positive change! God is a God of improvement!

I notice how people laugh at me when I suggest new ideas. I have observed with amazement how some architects, engineers, technicians, builders, lawyers, accountants and pastors are resistant to new concepts. I notice how they quietly sneer and giggle amongst themselves as they listen to me expound some new idea. "We don't do things this way." "It has not been done before!" "We are not in America." "If we had what they have in Europe, we could have done it." "You know, they have much more equipment abroad." "It is not possible in Ghana." "It's not realistic." I have *heard* these statements and *sensed* these messages even when they are not voiced out.

Africans sat on their continent whilst Europeans explored the world and discovered us. Why did we wait to be discovered in Africa? Why didn't we explore new horizons? Why didn't Africans explore new territories and discover the Europeans? Openness to new ideas is a secret to moving ahead as a leader. No wonder Europeans are ahead in almost every sphere of life (except spiritually).

God is a God of change. He is doing new things. Embrace new ideas with honesty. Try a new method. A new way of doing things may be the key to pushing you out ahead of everyone else in your field. When I practised the lay ministry I didn't do it because I saw others doing it. I did it because it needed to be done even though it was new. I am following my Heavenly Father who is a God of new things. Be like your heavenly Father. There is no better mentor.[1]

Five Examples of New Things That God Does

1. God embarks on new projects, new schemes, new ideas, new plans.

   Behold, I will do a new thing; now it shall spring forth; shall ye not know it? I will even make a way in the wilderness, and rivers in the desert.

   Isaiah 43:19

2. God gives new languages to his people.

And these signs shall follow them that believe; In my name shall they cast out devils; they shall speak with new tongues;

Mark 16:17

3. God gives brand new instructions to his servants.

Every instruction has an expiry date.

A new commandment I give unto you, That ye love one another; as I have loved you, that ye also love one another.

John 13:34

4. God makes us into brand new people who have never existed before.

Therefore if any man be in Christ, he is a new creature: old things are passed away; behold, all things are become new.

2 Corinthians 5:17

5. God makes new agreements and he issues fresh calls to service.

If you are open you will hear his voice.

In that he saith, A new covenant, he hath made the first old. Now that which decayeth and waxeth old is ready to vanish away.

Hebrews 8:13

Chapter 17

Value People

People are attracted to places where they are valued. Many organizations undervalue the people they have. Every person who feels undervalued will move away.

Every developed nation values its citizens. What you respect will come towards you. What you attack will run away from you. People are the most valuable thing a leader has. A nation that attacks its leaders will be void of leaders. A nation that attacks its wealthy citizens will be poor. All the rich people will run away to friendlier countries where wealth is not a hazard.

Why You Must Value People

1.   Because people are more valuable than money.

Invest in people financially and educationally. Pay people well and spend time teaching and training them.

2. Because people are more valuable than buildings.

See them as gifts from God.

3. Because people are more valuable than computers.

Try not to lose the people that God gives you. Do everything to prevent the loss of even one person. People can sense it when you value them.[1]

While I was with them in the world, I kept them in thy name: those that thou gavest me I have kept, and none of them is lost, but the son of perdition; that the scripture might be fulfilled.

John 17:12

4. Because people are more valuable than cars.

See people as being worth more to you than objects and projects. Jesus saw His followers as gifts from God. "I have manifested thy name unto the men which thou gavest me out of the world: thine they were, and thou gavest them me; and they have kept thy word" (John 17:6).

The Nation That Does Not Value Its Citizens.

I know a country that does not value its doctors and that is why most of them have left that country. I know a country that does not value its nurses and that is why many of them have left, and are still leaving to seek greener pastures elsewhere. I know a country that does not value its leaders and that is why almost every one of her former presidents is dead. I know a country that does not value its churches and that is why the government can attack the church.

If a country places more value on athletes and beauty queens than professionals and nation-builders, do you think that these professionals and nation-builders will be attracted to the nation?

The Church That Values Its Members

If you are a leader of a church you must value the different types of people that are in your congregation. If you place value on them, then you will attract more of their kind and your church will grow. Leadership is the art of valuing people that are given to you. Be like Jesus and see your followers as gifts from above.[2]

Chapter 18

Spend Any Amount of Money and Time to Get a Book

Eight Reasons Why a Leader Loves Books

1. **He knows that the information in a book may make the difference for his life's work.**

That is why a leader is prepared to pay any amount of money for a book.

2. **Reading a book puts you in direct contact with the author of the book.**

Authors are usually great men who have a lot to share. A leader knows that he may not have the opportunity to meet with certain people, so he makes use of the books they have written.

3. **A leader knows that authors are workers and researchers for him.**

4. **A leader knows that many years of experience can be transmitted through one book.**

5. **A leader knows that a book is a patient teacher.**

6. **A leader knows that he can catch an anointing from a book.**

7. **A leader knows that if you can't read you can't lead.**

8. **The greatest leaders of all time were readers.**

Biblical examples of this were Paul and Daniel. Daniel the prophet was a leader and he was an avid reader. Daniel was somebody who read Jeremiah's books.

> **In the first year of his reign I Daniel understood by books the number of the years, whereof the word of the Lord came to Jeremiah the prophet, that he would accomplish seventy years in the desolations of Jerusalem.**
>
> **Daniel 9:2**

An avid reader worth emulating was Paul. Paul sent for his books and his parchments. They obviously were very important to him.

> **The cloke that I left at Troas with Carpus, when thou comest, bring with thee, and the books, but especially the parchments.**
>
> **2 Timothy 4:13**

Reading is one of the most essential habits of every leader. If you do not read, please do not try to lead anyone. Reading is essential for leadership.

Ten Reasons Why Every Leader Must Be a Reader

1.	Read for intellectual growth.

You will develop your mind greatly as you read. Many minds need some more development.

2.	Read for spiritual growth.

As you read, you will find out that your spirit is affected greatly by the written Word of God. You must have communion with other great leaders through their books.

3.	Read to develop a preaching and teaching style.

You will definitely pick up some tips as you read from the messages of great men.

4.	Read to improve your language.

Whether you speak English or French, reading always improves your language. The best way to learn the English language is to read English books. If you want to improve your vocabulary, please start reading now!

5.	Read to have fellowship with great minds and great people.

Reading is a form of private interaction between yourself and another person. You can receive an anointing as you read a book.

6.	Read in order to learn how to write.

You may write a book one day. You will have to write letters to people. Learn how to write by reading.

7. Read to acquire new information.

Most people think that acquiring new information is the only reason why you should read a book. But this is only one of many reasons why you should be a reader. Ignorance is one of the greatest enemies of mankind. If you do not read, your ignorance is self-inflicted and inexcusable.[1]

8. Read to develop your leadership abilities.

Anyone who spends more money on books than on food and clothes is destined for leadership.

9. Read because a person who does not read is no better than a person who cannot read.

10. Read so that you will be in the top twenty per cent of society.

Do you know that the top twenty percent of every society buys all books? Join the top twenty percent of society today and be a winner and a leader.

Daniel Webster (1782-1852), a famous statesman and prominent lawyer once said,

"If religious books are not widely circulated among the masses in this country and the people do not become religious, I do not know what is to become of us as a nation. And the thought is one to cause solemn reflection on the part of every patriot and Christian. If the truth be not diffused, error will be; if God and His Word are not known and received, the devil and his works will gain the ascendancy; if the evangelical volume does not reach every hamlet, the pages of corrupt and licentious literature will."

Chapter 19

See Ahead! Prepare for the Future!

A prudent man foreseeth the evil, and hideth himself: but the simple pass on, and are punished.

Proverbs 22:3

A leader is someone who sees ahead. A leader is someone who has the future in mind. The leader can see the evil ahead. The leader can see growth and expansion ahead.

Three Things a Leader Should See Coming

1.   See the growth ahead.

A true leader knows that the population is going to grow. This means that potential souls are going to increase. This also means that we are going to need larger buildings and facilities. We will also need more workers. Build with the future in mind. Train people with the future in mind. Jesus predicted that His church would grow. He could see it coming!

> **And I say also unto thee, That thou art Peter, and upon this rock I will build my church; and the gates of hell shall not prevail against it.**
>
> **Matthew 16:18**

Ghana's first president saw many years ahead and built a huge hydroelectric dam for the nation. This dam produced electricity many times in excess of the needs of little Ghana. He was seeing ahead. Open your eyes and see ahead. Know that things will get better as the years go by.

2. See the evils ahead.

There are some evils that will come whether you want them to or not. Jesus promised that temptations would come.

> **Woe unto the world because of offences! for it must needs be that offences come; but woe to that man by whom the offence cometh!**
>
> **Matthew 18:7**

Betrayal will come as the years go by. Temptations will come. Satanic attacks will come. Know that good times and bad times are sure to come. The marriage vows say: "For better or for worse, in prosperity and in adversity". A real leader can virtually predict the ways things will go. Ask God for wisdom to see ahead. By wisdom, you can predict the future.[1]

3. See the changes ahead.

The Lord directed me to plant churches in different parts of my city years ahead. I realized that the city was expanding. It could take people more than two hours to move from one end of the city to the other. I felt that many of the people who lived far away would soon stop coming to church. So I began what I call the *Metropolitan Churches*. That was one of the most strategic moves I ever made. I have retained many of the people God gave me by establishing almost a hundred churches in the city.

Businessmen need to see ahead. Some of you are engaged in businesses that will soon be unprofitable. I have often advised businessmen to diversify because I could see a change coming which would make their current line of business obsolete. I have watched as people who owned great businesses deteriorated until there was nothing left. A leader is someone who sees ahead.[2]

Chapter 20

Always Learn New Things

Better is a poor and a wise child than an old and foolish king, who will no more be admonished.

Ecclesiastes 4:13

How can I stop learning new things? If what you know now is all that you will ever know, then I pity you. A true leader is a true learner. I learn so many new things every year that I get amazed. That is why the Bible teaches that to the making of many books there is no end.

Many people feel that they know everything. This is unfortunate! No true leader thinks like that. I sometimes listen to pastors criticizing other ministers and I marvel. I just listen quietly in amazement. Those they were criticizing were people I learnt great truths from. No wonder people are not promoted. I have realized that I can learn things from people in my own city. I can learn things from spiritual leaders as well as secular leaders.[1]

Do you consider yourself a leader? Then decide to never stop learning. What I want you to understand is that learning does not only take place by reading books. You can learn a lot from the things around you. You can learn a lot from the people that you see everyday. You can learn a lot from some fellow ministers. You can learn a lot from rival companies and businesses. Never stop learning new things![2]

Chapter 21

Know Your Strengths and Flow in Them!

No one was created "jack of all trades". I have tried almost every field of ministry. I realize that I can do well in many areas. I play musical instruments quite well. I think that I am not bad as a singer. I am good at leading worship. I am absolutely thrilled by evangelism. Prophecy and the prophetic ministry intrigue me. I pastor churches and train leaders. I have founded many things in my short life. But which of these is my real calling? I recently asked the Lord, "What do you want me to do?" The Lord made it clear to me that I was called to stand in the office of a teacher.

There are many things that I like to do, but I intend to stay with what God called me to do. A true leader knows where his strength lies. A leader can do many good things. *When you discover your strengths, flow in them and become a great leader.*[1]

Many people live and die without developing their strengths in ministry. Do not be a pastor because everyone is pastoring a church. Do not be a prophet because that is the latest fad in town.

I started my ministry as a lay person. Most of my workers are lay people. One of my strengths is the lay ministry. If I had followed what everyone else was doing, I would have destroyed my special ministry. You may be influenced by many people but make sure you do what God has called you to do.

Stay in the area which makes you unique. Develop it and become strong. I know many businessmen who jump from one thing to another without developing their strengths. By the time they have discovered the pitfalls and loopholes in one area of business, they are jumping into the next. They think the next business is going to bring a quick return. *There is no such thing as a quick fix.*

Most people who become millionaires are people who decided early in life what they were going to do and stayed with it. *Successful people are often people who have been doing the same thing for a long time.* Hopping around from country to country will not help you to prosper. Decide where you want to live and stay there until you become strong!

The Apostle Paul fought a good fight and ran *his* race. It is time for you to run *your* race.

> **I have fought a good fight, I have finished my course, I have kept the faith...**
>
> **2 Timothy 4:7**

Forget about somebody else's race. What does God have in store for you? What is your course? Is it the course of business? Then do not stray into politics! What is your course? Is it the course of ministry? Then do not stray into politics! Many ministers shorten their lives by doing things that they were not supposed to do. Are you a leader? Then stay on course and then everyone will see the gift of God upon your life. You will become a respected leader.[2]

Chapter 22

Be Ready for a Long Fight!

I have fought a good fight, I have finished my course, I have kept the faith:

2 Timothy 4:7

Leadership is one long fight. Paul said that he had fought a good fight. His whole life was full of fighting. I remember a conversation I had with a pastor. He told me what his wife had asked him the day before.

I asked, "What did she say?"

He said his wife asked him, "You at all, when will you have peace?"

His wife was wondering when the fight would be over!

Dear Christian friend, if you consider yourself to be a leader, get ready for one long fight! If you are not fighting the devil, you will be fighting demons. If you are not fighting demons, many unbelievers will fight you. If you are not fighting unbelievers, you will be fighting Christians who hate you.[1]

Do you call yourself a leader? Brace yourself for a long fight! It's a good fight. The fight for eternal crowns and the fight to hear Him say, "Well done, good and faithful servant."

I have fought a good fight, I have finished my course, I have kept the faith:

2 Timothy 4:7

Chapter 23

Count Your Pennies!

When they were filled, he said unto his disciples, Gather up the fragments that remain, that nothing be lost.

John 6:12

A frugal person is someone who counts his pennies. Every leader is going to need a lot of money to help him fulfil his vision. How is this money going to come? By being frugal! Years ago I wrote a book on frugality. It was something that I had taught in my church. I believed that it was a key that had helped me greatly in ministry.

I recently read a book on millionaires in America. I was surprised to find out that a study on millionaires had shown that the most common characteristic of wealthy people was frugality. I read this book many years after I had taught and written on frugality. You see, the principles are the same. A frugal person is someone who counts his pennies.

There is no limitless amount of money sitting anywhere. Many rich people are cash-strapped. Very few people have anything to spare. Years ago, when our church began a building project we asked a multi-millionaire to help us with some money. Someone even offered a building as security for a loan. But the millionaire was not moved by our request. He was not even moved by the offer of the building as security. No one helped us. The Spirit of God spoke to me and said, "You will accomplish this vision if you count your pennies." True to His word, we counted our pennies and we accomplished the vision.

Neither a wasteful person nor an extravagant person can accomplish much. Are you concerned about impressing people? Then you are not a good leader. Are you concerned about showing off expensive things? Then you are not a leader. A leader knows that in order to get to his goal he is going to have to count his pennies.

Why did Jesus ask the disciples to gather the crumbs? Was he trying to humiliate the disciples? Was he trying to keep the environment clean? No, he said very clearly that he was preventing losses. "When they were filled, he said unto his disciples, Gather up the fragments that remain, that nothing be lost" (John 6:12).[1]

The best way to become rich is to minimize your losses. If you are the leader of a company, your duty is to minimize your losses and prevent stealing. If you can do these two things, your company will prosper naturally. If you are a political leader, aim at reducing corruption. If the money stolen from African nations were to be recovered, we would no longer need loans from the IMF or the World Bank![2]

Chapter 24

Tell the Truth

And ye shall know the truth, and the truth shall make you free.

John 8:32

The very nature of leadership is truth. The truth will tell you where you are and where you are not! The truth will also tell you where to go. There are many pastors who need to start telling the truth about the size of their congregations. It is time to stop making wild guesses about the number of people in your church. When you realize the actual number of souls that you are ministering to, you will be motivated to work harder.

One day, I asked my data officer to tell me how many people were in church. When he gave me the figure, I was depressed for at least one week. But I realized that in spite of what I had achieved, I had a long way to go. If you cannot tell yourself the truth, you cannot be a good leader.[1]

It is unfortunate that there are many businesses that do not make any profit at all but are still operating! When they add up the real costs of operations, they realize that they are actually running at a loss. The wisest thing to do is to shut down the business or lay off some workers. That is true leadership.

Are you a leader? Do you want to know the truth? Do you tell yourself the truth?

Then said one unto him, Lord, are there few that be saved?...

Luke 13:23

Jesus answered and told him there is a narrow gate and few people are entering through that gate.

Chapter 25

Don't Lose Your Focus

Many people do not know that great achievers are people who have focused and concentrated on one thing for a long time. Concentration is the key to great achievement. Do you consider yourself a leader? You must learn the art of concentration. Concentrate on your vision. Concentrate on your church. Concentrate on your work and you will have great results.

Often when I begin to pray, I switch off all phones. This helps me to concentrate on the Lord. When I was in the university, I had the opportunity to join several Christian groups. I decided to flow with a particular ministry. I realized that I could not divide my time amongst the many Christian ministries on campus. By the time I left the university a new group had been formed which exists up until today.

When you concentrate on one thing, people will accuse you of being proud or unfriendly. They will say that you are inward-looking and unpatriotic. They will say that you are anti-social. Take no notice of them. Concentrate on what you are doing. Wisdom is justified of her children. Never forget that concentration brings growth and keeps you from strife. When Jesus went away he left clear instructions about what the Church was supposed to do.

Who then is a faithful and wise servant, whom his lord hath made ruler over his household, to give them meat in due season? Blessed is that servant, whom his lord when he cometh shall find so doing. Verily I say unto you, That he shall make him ruler over all his goods. But and if that evil servant shall say in his heart, My lord delayeth his coming; And shall begin to smite his fellowservants, and to eat and drink with the drunken; The lord of that servant shall come in a day when he looketh not for him, and in an hour that he is not aware of, And shall cut him asunder, and appoint him his portion with the hypocrites: there shall be weeping and gnashing of teeth.

Matthew 24:45-51

Not long after His departure, the Church had deviated into all sorts of things that were not instructed by Christ. In the name of good works and being socially acceptable, the Church has divided its attention into four main areas: health, education, relief services and Christian teaching. It is no wonder that other religions are said to be growing at a faster rate than Christianity. If the Church were to concentrate on their God-given goal, they would be called all sorts of names.

Some of my pastors and churches have come under criticism because we tend to concentrate on what we are doing. Statistics have proved, to the surprise of many, that excessive cooperation between churches does not lead to growth in the Body of Christ. This comes as a surprise to the proponents of unity in the Body. Remember that *unity* is different from *union*. What people often call unity is actually the physical union of congregations.

A leader understands the essence of concentrating on one thing until he has achieved it. A leader can distinguish between relevant and irrelevant issues. I have realized that the faster I work the more energy I have. Slow work makes you tired. I apply the principle of urgency and concentration to everything I do. I bring all my forces to bear until I conquer it. The more you suspend your projects for other things, the more depressed and unhappy and discouraged you will be.

Are you a leader? Decide to concentrate on one thing at a time. Put away useless socializing, empty chatting and excessive television watching. Concentration will bring you great success. Paul did it and so can you![1]

> **...but this one thing I do, forgetting those things which are behind, and reaching forth unto those things which are before...**
>
> **Philippians 3:13**

Chapter 26

Recognize the Small Beginnings of a Great Career

Many great careers begin in a small way. Unfortunately, many do not recognize the beginnings of greatness.

Though thy beginning was small, yet thy latter end should greatly increase.

Job 8:7

For who hath despised the day of small things? for they shall rejoice, and shall see the plummet in the hand of Zerubbabel with those seven; they are the eyes of the Lord, which run to and fro through the whole earth.

Zechariah 4:10

The Bible teaches us not to despise small beginnings. Countless Christians throw away great careers in the ministry because they cannot recognize the beginnings of a great career.

Never forget this! The greatest careers begin in the smallest ways.[1] A tiny mustard seed brings a mighty tree forth. There is no relationship between the size of the mustard seed and the size of the tree.

Six People Who Recognized the Small Beginning of a Great Career

1. Elisha began his career as a prophet by washing the hands of Elijah.

   But Jehoshaphat said, Is there not here a prophet of the Lord, that we may enquire of the Lord by him? And one of the king of Israel's servants answered and said, Here is Elisha the son of Shaphat, which poured water on the hands of Elijah.

   2 Kings 3:11

2. The great army general Joshua began his career as a servant to an old prophet.

   And Moses rose up, and his minister Joshua: and Moses went up into the mount of God.

   Exodus 24:13

3. King David began his career by playing instruments in the king's palace.

   And Saul sent to Jesse, saying, Let David, I pray thee, stand before me; for he hath found favour in my sight. And it came to pass, when the evil spirit from

God was upon Saul, that David took an harp, and played with his hand: so Saul was refreshed, and was well, and the evil spirit departed from him.

1 Samuel 16:22,23

4. Aaron began his career by holding up the hands of Moses.

But Moses' hands were heavy; and they took a stone, and put it under him, and he sat thereon; and Aaron and Hur stayed up his hands, the one on the one side, and the other on the other side; and his hands were steady until the going down of the sun.

Exodus 17:12

5. Ruth began her career by helping an elderly frustrated widow.

And Ruth said, Intreat me not to leave thee, or to return from following after thee: for whither thou goest, I will go; and where thou lodgest, I will lodge: thy people shall be my people, and thy God my God: Where thou diest, will I die, and there will I be buried: the LORD do so to me, and more also, if ought but death part thee and me.

Ruth 1:16,17

6. Jesus began his career as a carpenter.

Is not this the carpenter, the son of Mary, the brother of James, and Joses, and of Juda, and Simon? and are not his sisters here with us? And they were offended at him.

Mark 6:3

Chapter 27

Treat People as Equals but Make the Differences Clear

A good leader must strive to let people feel important. The reality is that you are the leader, so you are different.

Five Ways to Make Everyone around You Feel Important

1. **Mingle with all kinds of people.**

Jesus mingled with thieves (two thieves at the cross), tax collectors (Matthew), fishermen (Peter), foreigners (the Syro-Phoenician woman), demonised people (Mary Magdalene), madmen (the madman of Gadara), priests (Nicodemus) and noblemen (Joseph of Arimathea). There was no strata of society where Jesus did not interact freely. Do not restrict yourself to one group of the society.

2. **Do not call or describe your staff and subordinates as servants.**

> **Henceforth I call you not servants; for the servant knoweth not what his lord doeth: but I have called you friends; for all things that I have heard of my Father I have made known unto you.**
>
> **John 15:15**

Nobody likes to be called a servant even if that is the case. Jesus specifically said that he did not call his disciples servants.

3. **Describe your staff, subordinates and junior pastors as your friends.**

> **Ye are my friends, if ye do whatsoever I command you.**
>
> **John 15:14**

I enjoy the friendship of the people who work for me. If I did not have them I would be very lonely.[1]

4. **Describe the people who work for you as your family.**

> **But he answered and said unto him that told him, Who is my mother? and who are my brethren? And he stretched forth his hand toward his disciples, and said, Behold my mother and my brethren! For whosoever shall do the will of my Father which is in heaven, the same is my brother, and sister, and mother.**
>
> **Matthew 12:48-50**

This is one thing I have done all my life. I have never seen my pastors or workers as employees but as family. I actually hate being called *"boss"*. Create a family spirit in your organization. It is a hundred times better than a formal, stiff organization.[2] Let their family and personal problems be your personal problems!

5.   **Tell your pastors or juniors about yourself and your plans.**

> **…but I have called you friends; for all things that I have heard of my Father I have made known unto you.**
>
> **John 15:15b**

This is one thing that draws people close.

Six Ways to Make the Differences Clear

1.   Teach them.

Jesus taught his disciples all the time. When you teach someone you establish the authority to lead them. The authority to lead is found in the ability to feed.[3]

2.   Send them.

Jesus sent his disciples to buy food.

> **(For his disciples were gone away unto the city to buy meat).**
>
> **John 4:8**

Every time you send someone you establish the chain of command. You emphasize the chain of command that exists within the structure.[4]

104

3.   Bless them.

Pray for your followers and bless them. There is a faithful saying that the lesser is blessed of the greater.[5]

And without all contradiction the less is blessed of the better.

Hebrews 7:7

4.   Say who you are.

Jesus spoke of himself confidently. He said that he was the way, the truth and the life. He said that he was the door. He said he was the good shepherd. There are times I have had to declare that I am the leader and founder of my little church. It is important for people to know that you know who you are.[6]

5.   Don't be afraid of being different.

Jesus rode on a donkey whilst all his disciples walked. Garments were strewn on the floor for him to walk on.

And brought the ass, and the colt, and put on them their clothes, and they set him thereon. And a very great multitude spread their garments in the way; others cut down branches from the trees, and strawed them in the way.

Matthew 21:7,8

Accept privileges that are exclusively yours. When you refuse to accept your privileges, you create anomalies and disorder. The Bible calls this an evil and an error (mistake) that emanates from the ruler.

There is an evil which I have seen under the sun, as an error which proceedeth from the ruler: Folly is set in great dignity, and the rich sit in low place. I have seen servants upon horses, and princes walking as servants upon the earth.

Ecclesiastes 10:5-7

6. Allow yourself to be honoured.

Jesus allowed himself to be honoured by Mary. He permitted the expensive gift that was poured on his feet.

Then took Mary a pound of ointment of spikenard, very costly, and anointed the feet of Jesus, and wiped his feet with her hair: and the house was filled with the odour of the ointment.

John 12:3

Chapter 28

Predict the Future in a General Way

Behold, the hour cometh, yea, is now come, that ye shall be scattered, every man to his own, and shall leave me alone: and yet I am not alone, because the Father is with me. These things I have spoken unto you, that in me ye might have peace. In the world ye shall have tribulation: but be of good cheer; I have overcome the world.

John 16:32,33

    A leader is someone who sees ahead. Generally speaking, a good leader is able to predict what will happen in the future. Jesus said that the disciples would experience persecution. And they certainly did! You don't need to be a special prophet to know that the members of a new group will experience some trouble.[1]

Using *a combination of history, common sense, the Word of God and the Spirit of God, every leader can generally predict the way things will go.* The Bible teaches us that there is nothing new under the sun. The Bible says explicitly that what is going to happen is only what has happened already.[2]

The thing that hath been, it is that which shall be; and that which is done is that which shall be done: and there is no new thing under the sun.

Ecclesiastes 1:9

A good manager should be able to predict from the general trend of affairs that certain businesses are going to go out of date in the near future. Certain politicians must see that the course on which they are walking will only end in disaster. Ministers of the gospel must be able to predict the future in a general way. I am not talking about predicting events and dates. I am talking about using common sense!

A few years ago, I realized that members of my congregation were moving to different parts of the city. I also realized that the city was becoming very large. I predicted that many of the members who were living far away would stop coming to church because of the distance. I could predict it because I could predict human behaviour.

As a leader, I notice my people don't come to church when it rains. I notice how they come one week and they don't come the next. It is my duty to see that when it is very inconvenient the sheep will no longer follow. That is why I began metropolitan churches in the city of Accra.

Today, we have over fifty-five metropolitan churches in the city of Accra alone. We have thousands of members in these citywide churches. If I had not acted on my observation and predicted, I would have lost thousands of members. I am not talking about predicting when Jesus will return. I am talking about predicting the obvious and seeing ahead as a wise leader.

Chapter 29

Do Not Allow Yourself to Be Poisoned by Bitterness

A priest in the Old Testament was not supposed to have boils.

> **Speak unto Aaron, saying, Whosoever he be of thy seed in their generations that hath any blemish, let him not approach to offer the bread of his God. For whatsoever man he be that hath a blemish, he shall not approach: a blind man, or a lame, or he that hath a flat nose, or any thing superfluous, Or a man that is brokenfooted, or brokenhanded, Or crookbackt, or a dwarf, or that hath a blemish in his eye, or be scurvy, or scabbed, or hath his stones broken; No man that hath a blemish of the seed of Aaron the priest shall come nigh to offer the offerings of the**

Lord made by fire: he hath a blemish; he shall not come nigh to offer the bread of his God. He shall eat the bread of his God, both of the most holy, and of the holy. Only he shall not go in unto the vail, nor come nigh unto the altar, because he hath a blemish; that he profane not my sanctuaries: for I the Lord do sanctify them. And Moses told it unto Aaron, and to his sons, and unto all the children of Israel.

Leviticus 21:17-24

Boils represent unhealed wounds. Leadership is accompanied by wounds, offences and pain. You cannot allow the wounds of leadership to discolour your attitude.[1]

Four Dangers of Bitterness in a Leader

1.   A bitter leader can begin to mistrust God.

There are many unexplained events in the life of a Christian leader. Even in secular politics the good often do not win. The bad and ugly may win elections whilst the good lose out.

I remember when two of my young pastors died suddenly within three weeks of each other. One was twenty-seven years old and the other was thirty-eight years old. What possible explanation was there to such an event? As I comforted the wives of these two pastors I wondered to myself, "As a messenger of God what explanation could I give to a wife who had been married for only seven months?"

What explanation could the church give when James, the brother of John, was killed by Herod? Didn't the early church need the contribution of James to build a solid foundation for the church? Why did God allow James, the brother of John, to be taken away at such a time? Was soul winning not important? Was church planting not important? Was there not a need for more labourers? How could God allow such a thing?

In spite of the inexplicable occurrences of this life, a leader must continue to trust.

2. A bitter leader can begin to hate the people he leads.

As human beings manifest their nature of betrayal, ungratefulness and forgetfulness, a leader can gradually become bitter towards the flock. I have experienced many painful things. I have learnt that I *must* forgive and move on. Without a sweet spirit I will not be pleasing to God. Every bitter experience is a test of my ability to walk in love. I always pray that I will pass these tests.[2]

3. A bitter leader can hate his contemporaries and colleagues in ministry.

Unfortunately, it is your contemporaries in leadership who seem to wish you ill more than anyone else. Even unbelievers do not have some of the hateful attitudes that contemporaries and colleagues seem to have! God has given us all of these so that we may truly walk in love towards all men. If you fail to walk in love, your ministry will amount to nothing in the presence of God.

And though I have the gift of prophecy, and understand all mysteries, and all knowledge; and though I have all faith, so that I could remove mountains, and have not charity, I am nothing.

1 Corinthians 13:2

4. A bitter leader will have a distorted message.

Bitterness is described in Hebrews as a root which defiles many people. It is akin to poison in your drinking water. One of the things that bitterness poisons is your message. A bitter person has a discoloured and distorted message. Do not let your pain prevent you from ministering God's love to people.

Chapter 30

Change People's Minds

The art of changing people's minds is a very important skill that you must develop if you call yourself a leader. The art of persuasion is a basic art of leadership. When somebody has an opinion about something and you are able to change that opinion, then you are operating as a leader.

Thomas' opinion was that the resurrection was not real. Jesus worked on that and in the end Thomas believed in the resurrection. Do you care whether people believe in Heaven or Hell? If you do not care about what opinions people hold, you cannot be a leader. Perhaps, people have bad impressions about men of God. A leader can work on those people's minds until they are thinking aright!

The pastor often gets people to change their minds about life. His job is to make them love God and serve Him. Perhaps they were serving money, but through the ministry of a true pastor (leader) they believe that service to God is more important than anything else.[1]

Seven Ways to Make People Change Their Minds

1. **Teach them the Word of God.**

   And be not conformed to this world: but be ye transformed by the renewing of your mind, that ye may prove what is that good, and acceptable, and perfect, will of God.

   Romans 12:2

   This Scripture teaches that we will be changed or transformed when our minds have been renewed. The Word of God is the best tool for making people change their mind. There is power in the Word of God that is why Paul said, "I am not ashamed of the gospel of Jesus Christ for *it is the power of God..."*

2. **Make them go to church.**

   Church provides a regular mind-changing forum for anyone. Show me your church and I'll show you the way you think.

3. **Make them have certain friends.**

   Your company influences you more than your church. This is because you are with your friends for several hours a week whilst you may be in church for just a couple of hours a week. Like the saying goes, "Show me your friend, and I'll show you your character".

   Be not deceived: evil communications corrupt good manners.

   1 Corinthians 15:33

4. Introduce them to successful people who have the kind of mind you want them to have.

This is the secret of the Full Gospel Businessmen Fellowship International. They introduce successful Christian businessmen to sinners and show them that it is possible to be a successful businessman. Through this method many people are saved (In other words, change their minds).[2]

5. Share your own testimony.

A personal testimony is always a powerful instrument to change the mind. Paul used this method on King Agrippa. The entire chapter of Acts 26 describes Paul sharing his testimony to the king. At the end of this powerful personal testimony King Agrippa said,

> **...Paul, almost thou persuadest me to be a Christian.**
>
> **Acts 26:28**

6. Pray for them.

The state of the mind is a very spiritual thing. That is why Paul prayed that the Ephesians would be given a Spirit of revelation and wisdom. You may hear preaching and teaching but without revelation change never comes.

> **That the God of our Lord Jesus Christ, the Father of glory, may give unto you the spirit of wisdom and revelation in the knowledge of him:**
>
> **Ephesians 1:17**

7. Allow them to have certain experiences.

No matter what you say or preach, some people never change their minds. For such people the school of experience (and hard knocks!) may be the only teacher they will listen to. Allowing people to experience certain things is sometimes the only way to make their minds work in the right way. Sometimes I allow pastors to go through certain experiences. For instance, when people have the experience of starting a church, they often appreciate many of the things I teach.

I once had a pastor who did not appreciate the way I was handling another disloyal assistant. He thought I was not walking in love towards this rebellious fellow. No matter how much I explained the issues to this pastor, he still felt I was doing the wrong thing. In the end, I prayed that God would give him his own share of rebellious assistants. God really answered that prayer and he had one experience after another.

One day, he called me on the phone and told me that after having his own experience with disloyal people, he felt that I had been too lenient and kind with my rebellious pastor. I smiled to myself because I remembered his former attitude about that issue. This pastor's mind had really changed and now he felt that I was too loving to the rebel.

This is a very scriptural method to change people's minds. You will have to use it because there are many things that can only be learned by experience. The Father even trained Jesus by this method. The Bible says Jesus learned obedience through the things he experienced.

Though he were a Son, yet learned he obedience by the things which he suffered;

Hebrews 5:8

A leader is someone who uses all means at his disposal to make people change their minds. Have you been able to make someone change his mind about something?[3]

But Thomas, one of the twelve, called Didymus, was not with them when Jesus came. The other disciples therefore said unto him, We have seen the Lord. But he said unto them, Except I shall see in his hands the print of the nails, and put my finger into the print of the nails, and thrust my hand into his side, I will not believe. And after eight days again his disciples were within, and Thomas with them: then came Jesus, the doors being shut, and stood in the midst, and said, Peace be unto you. Then saith he to Thomas, Reach hither thy finger, and behold my hands; and reach hither thy hand, and thrust it into my side: and be not faithless, but believing. And Thomas answered and said unto him, My Lord and my God. Jesus saith unto him, Thomas, because thou hast seen me, thou hast believed: blessed are they that have not seen, and yet have believed.

John 20:24-29

Chapter 31

Know a Little about Everything That Goes on

The best leaders are people who know something about everything. A leader must know a little about everything. This is why many organizations train their leaders by taking them to every department.[1]

I know something about law, medicine, accounting, management, administration and carpentry. I know a bit about construction. I have learnt a lot about engineering and architecture. I also know a bit about electronics, music equipment, computers, and the list goes on. I engage in debates with all the professionals I deal with. They know that I know something about their field. They know that I cannot be pushed around like an ignoramus.

You will never be a good leader if you do not have an idea about what goes on. The fact that you are a layperson in a certain field means that you should read up and educate yourself.[2]

When a decision is taken in the field of accounting under your banner, you are responsible. That is why it is important to know a bit about everything. Never say, "Oh, that is medicine. I don't know, I don't care, and I don't want to know!" There is a lot that you can know and must know![3]

Chapter 32

Be a Leader with Emotion

People are attracted to people who show emotion. Don't be afraid of showing emotion. People will gather around you and listen to what you have to say because you are real. There is no need to live in pretence because you are a leader. Everyone born on this Earth laughs, cries, gets angry and becomes happy. There are highs and lows in everyone's life.

To be a leader you must exhibit reality. We live in a real world with lots of problems. A leader is a real human being with real emotions. A leader will experience all the emotions his followers feel. Most people don't know what to do with their emotions. If they find someone who is successful in spite of the real emotions he feels, they would like to relate with him.[1]

Eight Reasons Why People Who Show Emotion Are Attractive

1. People who do not show emotion are often boring and are not interesting to be with.

2. People who do not show emotion kill the atmosphere around them.

There is a lot of tension when you sit with a strict and unsmiling individual who makes no contribution or comment about the conversation going on.

3. Emotionless men and women are often strict, stern, authoritarian, exacting and rigorous.

4. Emotionless people may be phoney and artificial.

People simply do not want to deal with a pretender.

5. People feel that if someone reveals his true emotions, the things he says will also be true.

6. A show of emotion stirs up the emotions of others.

When people are stirred up emotionally, they become more committed.

7. People love to listen to a preacher who ministers varied emotions of joy, anger, sadness and suspense.[2]

8. Jesus, our great example-setter, showed emotion on many occasions.

Five Examples of Jesus Showing Emotion

1. Jesus was excited when he saw the man with great faith.

When Jesus heard these things, he marvelled at him, and turned him about, and said unto the people that followed him, I say unto you, I have not found so great faith, no, not in Israel.

Luke 7:9

2. Jesus wept over cities.

And when he was come near, he beheld the city, and wept over it,

Luke 19:41

3. Jesus was moved with compassion for lost and helpless people.

But when he saw the multitudes, he was moved with compassion on them, because they fainted, and were scattered abroad, as sheep having no shepherd. Then saith he unto his disciples, The harvest truly is plenteous, but the labourers are few;

Matthew 9:36,37

4. Jesus was angry with hypocrites.

And the Jews' passover was at hand, and Jesus went up to Jerusalem, And found in the temple those that sold oxen and sheep and doves, and the changers of money sitting: And when he had made a scourge of small cords, he drove them all out of the temple, and the sheep, and the oxen; and poured out the changers' money, and overthrew the tables;

John 2:13-15

5. Jesus wept over individuals.

Jesus WEPT. Then said the Jews, Behold how he loved him!

John 11:35,36

Chapter 33

Take Your Privileges at the Right Time and for the Right Reason

There is an evil which I have seen under the sun, as an error which proceedeth from the ruler. Folly is set in great dignity, and the rich sit in low place. I have seen servants upon horses, and princes walking as servants upon the earth.

Ecclesiastes 10:5-7

A leader must be a humble person but he must also be confident. The Bible teaches that it is foolishness when a leader refuses to sit in the appropriate place reserved for him. When it is time to take your privileges, you had better take them or you will be considered a fool. Leadership is not only sacrifice. Leadership is not only responsibility. Leadership goes along with certain privileges and blessings.[1]

Obedience Is More Important than Sacrifice

God's call is to obedience and not to sacrifice per se. There are times when obedience will mean you have to sacrifice. If you sacrifice when God has not asked you to do so, you will separate yourself from God. Do not forget how Saul was separated from God because he sacrificed things that God had not asked him to.[2]

And Samuel said, Hath the Lord as great delight in burnt offerings and sacrifices, as in obeying the voice of the Lord? Behold, to obey is better than sacrifice, and to hearken than the fat of rams. For rebellion is as the sin of witchcraft, and stubbornness is as iniquity and idolatry. Because thou hast rejected the word of the Lord, he hath also rejected thee from being king.

1 Samuel 15:22,23

When Princes Must Sit on Horses

There is a time when princes must sit on horses and servants must walk upon the earth. "I have seen servants upon horses, and princes walking as servants upon the earth" (Ecclesiastes 10:7). Do not be shy to earn money for all the hard work you put in. I feel sorry for ministers of the gospel who are treated like beggars who don't deserve anything. I know of churches where the pastors are not given money, but all of their domestic needs are taken care of. Church members come to inspect whether there is enough soap and toilet paper in the house. How pathetic! Do the pastors not have enough common sense to buy their own toilet paper?

The Error

I have watched church after church enter into crisis because a car was being bought for the pastor. Special funds were raised and the pastor's car became a controversial church matter. When people work at other institutions, is the purchase of a car a special project? Is it not their due? Why are pastors treated like undeserving idlers?

I work hard as a minister of the gospel. I deserve to be paid well. The Bible teaches that they that preach the gospel must live off the gospel.

Even so hath the Lord ordained that they which preach the gospel should live of the gospel.

1 Corinthians 9:14

Sowing Without Reaping

The husbandman that laboureth must be first partaker of the fruits.

2 Timothy 2:6

I must be able to have a good car for my safety and comfort. I must be able to build a house. There is nothing wrong with that! But there is something wrong when a man sows and does not reap. Everybody knows that! A leader must know when it is time to take his place and enjoy his benefits. It is a mistake to refuse your privileges and blessings when it is your turn to have them. I didn't call it a mistake, the Bible did! The Bible calls it the error that proceedeth from a ruler!

When Princes Eat in the Morning

Some nations have had leaders who begin their rule by drinking the lifeblood of the nation. Before a nation can blink, the leaders have siphoned out everything.

I recently visited a wealthy African nation that produces large amounts of oil. Would you believe that this nation, one of the largest producers of oil in the world, had severe petrol shortages? It was amazing! There were very long queues in every city I visited. Fuel was sold only on the black market.

It was later reported that the head of state of that nation had a billion dollars in petty cash. What is a president doing with a billion dollars of petty cash? These vampires have lined their pockets whilst the masses of the nation struggle to make ends meet. Is it not ironic that a nation that supplies a significant percentage of the world's oil, suffers from fuel shortages? This is what the Bible calls "princes eating in the morning". The prince represents the leader and the morning represents the wrong time.

Woe to thee, O land, when thy king is a child, and thy princes eat in the morning! Blessed art thou, O land, when thy king is the son of nobles, and thy princes eat in due season, for strength, and not for drunkenness!

Ecclesiastes 10:16,17

Dear friend, when a nation or church has an opportunist at the helm of affairs, get ready for frustration and poverty!

In our church, we have a policy that puts the church before the pastor. What do I mean by this?

We believe the church must come before the pastor's welfare. This means that the church building is constructed and the church is given a sound footing before the pastor's benefits are considered.

When Princes Eat in Due Season

Privileges become blessings only when they come at the right time. When they come too soon, everything is destroyed. Some people buy cars that they cannot even afford to maintain. Someone once said, "Don't buy a car unless you can afford to maintain three of the same thing." Some people live in houses that they cannot afford to maintain. Why worry yourself? Why do you try to impress people? Be yourself and do not rush to possess certain privileges. As the Lord lifts you up, you will receive everything you need at the right time.

He hath made every thing beautiful in his time…

Ecclesiastes 3:11

Beauty is only beauty within the context of the "right time". Have you ever noticed that when you look at pictures taken twenty years ago, you often look odd? Why is this? Because they have been taken out of their *"time"*.

His Time Is the Right Time

That car or home will only be a real blessing when it comes at the right time. If it comes too soon, it will not be a blessing. It will cause problems for you. Everyone is happy when a married woman gets pregnant. It is a blessing to be pregnant. However, when an unmarried teenager becomes pregnant, we are not happy. Why is this? Because the pregnancy has been taken out of its context of the "right time".

Are you a leader or a hungry vampire? Wait patiently to take your privileges at the right time. Do not rush; you will only destroy yourself, your business, your church or your nation. Do not kill the hen that lays your golden eggs. Keep it alive so that it can lay golden eggs for you for many more years![3]

Chapter 34

Relate with Individuals and Relate with the Crowd

There cometh a woman of Samaria to draw water: Jesus saith unto her, Give me to drink. Then saith the woman of Samaria unto him, How is it that thou, being a Jew, askest drink of me, which am a woman of Samaria? for the Jews have no dealings with the Samaritans. Jesus answered and said unto her, Whosoever drinketh of this water shall thirst again: But whosoever drinketh of the water that I shall give him shall never thirst; but the water that I shall give him shall be in him a well of water springing up into everlasting life. The woman saith unto him, Sir, give me this water, that I thirst not, neither come hither to draw.

John 4:7,9,13-15

Jesus was somebody who handled great crowds. He had a team of pastors he was training. Jesus also had a busy schedule. But when he met the woman of Samaria, he took a little time and spoke to her as an individual. A leader is someone who knows how to relate with individuals. Jesus did not know whether this woman was rich or poor. He just treated her as a human being who needed his help.

Every human being is a complex composition of spirit, soul and body. Every human being has his fears, mistakes and successes in the background. Jesus spoke to a woman with a whole lot of problems. He was able to help her. If God has called you to be a leader, you must help *individuals* with needs. Do not treat a human being as a mere number. Anyone who treats his members as "just one of the masses" will soon discover that he loses their support.

Jesus started his ministry fully aware that he was going to relate with poor people. He was going to minister to the broken-hearted and to people that were bound. Dear leader, remember that each individual needs special attention.

And Jesus said, Make the men sit down. Now there was much grass in the place. So the men sat down, in number about five thousand.

John 6:10

Jesus knew how to handle large groups of people as well as individuals. When you are handling a crowd, you must know how to behave. You must dress properly and speak wisely. Many people in the crowd want to know what the truth is. A good leader transmits appropriate information to the crowd.[1]

Keys for Relating with the Crowd

1.   Give them accurate and timely information.

Do not tell them that you will raise their salaries when you will not.

2.   Do not make useless promises.

People get tired of vain promises.

3.   Announce as much good news as you can.

If a new branch has started, announce it. If a miracle has taken place, tell the people. The people will not know until you tell them. Good news creates a good feeling in the crowd. Every wise government spends a lot of money informing the general population about what they want them to know. That is how they are able to keep the masses in check. Good news encourages everyone. That is how to control the crowds. Bad news discourages the followers.[2]

4.   Do not speak down at the people.

People like to feel respected. Even the tone of your voice can indicate whether you respect the people or not! As you sow love and respect you will reap admiration and many "following" hearts.

Chapter 35

Overcome the Disadvantages of Youthfulness and Inexperience by Studying History

The most important subject for a young leader is history. A young person does not have the benefit of experience. He has to tap into the experiences of others. His only chance of avoiding certain mistakes is to study those who went before him.

The thing that hath been, it is that which shall be; and that which is done is that which shall be done: and there is no new thing under the sun. Is there any thing whereof it may be said, See, this is new? it hath been already of old time, which was before us.

Ecclesiastes 1:9,10

Every good leader will learn a lot from history. History itself teaches us that most people do not learn from it. If you want to be a good leader, you must study church history and secular history.[1]

Seven Reasons Why Every Leader Must Study History

1. History is the greatest source of knowledge and wisdom, second only to the Scriptures.

2. The Scriptures themselves contain many history lessons that guide us.

3. God instructed his leaders to teach history so that people would not forget. Forgetting leads to a repetition of the same mistakes.

And these words, which I command thee this day, shall be in thine heart: And thou shalt teach them diligently unto thy children, and shalt talk of them when thou sittest in thine house, and when thou walkest by the way, and when thou liest down, and when thou risest up. And when thy son asketh thee in time to come, saying, What mean the testimonies, and the statutes, and the judgments, which the Lord our God hath commanded you? Then thou shalt say unto thy son, We were Pharaoh's bondmen in Egypt;

> **and the Lord brought us out of Egypt with a mighty hand: And the Lord shewed signs and wonders, great and sore, upon Egypt, upon Pharaoh, and upon all his household, before our eyes:**
>
> **Deuteronomy 6:6,7,20-22**

4. History repeats itself.

You are walking where others just like you, have walked. If you know what happened to them, then you will know what will happen to you. There is a proverb that states: "Those who do not know history are doomed to repeat it."

5. Because many things are programmed in cycles.

There is an in-built cyclical system of the world. The planets revolve around the sun. The moon circles around the earth. The human body has numerous biochemical and hormonal cycles within it. The Krebs cycle and the menstrual cycle are examples of these. Your life may be part of an evil cycle that is playing itself out. You can break every terrible cycle of your life and ministry by studying history.

6. A student of history can predict the future.

Your prophetic insights will be greatly enhanced as you study church history.

7. Boldness and confidence are fruits of studying history.

You can lead the way with greater confidence by using the lessons you learnt from history.

One day I was standing with an old wise man in front of my house. I told him about a crisis I had experienced in my fellowship. He smiled to himself and said something that I will never forget. He said, "The devil has just a few tricks.

And he keeps using them over and over."

He continued, "I am always surprised that the same trick works every time."

He explained, "Because people do not know what happened in the past, they keep falling for the same old tricks."

Dear friend, will you fall for the same trick that your senior brother fell for? Why don't you read about what happened yesterday? Dear politician can you not see how your predecessor ended up. It's time to glean the lessons of wisdom and knowledge from history.

> **The thing that hath been, it is that which shall be; and that which is done is that which shall be done: and there is no new thing under the sun.**
>
> **Ecclesiastes 1:9**

Chapter 36

Take Responsibility and Give Account

What you must realize is that every leader will give account for what he or she is doing. Are you ready to account to God for the sheep he gave you? Jesus kept on saying that he had lost none of the sheep except the son of perdition. Paul kept saying that he would have to give account.

Obey them that have the rule over you, and submit yourselves: for they watch for your souls, as they that must give account, that they may do it with joy, and not with grief: for that is unprofitable for you.

Hebrews 13:17

Leadership is a great responsibility. I remember years ago, I watched as several heads of state and ministers of state were executed by a firing squad. It was pathetic to see important people being humiliated and murdered. The ordinary citizen in his home received no such treatment. This was because the ordinary man had not taken up the responsibility of ruling the country. However, those who had taken up responsibility had to pay with their lives.

If you are conscious of the reality that you will account for your leadership you will discover that you will become a better leader. Always remember that the day of accountability is coming. This will make you do the right thing. I am constantly aware that I will give account for the call of God on my life. I know that I will have to account for the sheep in my churches. This is why I make great efforts to look after them.

Are you a leader? Are you constantly thinking of your day of accountability? Please do! You will be transformed into a natural and effective leader.[1]

Chapter 37

Don't Give up Your Source of Power!

Every leader derives power from something. Jesus knew that his source of power was prayer. That is why he never stopped praying. That is why he prayed so earnestly in the garden of Gethsemane.

The apostle Peter knew that his source of power was in prayer and in the Word. That is why he refused to give it up![1]

> **...It is not reason that we should leave the word of God, and serve tables. But we will give ourselves continually to prayer, and to the ministry of the word.**
>
> **Acts 6:2,4**

Every leader must know the source of his power. Many politicians know that their source of power is popular opinion. That is why they will sacrifice everything to maintain popular opinion. I have watched many politicians sacrifice their families and friends so they could have popular support.

Years ago, I spoke to a Christian who was involved in politics. He was helping our church. He did help us to a point. Then one day he told me, "Bishop, the way this matter is going I cannot help you anymore."

This was a born again, tongue-speaking Charismatic Christian. He was even a leader in his church. He continued, "If this matter goes any higher, I'm afraid I cannot support the church anymore."

I looked at him as he explained, "You know, politics is my life. If this goes against me politically, I will lose my job. And that means a lot to me."

A few weeks later, the matter escalated. This Christian politician took sides against the church and helped politicians to attack the church. This was unfortunate, but it reflected a deep truth. This man thought his power came from politics and not from God. He remained loyal to what he thought was giving him power.

Many politicians think that the secret of their power is in popular support. This makes them sacrifice their principles, morals and even their faith. A Christian leader must know that his strength comes from God. Even politicians are mistaken when they think that their strength comes from people. Ultimately, God rules in the affairs of men.

Every minister of the gospel must be aware that his strength is from the Lord and not from money or people.[2]

When a leader does not treasure his source of power, he will lose it. Samson played around with his source of power. Eventually, he lost everything.

That he told her all his heart, and said unto her, There hath not come a razor upon mine head; for I have been a Nazarite unto God from my mother's womb: if I be shaven, then my strength will go from me, and I shall become weak, and be like any other man.

Judges 16:17

Are you a leader? Find out what is the source of your strength, treasure it, protect it and do not give it up for anything!

Chapter 38

Be Decisive! It Is the Greatest Attribute of a Leader

Decisiveness is truly the greatest attribute of a leader. Many people cannot take decisions. Only real leaders face up to realities and take important decisions. *The failure to take a decision is the failure to lead.* Well-run businesses often take hard decisions to lay off employees when they realize that they have to. This type of decision is not easy and has far reaching consequences. Failure to take a decision can lead to the destruction of all that you are building.[1]

Four Reasons Why You Must Be Decisive

1. God is a decisive God.

We are supposed to be imitators of God, who is known for his ability to take far-reaching decisions.

> **Be ye therefore followers of God, as dear children;**
>
> **Ephesians 5:1**

2. All great leaders are decisive.

We are to follow the example of people who through faith and patience have accomplished great things.

> **That ye be not slothful, but followers of them who through faith and patience inherit the promises.**
>
> **Hebrews 6:12**

3. A failure to decide is a failure to lead.

Leadership is eighty per cent decision taking and twenty percent implementation. That is why the failure to decide is a failure to lead.

4. Failure to decide is the same as a decision to do nothing.

How can you follow someone who has decided to do nothing? You might as well follow a little child around the playground. That is the same as doing nothing.[2]

Ten Decisions of Jehovah

1. When the Earth was without form, void and covered with darkness, God took a decision to create Heaven and Earth.

   And the earth was without form, and void; and darkness was upon the face of the deep. And the Spirit of God moved upon the face of the waters.

   Genesis 1:2

2. When God realized that man was lonely, he took a decision to create a woman.

   And the Lord God said, It is not good that the man should be alone; I will make him an help meet for him.

   Genesis 2:18

3. When the Earth was full of wickedness, God took a decision to kill all the human beings and leave only Noah and his family alive.

   And God saw that the wickedness of man was great in the earth, and that every imagination of the thoughts of his heart was only evil continually. And it repented the Lord that he had made man on the earth, and it grieved him at his heart.

   And the Lord said, I will destroy man whom I have created from the face of the earth; both man, and beast, and the creeping thing, and the fowls of the air; for it repenteth me that I have made them.

   Genesis 6:5-7

4. When God saw Noah's sacrifice, he took a decision not to destroy all living things anymore.

And the Lord smelled a sweet savour; and the Lord said in his heart, I will not again curse the ground any more for man's sake; for the imagination of man's heart is evil from his youth; neither will I again smite any more every thing living, as I have done.

Genesis 8:21

5. When God saw the homosexuality in Sodom and Gommorah, he took a decision to eliminate that city forever.

And the Lord said, Because the cry of Sodom and Gomorrah is great, and because their sin is very grievous; I will go down now, and see whether they have done altogether according to the cry of it, which is come unto me; and if not, I will know.

Genesis 18:20,21

6. When God saw that the Israelites were suffering so much in Egypt, he took a decision to rescue them from the hand of Pharaoh.

And it came to pass in process of time, that the king of Egypt died: and the children of Israel sighed by reason of the bondage, and they cried, and their cry came up unto God by reason of the bondage. And God heard their groaning, and God remembered his covenant with Abraham, with Isaac, and with Jacob. And God looked upon the children of Israel, and God had respect unto them.

Exodus 2:23-25

7. When God was taking the children of Israel out of Egypt into Canaan and they began to complain, God immediately took a decision to keep them in the wilderness for forty more years.

(When your fathers tempted me, proved me, and saw my works forty years. Wherefore I was grieved with that generation, and said, They do alway err in their heart; and they have not known my ways. So I sware in my wrath, They shall not enter into my rest).

Hebrews 3:9-11

8. When God saw that Lucifer was rebellious, he took a decision to cast him out of Heaven.

Thine heart was lifted up because of thy beauty, thou hast corrupted thy wisdom by reason of thy brightness: I will cast thee to the ground, I will lay thee before kings, that they may behold thee.

Thou hast defiled thy sanctuaries by the multitude of thine iniquities, by the iniquity of thy traffick; therefore will I bring forth a fire from the midst of thee, it shall devour thee, and I will bring thee to ashes upon the earth in the sight of all them that behold thee.

Ezekiel 28:17,18

9. When God realized that the Israelites did not want to be ruled by a prophet, he took a decision to change the style of leadership from judges to kings.

And the Lord said unto Samuel, Hearken unto the voice of the people in all that they say unto thee: for they have not rejected thee, but they have rejected me, that I should not reign over them.

1 Samuel 8:7

10. When God saw that all of his creation was going to be lost through sin, he took a decision to send his Son to win them back.

For God so loved the world, that he gave his only begotten Son, that whosoever believeth in him should not perish, but have everlasting life. For God sent not his Son into the world to condemn the world; but that the world through him might be saved.

John 3:16,17

Many pastors fail to get rid of disloyal elements within their ranks. When you fail to take the hard decision to remove traitors you will be destroyed. Are you a leader? Are you aspiring to be a leader? If so, then welcome to the world of taking difficult decisions.

Six Keys for Decision-Taking

1. Be brave.

You need courage to take good decisions. King David instructed Solomon to be strong. He knew that Solomon would need strength to be decisive. David knew that decisiveness was the greatest attribute Solomon would need.

I go the way of all the earth: be thou strong therefore, and shew thyself a man;

1 Kings 2:2

Because I am a leader, I understand the importance of this instruction. Without strength, you cannot be decisive. A church needs a strong leader to move it forward. Democracy and committees are not helpful; what you need is strong leadership.[3]

Solomon went ahead and eliminated his brother Adonijah, who had earlier tried to take the throne from him. The first act of strength that Solomon performed was to eliminate all possible traitors and wicked elements in his kingdom.

Some of you are too weak to get rid of that bad man in your life. That is why you will never be a successful leader. Decisiveness is the greatest attribute of a leader. You need strength to obey the voice of the Lord.

When God told me to be a pastor, it took a lot of strength to forge ahead into God's will. No one supported or helped me. When I started out in ministry, I found myself surrounded by people who didn't believe in me. I had to get rid of the scoffers in my life and I did just that! I remember telling one gentleman, "From today, you are no longer part of this church."

I continued, "Do not come to the church anymore. Your services are not needed!"

This brother was taken aback but it was a very necessary step for my own survival. No one can prosper if disloyal scorners surround him. You need an environment of encouragement and peace.

2.　　See ahead.

Know that the decision you are taking now will turn out for good. Solomon knew that eliminating his brother Adonijah would turn out for the good of the whole nation. If Solomon had not seen ahead he would not have taken that decision. A bad manager cannot see that if he does not take the hard decision of cutting the work force, for instance, the whole company will close down.[4]

3.   **Consider the consequences of failing to take a decision.**

Abraham was very close to his nephew Lot. One day, he had to face the painful reality that his nephew's presence in his life was causing more harm than good. Being a good leader, he took the decision and separated from his nephew. The consequence of failing to take this decision would have been strife. And it was not worth it.

> **And Abram said unto Lot, Let there be no strife, I pray thee, between me and thee, and between my herdmen and thy herdmen; for we be brethren. Is not the whole land before thee? separate thyself, I pray thee, from me: if thou wilt take the left hand, then I will go to the right; or if thou depart to the right hand, then I will go to the left.**
>
> **Genesis 13:8,9**

Notice that it was after this decision that God gave him specifications of the lands and blessings that were his.

> **And the Lord said unto Abram, after that Lot was separated from him...**
>
> **Genesis 13:14**

4.   **Move quickly when all the relevant information has come in.**

Do not take decisions based on part of the available information. You will make disastrous mistakes when you do that. Solomon was advised by his father to get rid of Joab. The only information that Solomon needed was his father's instruction. Joab was someone who had disobeyed David on several occasions. David asked Solomon to eliminate Joab.[5]

> **...let not his hoar head go down to the grave in peace.**
>
> **1 Kings 2:6**

When the opportunity presented itself, Solomon executed Joab. When the information came in, Solomon took the decision to immediately execute Joab. David also asked Solomon to deal with Shimei. Shimei was someone who cursed King David when he was running away from Absalom.

> ...thou hast with thee Shimei... hold him not guiltless...
>
> 1 Kings 2:8,9

You will notice that after Solomon fulfilled his father's instructions the kingdom of Israel became established under his rule. The decisiveness of Solomon at the beginning of his reign took him very far.

> ...And the kingdom was established in the hand of Solomon.
>
> 1 Kings 2:46

Because Solomon was decisive, his kingdom was established. Once the information came in, he took the decision and implemented it.[6]

5. Implement decisions that have been taken.

Solomon asked Shimei not to cross the brook Kidron. He told Shimei that if he crossed the brook, that would be his last day on Earth. When the information came that Shimei had crossed the boundary, Solomon implemented the hard decision that he had already taken. The decisiveness of Solomon was at work.

6. Surround yourself with godly people who give good advice.

Don't make the mistake of Rehoboam.

And Rehoboam went to Shechem: for all Israel were come to Shechem to make him king. And it came to pass, when Jeroboam the son of Nebat, who was yet in Egypt, heard of it, (for he was fled from the presence of king Solomon, and Jeroboam dwelt in Egypt;) That they sent and called him. And Jeroboam and all the congregation of Israel came, and spake unto Rehoboam, saying, Thy father made our yoke grievous: now therefore make thou the grievous service of thy father, and his heavy yoke which he put upon us, lighter, and we will serve thee. And he said unto them, Depart yet for three days, then come again to me.

And the people departed. And king Rehoboam consulted with the old men, that stood before Solomon his father while he yet lived, and said, How do ye advise that I may answer this people? And they spake unto him, saying, If thou wilt be a servant unto this people this day, and wilt serve them, and answer them, and speak good words to them, then they will be thy servants for ever. But he forsook the counsel of the old men, which they had given him, and consulted with the young men that were grown up with him, and which stood before him: And he said unto them, What counsel give ye that we may answer this people, who have spoken to me, saying, Make the yoke which thy father did put upon us lighter?

And the young men that were grown up with him spake unto him, saying, Thus shalt thou speak unto this people that spake unto thee, saying, Thy father made our yoke heavy, but make thou it lighter unto us; thus shalt thou say unto them, My little finger shall be thicker than my father's loins. And now whereas my father did lade you with a heavy yoke, I will add to your yoke: my father hath chastised you with whips, but I will chastise you with scorpions. So Jeroboam and all the people came to Rehoboam the third day, as the king had appointed, saying, Come to me again the third day. And the king answered the people roughly, and forsook the old men's counsel that they gave him; And spake to them after the counsel of the young men, saying, My father made your yoke heavy, and I will add to your yoke: my father also chastised you with whips, but I will chastise you with scorpions. Wherefore the king hearkened not unto the people; for the cause was from the Lord, that he might perform his saying, which the Lord spake by Ahijah the Shilonite unto Jeroboam the son of Nebat.

So when all Israel saw that the king hearkened not unto them, the people answered the king, saying, What portion have we in David? neither have we inheritance in the son of Jesse: to your tents, O Israel: now see to thine own house, David. So Israel departed unto their tents.

1 Kings 12:1-16

Two Common Mistakes of Leaders

1. Failure to take an obvious decision.

2. Failure to implement a decision that has been taken.

Chapter 39

Know about the Power of Habits and Develop Good Habits

A habit is something that you do without thinking about it or intending to do it. Every good leader has many good habits. These good habits are what has made him into what he is.[1]

Two Habits of Jesus

1.　Going to church regularly.

Did you know that Jesus had good habits? The Bible teaches us that he had a habit of going to church on the Sabbath day.

> And he came to Nazareth, where he had been brought up: and, as his custom was, he went into the synagogue on the sabbath day, and stood up for to read.
>
> **Luke 4:16**

2.   **Going on prayer retreats.**

Jesus also had a habit of going to a particular garden for retreats. It was a place that he often went. And everyone knew his habit of praying in the garden.

> When Jesus had spoken these words, he went forth with his disciples over the brook Cedron, where was a garden, into the which he entered, and his disciples. And Judas also, which betrayed him, knew the place: for Jesus ofttimes resorted thither with his disciples.
>
> **John 18:1,2**

Daniel's Habit

Daniel prayed at specific times of the day. It was something he was used to. It was one of the greatest secrets of his life.

> Now when Daniel knew that the writing was signed, he went into his house; and his windows being open in his chamber toward Jerusalem, he kneeled upon his knees three times a day, and prayed, and gave thanks before his God, as he did aforetime.
>
> **Daniel 6:10**

Ten Things Every Leader Should Know about the Power of Habits

1. A habit is an act that is repeated easily without thinking about it or planning to do it.

2. A habit is an act that becomes your custom whether you are conscious of it or not.

3. A habit is often an insignificant act that seems to have no power to affect the future.

This is why many people do not recognize the concept of having good habits as a powerful tool for future accomplishments.

4. A habit can either be good or bad, natural or spiritual.

Spiritual habits are things like morning prayer and having a daily quiet time. Natural habits are things like brushing your teeth and having your daily bath.

5. Good habits are repeated as easily as bad habits.

6. Bad habits lead to consistent failure and defeat without the person realizing what is happening.

7. Good habits lead to consistent success and victory without the person even realizing what he is doing.

8. Bad habits are easy to form but difficult to live with. Good habits are difficult to form but easy to live with.

9. Every successful leader has a number of good HABITS that have brought him to success.

Many years ago, a friend of mine taught me how to have a quiet time with God every morning. I developed that as a personal habit and it has been my greatest secret as a Christian and later as a minister. Almost all the things I preach about come as a result of this good habit.

10. Habits are a safety procedure for leaders.

This is because even when a leader is under pressure, he will do certain good things habitually, naturally and easily. When under pressure, the leader may not have time to think of what to do or how to act. It is a good habit of prayer or quiet time that may lead him out of difficulty. Just like Jesus, I also have a place I often go to pray. I also often go with my pastors. This habit helps keep me spiritually protected even when I am not aware of danger.

Twenty Good Habits Every Leader Should Develop

1. Read your Bible everyday of your life.

In the day of crisis it is that Bible reading that may save you.[2]

2. Have a personal quiet time with God everyday.

Let *NBNB* (No Bible, No Breakfast) be a principle that you adopt.[3]

3. Pray for a minimum of one hour everyday of your life.

Develop the habit of praying before you eat.[4]

4. Fast at least once a week.

For example, you could choose Fridays as a day of fasting.

5. Constantly listen to preaching tapes in your car or in your home.

6. Constantly have a book that you are reading.

As soon as you finish one book, immediately begin reading another. This is a very good habit that will unconsciously increase your knowledge and learning.[5]

7. Play only Christian music in your house or car.

Never allow worldly music to be played in your presence, even if it is coming from the radio. This habit will make you create a Holy Spirit-friendly-environment around you all the time. The Holy Spirit will come to you because God inhabits praise and worship. You will also unconsciously drive away evil spirits without intending to do so. "And it came to pass, when the evil spirit from God was upon Saul, that David took an harp, and played with his hand: so Saul was refreshed, and was well, and the evil spirit departed from him"(1 Samuel 16:23).

8. Do a lengthy fast at the beginning of the year to commit the rest of the year into God's hands.

9. Have at least one long prayer time at least once a week.[6]

10. Let your closest friends be members of the same sex.[7]

11.   Chat with your wife everyday.

I have discovered that a woman's greatest need is to be talked to, even if it is about "nothing". Women are born with a gift of talking. One of their gifts is chatting. Fifteen minutes of chatting would do every woman a world of good.[8]

12.   Play and talk with your children.

If you spend half as much money on your children and twice as much time with them they will turn out better.[9]

13.   Have sex regularly with your spouse.

You can do this at least every other day or as your strength permits.

14.   Rest once a week.

I rest on Mondays. I have learned that it is an important day for me. I have discovered that the work never ends.[10]

15.   Witness to every unbeliever you meet.

Do this whether you have prayed or not. Do not let an unbeliever get away from your presence without hearing the gospel. This habit will lead to many people being saved without you ever planning a salvation crusade.[11]

16.   Do not borrow money.

Some people have the habit of borrowing money every time they are in need. You must develop the habit of not borrowing money.[12]

17. Set aside some time to specially wait on God every few months.

Whenever I do this, I go away for a few days and spend time with the Lord. This is one of the great secrets of my life.[13]

18. Saving money.

Save a little money every month.

19. Develop the habit of not watching much television.

Television takes up the time that would have been used reading, praying, having a quiet time, talking with God, chatting with your wife or children. Television is also a bad influence. People get ideas of divorce and other evils from watching television.[14]

20. Pay your tithes every month.

Let the first ten per cent of your income be assigned to God.

Do you consider yourself to be a leader? What good habits do you have? Develop a life filled with many good habits. Don't forget that every successful leader has some secret good habits that make him lead successfully.[15]

Chapter 40

Know Where You Are! Know Where You Are Not! And You Will Know Where to Go!

And ye shall know the truth, and the truth shall make you free.

John 8:32

The truth will tell you where you are and where you are not! The truth will also tell you where to go. Many pastors need to start telling the truth about the size of their congregations. It is time to stop making wild guesses about the number of people in our churches. When you know the actual number of souls you are ministering to, you will be motivated to work harder.

One day, I asked my data officer to tell me how many people were in church. When he gave me the figure, I was depressed for one week. I realized that our church was very small. I had a long way to go! If you cannot tell yourself the truth, you cannot be a good leader.

Many businesses do not make any profit at all! When you add up the real costs of their operations, you discover that they are actually making a loss. If managers were honest, they would take the necessary hard decisions. That is what leadership does.[1]

Then said one unto him, Lord, are there few that be saved?...

Luke 13:23

Jesus answered and told him that there is a narrow gate and few people are entering through that gate. This was the truth. Leaders need to deal with reality. Without real figures, a Chief Executive cannot take sound financial decisions. Every leader must ensure that he has the real picture.[2]

Chapter 41

Become Self-Motivated. Do Not Expect Direction or Encouragement from Outside

…but David encouraged himself in the Lord his God.

1 Samuel 30:6

Everyone looks up to the leader for encouragement, but who encourages the leader? A true leader is someone who knows how to encourage himself whenever it is necessary. I do not look to the outside for motivation. I have learnt that I have to motivate myself. I cannot depend on external factors to encourage me.

There are many times I have been absolutely discouraged and dejected in ministry. There are times I have problems that

I have no one to talk to about. Like David, I have had to learn to encourage myself in the Lord.

You cannot encourage your followers until you have learnt to encourage yourself. David experienced a crisis and he had no one to talk to. He had no choice but to encourage himself.

And David's two wives were taken captives, Ahinoam the Jezreelitess, and Abigail the wife of Nabal the Carmelite. And David was greatly distressed; for the people spake of stoning him, because the soul of all the people was grieved, every man for his sons and for his daughters: but David encouraged himself in the Lord his God.

1 Samuel 30:5,6

Seven Steps to Encouraging Yourself

1. Develop a personal relationship with the Holy Spirit.

Hear him speaking to you personally. You will do this by faith. You must be able to say that God has spoken to you. When you are all alone and there is no one to speak to, the Holy Spirit will be the guide that you need. That is what he is there for! Be constantly aware of the Greater One in you. You have overcome because he is in you.[1]

Ye are of God, little children, and have overcome them: because greater is he that is in you, than he that is in the world.

1 John 4:4

In my darkest moments, I have found the Holy Spirit to be someone who speaks to me personally. Jesus described the Holy Spirit as *another* Comforter.[2]

> **And I will pray the Father, and he shall give you another Comforter, that he may abide with you for ever;**
>
> **John 14:16**

Jesus was the first comforter. He was available to speak to. He was there to answer questions. He was there to give guidance. Today, the Holy Spirit does this job. Leaders are often lonely people. I pity any leader who does not have the Holy Spirit as a personal friend to talk to.[3]

2. Receive living messages from God by the simple reading of Scriptures.

When the Bible becomes a living message from God to you, you will always have a source of direction and encouragement. When I'm in need of encouragement or direction, I believe that whichever part of Scriptures I read at that time will be God's message to me. This makes the Bible my greatest tool of self-encouragement and motivation.[4]

3. Remember other problems that God has delivered you from.

When you remember what the Lord has done in the past you will be encouraged. Jesus expects us to remember the things he has done for us in the past to encourage ourselves. Notice how he was angry with the disciples for not remembering the past miracles.[5]

Having eyes, see ye not? and having ears, hear ye not? and do ye not remember? When I brake the five loaves among five thousand, how many baskets full of fragments took ye up? They say unto him, Twelve. And when the seven among four thousand, how many baskets full of fragments took ye up? And they said, Seven. And he said unto them, How is it that ye do not understand?

Mark 8:18-21

4.   Make positive confessions.

Your faith must speak when you need encouragement. Faith is the opposite of depression. Faith is a shield. Your faith is a God-given weapon meant to stop attacks. That is why the Bible calls faith a shield that quenches the fiery darts. In my book, *Name it! Claim it! Take it!* I have written a whole lot of positive confessions that will help every leader. (See *Name it! Claim it! Take it*! by Dag Heward-Mills).

5.   Learn to listen to appropriate tapes and get fired up again.

6.   Play the right music at the right time.

7.   Avoid depressive and discouraging personalities who only draw you back into the darkest gloom.

Remember that joy cometh in the morning.[6]

Chapter 42

Be Flexible, Rigidity Is Costly!

To the weak became I as weak, that I might gain the weak: I am made all things to all men, that I might by all means save some.

1 Corinthians 9:22

A true leader exhibits flexibility. Being flexible does not mean that you compromise in things you believe in. A leader must not be rigid. An old rigid tree will be broken, but a young supple tree can be bent over. Paul said that he became all things to all men so that he might save them all. Are you prepared to do anything to achieve good results? There are times that you may have to vary your dressing to flow with the people around. You are not always right, you know![1]

In certain cultures, people are not punctual. When you say the programme starts at six o'clock, they will leave their homes at six and be there for seven. If you are very rigid with your timing, you may end up preaching to empty chairs and closing your service as the majority of people walk in.[2]

A pastor must be flexible with ignorant baby sheep. Sometimes, sheep will ask you to counsel them about things you have just preached about. The message is very clear but they still want you to talk to them. There are times you have to be flexible and accommodate these sheep. Without being flexible you will not be able to flow in a miracle service where the Holy Spirit has the liberty. If you really want to keep your service to two hours, you may miss certain moves of the Spirit.

A leader tries new things. Try new ways of evangelism. Be open to methods that you did not invent. Listen to young people who have fresh ideas. Do not rigidly think that God only speaks through a grey-haired sixty-year-old prophet. Flexibility will allow you to receive from a twenty-year-old anointed youth.[3]

Are you a leader? Then you must be flexible and open to new ideas.[4]

Chapter 43

Command Your Troops!

For if the trumpet give an uncertain sound, who shall prepare himself to the battle?

1 Corinthians 14:8

There are times that making suggestions and giving advice will not work. You must give a clear command to the troops. The Centurion said to Jesus, "I say to one 'Go', and he goeth. I say to another 'Come', and he cometh." He was just showing Jesus that he was a leader. A leader is often a commander. If you are too weak to give a command you cannot be a leader. Leaders must give advice and make suggestions. But a leader must also give commands. There are times that you have to say, "Go!"[1]

I Gave a Command

One night, the Lord revealed that a certain pastor in my outfit was disloyal to me. He said to me, "Give a clear command." I will never forget that night, as the Spirit of God ministered very clearly to me. I could not sleep because the Spirit of God was talking to me. I was wide awake in the middle of the night. All that the Lord told me was to give a clear command. He told me that after I give the command, the disloyal element would be made manifest.

The next day, I called two pastors to my office. I told them, "I have given you suggestions and advice before. But now I am explicitly instructing you to move out of this city into the following towns." I continued, "In other words I am transferring you."

You see, I had taken my place as a strong leader of my church. I said to them, "I am transferring you out of this city."

One of the pastors agreed to go after clarifying a few points. The other pastor smiled and said, "Well, I have been to that town before and I have even worked there. I would be happy to go there, but I think that this is a good opportunity to inform you of my decision to resign."

When I heard that, I said to myself, "The cat is out of the bag."

This young man had been hatching a plan for some time. He had not had the courage to disclose it. I had known that his heart was not with me. Giving the strong command had brought out what was in him.[2]

Be strong and of good courage...

Joshua 1:6

Pray for strength and courage to be a good leader. Giving advice is very different from giving commands. Giving suggestions is very different from giving commands. There is a time to advise and a time to command. Giving commands will establish your position as a leader and will expose disloyal elements within your ranks. Develop the art of commanding. Of course, you must not go about commanding everyone. You can only command your own troops.[3]

Chapter 44

Balance Your Priorities

A false balance is abomination to the Lord: but a just weight is his delight.

Proverbs 11:1

Leadership is the ability to know what comes first and what comes second. Every leader has a home, a family, a church, a business, a school and the list goes on. What comes first? A leader knows that God always comes first. Almost every seasoned leader will tell you that the family is of utmost importance. Some people place so much emphasis on the family that they neglect God. Others neglect their families in the name of serving God. Both of these are wrong. And the leader is the one who rises up and creates the perfect balance.[1]

Maintain the right balance between all the priorities that God has given you. Nobody wants to get to Heaven only to hear that they neglected a whole area of ministry.[2]

Do you consider yourself a leader? Then maintain the right balance between all the priorities that God has given to you. We will be glad to follow your example. Nobody wants to get to Heaven only to be told that they neglected a whole area of ministry. Even within the offices of ministry, it is important to balance your different callings. Perhaps you are an evangelist and a pastor, you must balance the two and ensure you fulfil each one to its utmost. I believe God has put me in the office of a teacher. That is my first priority! I love evangelising and I love to pastor. But God has directed me to put the first things first![3]

Chapter 45

Live by the Logical Laws of Teamwork

Fourteen Laws of Teamwork

1. **Everybody in the ministry team should know what you are trying to do.**

   When people understand what you are trying to do, it helps them to flow in the vision.[1]

2. **Everyone in the ministry team must know what he is expected to do.**

   This allows you to know who to blame when things go wrong and who to praise when things work out.[2]

3. **Everyone in the ministry team must know what every other member of the ministry team is supposed to be doing.**

That is why you must have meetings with individuals and then meet them in a group so that others would know what is going on.[3]

4. **Everyone must have a complete section in which he has full control.**

Delegate people to do things. Give them control over the section you have delegated to them.[4]

5. **Give a lot of praise and recognition to your ministry team members in public.**

If you want somebody to repeat something good, praise him for that thing.[5]

6. **Give criticism and rebuke to your people in private.**

If you want to correct somebody, do not do so in front of their subordinates. It will weaken their position of authority in the sight of their subordinates.[6]

7. **As a ministry team leader, my criticism must be constructive.**[7]

8. **As a ministry team leader, accept responsibility for everything and anything that goes wrong.**

Take the blame and share the glory.[8]

9. **Do not complain about or condemn your team members.**[9]

10.   Decide always to give advice on how to do things better.[10]

11.   Treat everybody as very important.

When you see someone who doesn't look important, be nice to them. They may not look important but treat them as important.[11]

12.   Reposition and relocate people until they are in the place they function best.[12]

13.   Give people jobs according to their personalities.

Some people are light-hearted and merry, others are moody and strict. There is a job that suits everyone.

14.   Forgive and overlook the mistakes of team members.

Chapter 46

Get Angry Sometimes

And Jesus went into the temple of God, and cast out all them that sold and bought in the temple, and overthrew the tables of the moneychangers, and the seats of them that sold doves, And said unto them, It is written, MY HOUSE SHALL BE CALLED THE HOUSE OF PRAYER; but ye have made it a den of thieves.

Matthew 21:12,13

If you are a leader, you will become happy with the things that make God happy. You will also become angry with the things that make God angry. You see, Jesus got angry when he saw the evil that was being perpetrated by backslidden worshippers. They had converted the church into a business centre.

Most people are only capable of natural fleshly anger. But the Bible speaks of anger that is different. That is what I call holy anger.[1]

BE YE ANGRY, AND SIN NOT: let not the sun go down upon your wrath:

Ephesians 4:26

In this Scripture, Christians are actually instructed to get angry sometimes. The important thing is not to sin whilst you are angry. Holy anger is the anger that rises within you against the devil, sin and wickedness in the world. Holy anger is the anger that rises against injustice and oppression.[2]

When holy anger comes upon you, you are expected to take certain decisions. Just as Jesus threw out the moneychangers from the temple, there is a time to throw certain people out of your organizations. Many businesses and companies fail because they fail to act appropriately in righteous anger. Leaders must know how to operate in righteous biblical anger.

Chapter 47

Control the People You Lead by the Power of Teaching

Do you consider yourself to be a leader? I advise you to study the art of communicating, teaching and preaching. Even a businessman needs to make his subordinates understand what he is trying to achieve. You see, people relate with you on the basis of your words.

Solomon was a king but he taught the people. He knew that his control over the people would be through his teaching.

And moreover, because the preacher [King Solomon] was wise, he still taught the people knowledge; yea, he gave good heed, and sought out, and set in order many proverbs.

Ecclesiastes 12:9

Teaching is the art of shaping people into what you want. People are not easy to lead. Everyone comes around with his own opinion and his own set of ideas. Teaching moulds the people into what you want. Through the power of teaching, you can get people to do almost anything. *Without the power of teaching, you would hardly be able to lead anyone anywhere.*[1]

A bishop then must be… apt to teach;

1 Timothy 3:2

The authority to lead people is found in your ability to teach them. A leader must be able to impart information in a simple and easy to understand style. Even if your office is not that of a teacher, you must learn how to teach.[2]

How I Led My People into the Miracle Ministry

When I began operating in the miracle ministry, I realized that many of the pastors were not flowing with me. It was something new. Without even knowing what I was doing, I launched into a series of teachings on the power of the Holy Spirit. I taught about the anointing! I taught about healing! I taught about why miracles were necessary! These teachings helped tremendously. Today, the whole church is ever ready for a miracle session.

If you want to lead people along a certain road, you often have to teach them first. King Solomon was wise, that is why he taught his people knowledge. Are you a wise leader? Then teach your people knowledge![3]

Chapter 48

Be a Great Leader, Go the Extra Mile

And whosoever shall compel thee to go a mile, go with him twain.

Matthew 5:41

Every true leader goes the extra mile for his followers. This may mean a little more sacrifice and a little more time. One extra mile for somebody you love is never too much. It is not uncommon to find the leader of a company in his office well after his closing hours. He is going the extra mile.

When I became a pastor, I often went the extra mile without being asked to. The extra mile is the mile you are not supposed to go. The extra mile is the mile you are not really required to do. That is why it is called the extra mile![1]

My car was used as the church bus. My stereo sound system was used as the church equipment. My private room was used as the church office. These were not things that I was required to do, but I did them gladly because that is what a natural leader does. Without even being asked, you will do extra things.

For your church or business to work, somebody has to put in the extra effort. Do you consider yourself a leader? Are you going the same number of miles that everybody else does? Remember that a true leader is often doing extra miles.[2]

Chapter 49

What Have You Survived?

All leaders can be sure of having some level of disloyalty within the ranks of their followers. Jesus' ministry survived the betrayal by Judas. Betrayal is part of life. No matter who you are or what type of leadership you have, you will experience betrayal. But you must be a survivor![1]

> The Lord is my shepherd; I shall not want. He maketh me to lie down in green pastures: he leadeth me beside the still waters. He restoreth my soul: he leadeth me in the paths of righteousness for his name's sake. Yea, though I walk through the valley of the shadow of death, I will fear no evil: for thou art with me; thy rod and thy staff they comfort me.

Thou preparest a table before me in the presence of mine enemies: thou anointest my head with oil; my cup runneth over. Surely goodness and mercy shall follow me all the days of my life: and I will dwell in the house of the Lord for ever.

Psalm 23:1-6

King David spoke of surviving the valley of the shadow of death. Survival is a central theme of the ministry. All true ministers must have a survival mentality. God did not promise us an easy road when we chose to serve Him. God expects us to survive after the attacks are over.[2]

...and having done all, to stand.

Ephesians 6:13

If you cannot survive you cannot be a leader because leadership involves surviving.

Ten Things Every Survivor Must Do

1. A survivor must continue to exist or function in spite of adverse conditions.

We are in a battle with a real enemy. The conditions are not good. Satan is the god of this world and in a sense we are on his turf.

2. To come through.

Every survivor must come through and pull through. After I had preached in one church, the pastor told me, "It seems you have been through hell." Certainly, I have been through a lot, but I am still around.

3. Every survivor must carry on and carry through.

4.	Every survivor must continue.

> Then said Jesus to those Jews which believed on him, If ye continue in my word, then are ye my disciples indeed;
>
> John 8:31

5.	Every survivor must remain alive after the challenges of life.

6.	Every survivor must last.

Paul was a leader who lasted.

7.	Every survivor must outlive the storms.

When the storm is over you must still be around.

8.	Every survivor must recover and revive.

9.	Every survivor must live to fight again.

10.	Every survivor must continue to live or exist in spite of danger.

Fifteen Things Paul Survived

1.	Paul survived frequent imprisonments.
2.	Paul survived five beatings from the Jews.
3.	Paul survived three beatings with rods.
4.	Paul survived stoning.
5.	Paul survived three shipwrecks.
6.	Paul survived forty-eight hours in the deep sea.
7.	Paul survived several journeys.

8. Paul survived dangers from robbers.

9. Paul survived dangers in the city.

10. Paul survived dangers from his own countrymen.

11. Paul survived dangers in the wilderness.

12. Paul survived dangers from disloyal people.

13. Paul survived extreme exhaustion.

14. Paul survived a lot of pain.

15. Paul survived the cold and nakedness.

Are they ministers of Christ? (I speak as a fool) I am more; in labours more abundant, in stripes above measure, in prisons more frequent, in deaths oft. Of the Jews five times received I forty stripes save one.

Thrice was I beaten with rods, once was I stoned, thrice I suffered shipwreck, a night and a day I have been in the deep; In journeyings often, in perils of waters, in perils of robbers, in perils by mine own countrymen, in perils by the heathen, in perils in the city, in perils in the wilderness, in perils in the sea, in perils among false brethren; In weariness and painfulness, in watchings often, in hunger and thirst, in fastings often, in cold and nakedness.

2 Corinthians 11:23-27

Six Things Every Leader Must Survive

1.   Survive persecution.

I have been strongly persecuted for my beliefs. I have been persecuted for starting a church. I have been ridiculed for starting a ministerial association. In 1988 and 1989, two different people called me "Jim Jones"! One of them was my classmate, a fellow medical student. The other person who called me "Jim Jones" was a professor in the medical school and a family friend. By the grace of God I have survived these persecutions.

I needed a church hall for my wedding, but this professor told my parents that he would only help if I promised to close down my church. He was so convinced that I was another "Jim Jones". Who was Jim Jones? He was a cult leader who led thousands of people to their deaths. I was portrayed as a cult leader and a lunatic. Those were difficult moments, but I came through. I have survived these hateful persecutions and I am still around by the grace of God.

Don't be discouraged because of your persecutions. A leader is supposed to be a survivor.[3]

2.   Survive rejection.

I have survived rejection as a minister of the gospel. When I was getting married, there was no external minister I could trust to officiate my wedding. My associate pastor had to officiate my wedding. I invited all the pastors in the city but no one turned up. These ministers were not interested in my wedding. When it was time to take pictures with all pastors, none were present. The MC called for all pastors but no one came forward. I was completely rejected. But I have survived and many of the people who rejected me then, show respect to me today. Do not allow rejection to kill your vision for leadership. Leadership includes surviving everything that is thrown at you.

3. Survive bad stories.

A leader is someone who survives bad stories. When Jesus rose from the dead some people spread a rumour about his disciples. They claimed that the disciples were grave looters who had stolen the body of Jesus. In other words, their claim was that he did not really rise from the dead. But the gospel has survived this story.

> **And when they were assembled with the elders, and had taken counsel, they gave large money unto the soldiers, Saying, Say ye, His disciples came by night, and stole him away while we slept. And if this come to the governor's ears, we will persuade him, and secure you. So they took the money, and did as they were taught: and this saying is commonly reported among the Jews until this day.**
>
> **Matthew 28:12-15**

Before Peter could begin his ministry, many people saw him as a liar and a thief. Others saw him as the greatest deceiver to live in Jerusalem for centuries. Yet, he was a genuine minister of the gospel, proclaiming only what he had seen and heard.

This is the lot of all true leaders or ministers of the gospel. You will have to survive the unbelievable stories that go on around you. I have heard people say amazing things about me. Once, somebody said we were printing money in our church. Someone even accused us of dealing in drugs. How do we explain all these stories?

Government officials sometimes describe church leaders as charlatans who rip and rape the people. This is the impression that many people have of us. What can we do about it? *We can only survive!* To survive means to outlive and outlast every storm. A leader is a survivor. To survive, you need determination and a whole lot of faith. You need to believe in yourself and you need to believe that what you are doing is the right thing. You need to believe that God will help you.

4. Survive every crisis.

A leader survives every crisis. You've got to hold on in the midst of your crisis. I know we all want peace and perfect harmony. That is the way it should be, but life has its twists and turns. You have to survive. You need self-confidence and self-determination. You can do it! If you believe, you can conquer it all! A leader needs friends and family in times of crisis. I have found that God is your best friend in such times.

Jesus was a survivor. He met with stiff rejection and hatred. People wanted him killed from day one, but he survived. When Jesus announced that he was anointed and had a healing ministry, many people rejected him outright.

And there was delivered unto him the book of the prophet Esaias. And when he had opened the book, he found the place where it was written, The Spirit of the Lord is upon me, because he hath anointed me to preach the gospel to the poor; he hath sent me to heal the brokenhearted, to preach deliverance to the captives, and recovering of sight to the blind, to set at liberty them that are bruised, To preach the acceptable year of the Lord. And all they in the synagogue, when they heard these things, were filled with wrath, And rose up, and thrust him out of the city, and led him unto the brow of the hill whereon their city was built, that they might cast him down headlong. But he passing through the midst of them went his way,

Luke 4:17-19,28-30

Jesus survived! I see you surviving! Your children will survive! Your family will survive! Jesus survived and so will you! A leader cannot please everyone; he has to do what God has told him to do!

5. Survive envy, jealousy, disloyalty and betrayal.

(Now the man Moses was very meek, above all the men which were upon the face of the earth).

Numbers 12:3

As you go higher in ministry, you will attract lots of envy and jealousy. Most of that will come from your own brothers and sisters.

Now Israel loved Joseph more than all his children, because he was the son of his old age: and he made him a coat of many colours. And when his brethren saw that their father loved him more than all his brethren, they hated him, and could not speak peaceably unto him.

Genesis 37:3,4

Joseph obtained favour and was given a coat of many colours. Soon he attracted the hatred of his own brothers. A leader must survive the envy and jealousies of his brothers.

The people who have said some of the nastiest things about me are ministers of the gospel in my own city. Things have a way of getting round to you. One minister told me, "If you knew what one pastor said about you, you would never ever go to his church again."

A leader thrives in the midst of petty jealousies and hatred. Joseph survived the test of slavery. He survived going to prison. He survived the lies and bad stories of Potiphar's wife. A leader is a survivor! Joseph's ability to lead Egypt in a time of crisis was partly because of his ability to survive the envy and jealousy of everyone around him.

Sometimes people want you to apologize for being blessed. How can I apologize for the blessing of God upon my life? Many of the things I have today, I did not even ask for. They just came my way. Are you a leader? Do not be intimidated by the hatred of those around you. David's first problem began when he killed Goliath. The Bible says that Saul eyed David after that victory.

> **And the women answered one another as they played, and said, Saul hath slain his thousands, and David his ten thousands. And Saul was very wroth, and the saying displeased him; and he said, They have ascribed unto David ten thousands, and to me they have ascribed but thousands: and what can he have more but the kingdom? And Saul eyed David from that day and forward.**
>
> **1 Samuel 18:7-9**

Are you a leader? Get ready for envy, jealousy and betrayal as you rise to prominence. To survive all these, you need determination and a great deal of faith.

Jesus' ministry survived the betrayal by Judas. Betrayal is part of life. No matter who you are or what type of leadership you have, you will experience betrayal. If Judas is anything to go by, then one out of twelve people may be disloyal.

I recently heard of a church that voted for a new pastor. This new pastor received ninety-one percent of the votes. What did that mean? It meant that nine percent of the people did not really want the new pastor. This poor pastor will not even know who voted against him. However, he can be sure that the disapproving group will be within the congregation.

All leaders can be sure of having some level of disloyalty within the ranks of their followers. Keep disloyalty to a minimum and survive the rebellion that comes against your leadership. Do not cry about it. Do not moan about it. That is leadership. Jesus was betrayed. And Paul was betrayed. How can it be that you will not experience the same?

I have had friends who were very close to me, turn around against me. People I ate with, slept with and played with turned against me in bitter hatred.

Yea, mine own familiar friend, in whom I trusted, which did eat of my bread, hath lifted up his heel against me.

Psalm 41:9

At one point, I thought I would not survive the betrayal. The betrayal of one friend cut me like a knife through the heart. I became ill for two weeks as I endured the lies and slander of an old friend. But I survived! A leader is a survivor! A leader is not someone who has had things rosy. Be determined, dear friend, to be a survivor. You will live through whatever storm you are experiencing!

6.   Survive pressure.

Real leaders often come under extreme and varied pressures because they are out there in the front. They are the ones who receive all the blows. The pressure is always on them. If you cannot stand pressure then you cannot be a leader.

Develop a hard forehead. Do not go mad. Do not go crazy. Some people break down under pressure. God told Ezekiel not to be afraid of the people's faces. Be harder than everything that comes against you.

Confess boldly, "I can do all things through Christ who strengthens me." Say aloud, "I am able, more than able to prevail and to win this battle. Though a thousand fall at my side and ten thousand at my left hand, I shall survive. I am a survivor in the name of Jesus. God will strengthen and keep me in all my ways!"

Chapter 50

Acknowledge the Gifts of Others

But contrariwise, when they saw that the gospel of the uncircumcision was committed unto me, as the gospel of the circumcision was unto Peter...

Galatians 2:7

Peter acknowledged that the ministry to the Gentiles was clearly in the hands of the apostle Paul.

Can you acknowledge that God has given something to someone else? If you can, then you are a leader. A leader is someone who is able to acknowledge the special grace on another person's life. My library is made up of books of other ministers. I have the books of every pastor in my city. I acknowledge that God is using other people apart from me. I want to learn what they know. I privately and publicly acknowledge that they are doing great things for the Lord.[1]

Instead of acknowledging the gifts in others, pastors often find themselves criticizing and maligning one another.

Years ago, I realized that there were many people I could not reach. Many people cannot relate to the way I preach. That is why God has raised up other ministers. There are also many people who could not relate to the way others preach. That is why they joined my church. I am often amused as I observe how reluctantly some ministers acknowledge my gift. They fear to acknowledge the gifts of others.

Peter acknowledged Paul's ministry to the Gentiles. Paul also acknowledged Peter's ministry to the Jews. You must recognize what God recognizes and honour what God honours. That is true leadership!

Chapter 51

Be a Creative Leader

In the beginning God created the heaven and the earth.

Genesis 1:1

The universe is ruled by a creative God. This world is ruled by creative people. To be able to think of something new and greater and to achieve it is creativity. An ordinary person wants to do what everyone else is doing. A leader is someone who is prepared to be creative and to chart new territories.

There are two groups of people in this world. One group have created new things. The other group have created nothing. *Creative people dominate non-creative people.* You don't have to look far to see this truth.[1]

The creative rule the non-creative. Be creative in your business. Be creative in your work. Be creative as a minister of the gospel. The fact that something has not been done before does not mean that it's wrong. You will dominate in your sphere of life. The ministry I oversee is made up of mainly lay people. I myself, started out in ministry as a layperson. When I did, people preached about me in their pulpits saying I was not concentrating on my studies. They had never seen the lay ministry in operation. They could only criticize. Today, this creative lay ministry has led to much growth in my ministry. Decide to be a creative leader![2]

Seven Steps to Becoming a Creative Leader

1. Ask the Holy Spirit to teach you what to do.

Realize that you may be in a non-creative environment. You may have to fight a spirit of non-creativity all your life.

2. Admire nature.

Be interested in animals, nature and the human body. As you become interested in things God has created, the spirit of creativity will be stirred up in you. Non-creative people are usually uninterested in nature.

3. Overcome the natural resistance to change.

Most people do not like change. Be honest, and deal with every streak of non-creativity and the "anti-change" spirit in your life.

4. Be interested in the amazing creations of ordinary men.

Be interested in medicine, surgery, cars, planes, computers, etc. Non-creative people are usually not interested in such things.

5. Be open to new and unusual ways of doing things.

Do not have a blackout attitude towards every new suggestion. I have often been laughed at when I have made new suggestions. In the end, it is these same suggestions that have been a blessing to many people. Creative people are often laughed at because of their ideas.

6. Be ready to embark on adventure.

Adventure is the sister of creativity.

7. Try introducing variations to already existing models.

Variation is the brother of creativity.

A creative leader is someone who is able to come up with new ideas. New ideas often contain the solutions we need. Are you someone with new ideas?

Chapter 52

Respect Principles and You Will Build a Great Organization

Three Definitions of a Principle

1. A principle is a fundamental rule which becomes the basis of an action.

2. A principle is the fundamental truth which is the basis of our reasoning.

3. A principle is a general law which is the foundation for a decision.

Seven Types of Organizations That Do Not Last

Organizations are destroyed by leaders who do not base their decisions and reasoning on principles. To build a lasting organization, church or nation, you must base your reasoning, actions and decisions on principles. Principles outlive favouritism, partisanship and political expediency. If you break principles, the principles will break you.[1]

1. **An organization that is governed by political expediency rather than principles is doomed.**

"It is not politically expedient!" is what many political leaders say. These leaders take bad decisions that destroy entire nations. When decisions in a country are taken to gain political favour rather than to get the right thing done, the country is often doomed.

2. **An organization that is run mainly by giving favours to relatives rather than principles will be destroyed.**

When a leader decides to place members of his family in certain positions they do not qualify for, he has set aside principles and is governing his organization by emotions. The Bible teaches that partiality and hypocrisy are not wisdom.

But the wisdom that is from above is... without partialit, and without hypocrisy.

James 3:17

Your nation, business or church will break up when you deal with people based on family relationships rather than on important principles.

3. **An organization ruled by a leader who takes decisions to gain personal financial advantage will eventually collapse.**

I know of a project that should have cost an organization only forty million dollars. However, it ended up costing fifty million dollars. Why? Because somebody was bribed to agree to a higher figure. Such an organization will only end up becoming highly indebted and poor. It is not governed by principles but by leaders who seek to line their pockets. If I sought to make myself rich rather than to build the church, I would see the church collapse.

4. **When a nation is governed by greed rather than by principles, it will end up in deep poverty.**

This is the story of Africa. It is the story of greedy leaders who have drunk the blood of the nations they have governed. Instead of principled leadership, we have had greedy vampires and vultures who sucked up every drop of blood. Despotic African leaders have left their countries desolate while they have amassed millions of dollars that they can never spend in their lifetime.

5. **A nation governed by selfishness rather than by rules and principles is doomed.**

Selfish African leaders send their children to schools in Europe and America whilst the educational system of their own country crumbles. These selfish government ministers do not care two hoots if ten million children are not educated. The hospitals of developing Ghana decay, whilst government officials seek medical help for themselves and their favourites in London's Cromwell Hospital. Selfishness is not a basis for good leadership.

Democracy is a political system or government based on giving power to the people through elections. The very nature of this system corrupts leaders. Selfishness drives them to remain in power indefinitely. So-called democratic leaders try to please the masses with sweet words. This is why many democratically elected leaders are liars and hypocrites. Many promises are never fulfilled.

6. An organization ruled by favouritism and partiality rather than by principles is doomed.

When a leader favours one or two people he likes because they are friends or schoolmates, he rules his organization by favouritism rather than by principle. People must be promoted on merit and not on the basis of favouritism. When everything depends on who you know and whose friend you are, the organization deteriorates.

7. An organization ruled by ethnicity rather than by principles is destined for division and war.

A leader whose mind works along ethnic lines rather than in accordance with principles is destroying his organization. Those who are not of his ethnic origin will gradually hate him. This is the basis of many of the civil wars in Africa and Europe. Many African leaders reason along ethnic lines rather than along the lines of principle. Many countries have degenerated into war zones because of this kind of leadership. The Second World War developed as Hitler tried to eliminate Jews and other groups he considered undesirable. The Balkans conflict grew as Muslims, Croats and Serbs tried to get rid of each other. The Tutsis and Hutus of Rwanda are another sombre reminder of how leadership based on ethnicity can destroy an entire region.

Three Principles You Need to Build Your Organization

1. Everybody must have an equal opportunity to make the best of his life in your organization.

2. Everyone must be promoted and rewarded based on merit rather than on anything else.

3. The achievement of results, hard work, loyalty, productivity and a good attitude must always be rewarded.

Chapter 53

Don't Think of How Much Money You Can Get from the People You Lead. Think of How Much You Can Help Them

But when he saw the multitudes, he was moved with compassion on them, because they fainted, and were scattered abroad, as sheep having no shepherd.
                              Matthew 9:36

Jesus had a reason for praying. He had reasons for doing the things he did. He wanted to help people. He was moved with compassion. This means that Jesus felt pity, mercy, kindness and tenderness towards the people. Obviously, Jesus was not thinking about getting any money from them. He was thinking about helping them.[1]

Are you a leader? What thoughts go through your mind? Are they thoughts of how much money you can get from the people you lead? Are they thoughts of how much you will be paid for each move you make? Is your mind filled with thoughts of personal gain and personal profit? If that is the case, then you are not the Jesus type of leader! Your motives are very important.[2]

The Apostle Paul described how he was burdened for his people, the Israelites. If you are leading people for any other reason other than a desire to help them, I'm afraid you are in the wrong job. You must be concerned about other people and their problems even if you do not have those problems.[3]

I say the truth in Christ, I lie not, my conscience also bearing me witness in the Holy Ghost, That I have great heaviness and continual sorrow in my heart. For I could wish that myself were accursed from Christ for my brethren, my kinsmen according to the flesh:

Romans 9:1-3

Since God looks on the heart, your motives are very important. God has made it clear that ministers should not be in the ministry for the money.

Feed the flock of God which is among you, taking the oversight thereof, not by constraint, but willingly; not for filthy lucre, but of a ready mind;

1 Peter 5:2

This is why I encourage the lay ministry so much. The lay ministry serves as a filter. If you are in the ministry for financial reasons, you will not be happy to be a lay minister. Faithful lay people who desire to serve God at the highest level should be the ones to come into full-time ministry.

Chapter 54

Grow in Your Influence

…behold, the world is gone after him.

John 12:19

Jesus had influence over a large number of people. A leader increases his scope of influence as he grows in the art of leadership. The Bible tells us that the whole world went after Jesus. The Pharisees were very disturbed over this. The devil will be afraid of the influence of a true leader. This is why governments become afraid of pastors who are true leaders. They know that a true leader influences a large number of people.[1]

The key to growing in your influence is to grow in your influence over smaller sub-groups of people. The cumulative effect of your influence and control over these sub-groups will give you a larger sphere of influence.[2]

When a person is a leader at heart, people who are even senior to the leader will follow him. The Apostle Paul taught Timothy to establish his influence over sub-groups in his church. In our church we call these Timothy Groups.

Eight Groups of People You Must Influence

1. Older men.

   Rebuke not an elder, but intreat him as a father; and the younger men as brethren;

   1 Timothy 5:1

2. Younger men.

   Rebuke not an elder, but intreat him as a father; and the younger men as brethren;

   1 Timothy 5:1

3. Older women.

   The elder women as mothers; the younger as sisters, with all purity.

   1 Timothy 5:2

4. Younger women.

   The elder women as mothers; the younger as sisters, with all purity.

   1 Timothy 5:2

5.   Servants.

Let as many servants as are under the yoke count their own masters worthy of all honour, that the name of God and his doctrine be not blasphemed.

1 Timothy 6:1

6.   Poor people.

Honour widows that are widows indeed.

1 Timothy 5:3

7.   Rich people.

Charge them that are rich in this world, that they be not highminded, nor trust in uncertain riches, but in the living God, who giveth us richly all things to enjoy;

1 Timothy 6:17

8.   Leaders.

Let the elders that rule well be counted worthy of double honour, especially they who labour in the word and doctrine.

1 Timothy 5:17

Timothy grew in his ministry until all sorts of people were part of his church. Apostle Paul had to show him how to handle all the different types of people who were responding to his gift of leadership.

Rebuke not an elder, but intreat him as a father; and the younger men as brethren; The elder women as mothers; the younger as sisters, with all purity.

1 Timothy 5:1,2

I see you developing in the art of leadership until all sorts of people respond to your influence.

Keys to Influencing Different Groups of People

1.   Show respect to those that particularly deserve it.

Elderly people for instance, deserve more respect due to their age and experience. Do not expect the same output of energy that you would receive from younger ones. Regard the honourable citizens that God brings into your midst. The fact that Nicodemus and Joseph of Arimathea were mentioned in the Bible tells us that their support for Jesus was unusual and therefore given special recognition. This does not mean you must be prejudiced and biased towards the rich and powerful. What it means is that you must give honour to whom honour is due.

Render therefore to all their dues: tribute to whom tribute is due; custom to whom custom; fear to whom fear; honour to whom honour.

Romans 13:7

2.   Study the peculiarities of different groups.

There are vast differences between men and women. These must be appreciated by anyone who wants to minister to them. There are also vast differences between older and younger women. The vision of younger women is marriage, husbands and children. The disillusionment of older women is often marriage, husbands and sometimes children. I have found that older women have fewer delusions about what marriage and husbands can offer. They are more inclined to the service of God than younger women. That is why the Bible says that older women should teach younger women.

3. Respect the differences that exist between different groups of people.

Do not despise the peculiarities or weaknesses of each group. Very generally speaking, women are more interested in things like chatting, shopping and clothes whilst men are more interested in their jobs, money, cars, sex, etc. You cannot have a successful women's ministry if you despise women's God-given traits. You must respect them and celebrate womanhood.

4. Develop teachings that are specific to each group.

Bishop T.D. Jakes is an example of a minister who shows a lot of understanding for women's needs. That is why he is a successful women's minister. He has developed teachings and written books specifically for women.

5. Develop a strong influence over leaders.

Every pastor must develop a strong teaching ministry towards leaders. There are pastors who do not know what to tell their leaders. I enjoy teaching my leaders. The more I teach leaders, the more influence I have because each leader has a sphere of authority.

Chapter 55

Develop Personal Proverbs and Dark Sayings

And moreover, because the preacher was wise, he still taught the people knowledge; yea, he gave good heed, and sought out, and set in order many proverbs.

Ecclesiastes 12:9

This preacher was someone who developed many proverbs. What is a proverb? It is a wise saying with a deep meaning. I once heard an old man say, "It is not money you need to build a house; it is wisdom." This was a wise saying from a man who had led the way to build many houses.

As you become a successful leader, you will develop wisdom through experience. This wisdom will be transmitted through your proverbs.

A wise man will hear, and will increase learning; and a man of understanding shall attain unto wise counsels: To understand a proverb, and the interpretation; the words of the wise, and their dark sayings.

Proverbs 1:5, 6

Chapter 56

Negotiate with Authorities on Behalf of Your Followers

This is a vital part of leadership. You will always have to deal with authorities. Learn to be someone who solves problems. Pray for wisdom to deal with unreasonable and difficult authorities. God will give you wisdom every time.

If any of you lack wisdom, let him ask of God...

James 1:5

Getting approval from various authorities is one of the tasks of a good leader. When I was a student, I had to get permission from principals of schools in order to use their classrooms for meetings I wanted to hold. Getting permission for what you want to do is not always as simple as it may sound. You may need to deal with city planners, the police and local authorities.

A good leader is able to make higher authorities trust you enough to grant you what you need to accomplish your vision.

Five Ways to Deal with Authorities

1. **Recognize that you have to deal with authorities.**

There is no way you are going to do anything in this secular world without dealing with the authorities that be. You have to recognize this fact and prepare yourself to deal with them. You cannot avoid them or go around them.

> **Then the king said unto me, For what dost thou make request? So I prayed to the God of heaven. Moreover I said unto the king, If it please the king, let letters be given me to the governors beyond the river…**
>
> **Nehemiah 2:4,7**

Notice how Nehemiah was able to acquire permission from the king to do what he wanted. Some people are not able to get approval or permission for anything. A good leader must be successful in this area of leadership; otherwise, you will build nothing for God.

2. **Decide to comply with existing laws and regulations.**

The Bible says that these authorities are there for our good.

> **Obey the government, for God is the one who put it there. All governments have been placed in power by God.**
>
> **Romans 13:1 (New Living Translation)**

3.   Use the appropriate people to help you to deal with these authorities.

For instance, if you are dealing with legal issues involving the government, you will have to employ good lawyers or people with legal minds.

4.   Develop and maintain personal and cordial relationships with every relevant authority.

Remember them at Christmas and other important occasions.

5.   Deal with them spiritually.

It is important to deal with authorities by praying for them. Over the years, I have learnt to deal with authorities by praying for them. There is a direct promise in the Word for those who pray for authorities. The promise is that you will be able to live in godliness, honesty and contentment.

> **I exhort therefore, that, first of all, supplications, prayers, intercessions, and giving of thanks, be made for all men; For kings, and for all that are in authority; that we may lead a quiet and peaceable life in all godliness and honesty.**
>
> **1 Timothy 2:1,2**

Chapter 57

Convince People to Make Great Sacrifices

If any man come to me, and hate not his father, and mother, and wife, and children, and brethren, and sisters, yea, and his own life also, he cannot be my disciple.

Luke 14:26

Under the leadership of Jesus, many people gave up their lives for a great cause. Many people lost their lives because they believed in Him. I know of many missionaries who died as they served the Lord on mission fields. A leader is someone who can convince people to make sacrifices towards a great cause.[1]

I once told a young medical doctor to go and live in a remote town of Ghana and begin a church there. This medical doctor had the option of going to the USA to become a rich consultant. He made a great sacrifice and went to that town because I had asked him to. I believe that one day, when we get to Heaven, he will be very glad that he made that sacrifice!

I remember some time ago when our church was in a crisis and we needed a huge financial input. I had to speak to many individuals and ask them to sacrifice their building projects and large amounts of money for the gospel. They did it gladly. God has also blessed them with more than they can carry because of the sacrifices they made!

The Master Key to Leading People into Sacrifice

Are you the type of leader that people would make sacrifices for? Let me give you a key to becoming this type of leader. It is simple. You must be someone who has made great sacrifices yourself. People assess you as you speak! They are convinced when they realize that you practise what you preach.[2]

Verily, verily, I say unto thee, When thou wast young, thou girdedst thyself, and walkedst whither thou wouldest: but when thou shalt be old, thou shalt stretch forth thy hands, and another shall gird thee, and carry thee whither thou wouldest not.

This spake he, signifying by what death he should glorify God. And when he had spoken this, he saith unto him, Follow me.

John 21:18,19

Jesus told Peter very clearly that following him would lead to a horrific death on the cross. Peter was prepared to die because Jesus was leading him.

By 1840, twelve missionaries had been sent to the Gold Coast (Ghana) from the Basel Mission in Switzerland. Only two survived. The story is told of how a class of the Basel Mission were asked, "Who will volunteer to go to the Gold Coast?" No one responded. Another question was asked, "Who is prepared to be sent to the Gold Coast?" Several people responded to that. These missionaries were prepared to die if someone would send them.

You see, people are prepared to make sacrifices if they are led into it. You need a strong leader to send people to a place that has swallowed up the lives of others. Thank God for strong leadership. Be a leader who convinces people to make sacrifices for a good cause.

Chapter 58

Take Everyone to the Top with You

As God blesses your leadership, you will find yourself rising to the top. It is important not to go to the top alone. If you go up there alone you will become isolated. You will be the only one who has prospered and has tasted the fruits of success.[1]

Three Reasons Why You Must Take Everyone to the Top with You

1. **To avoid isolation.**

When you are isolated, you are lonely and have no one to share your joys with. Joy shared is double joy and sorrow shared is half-sorrow. I am glad I have people to share my nice things with. I can speak freely about God's blessings on my life because I am not the only one who is blessed. The people around me can relate to those blessings because they experience them as well.

When I began playing golf, I tried to get all my full-time pastors to play as well. I'm glad that today I have people to play with and to have fun with. I would have been very lonely out there on my own![2]

2. To avoid becoming an easy target.

When you are isolated at the top you become an easy target. You are easy to spot because you are the only one who has certain benefits. When you are the only one with a nice car or house, you are easy to pick out. Many of my staff have just as nice a house or car as I have. I am not the only one in my church who travels around the world. Many of my pastors travel around the world whilst I stay home. They ring me from different parts of the world while I hold the fort in Africa.

3. To avoid being pulled down.

When you are the only one at the top you are surrounded by desperate people. Desperate people are dangerous and could harm you at any time. They will try to pull you down to their level of frustration. However, if you are all at the top, they can only pull you sideways and not downwards.

Six Attempts by Jesus to Take Everyone with Him to the Top

1. Jesus took his disciples to nice places like weddings.

He didn't just take them to the synagogues, prayer meetings in the garden of Gethsemane or Great Commission staff meetings.

And both Jesus was called, and his disciples, to the marriage.

John 2:2

2. Jesus always took his disciples to high society engagements.

And both Jesus was called, and his disciples, to the marriage.

John 2:2

3. Jesus always ate with his disciples.

He took his disciples along with him to dinners and luncheons held in his honour.

And as they were eating, Jesus took bread, and blessed it, and brake it, and gave it to the disciples, and said, Take, eat; this is my body.

Matthew 26:26

4. Jesus asked his Father if his staff could come to Heaven with him.

Father, I will that they also, whom thou hast given me, be with me where I am…

John 17:24

5. Jesus invited all sorts of people to the famous banquet of Luke 14.

He tried to get cripples, beggars, prostitutes and anyone who was interested to come with him to the banquet.

Then said he unto him, A certain man made a great supper, and bade many:

Luke 14:16

6. Jesus invited the thief on the cross to come to paradise with him.

Truly, Jesus wanted to take everyone to the top with him.

And Jesus said unto him, Verily I say unto thee, to day shalt thou be with me in paradise.

Luke 23:43

Chapter 59

Build Something if You Are a Leader!

Many people think that it takes wealth and riches to build a house. From experience, I know that it does not require money per se, but wisdom. People who are able to rally their resources together and use them wisely often become builders. Often such a person is a leader. Have you built a house? Have you built a church? What you build will testify of your leadership. Decide to build something for God in your lifetime.

Through wisdom is an house builded; and by understanding it is established: And by knowledge shall the chambers be filled with all precious and pleasant riches.

Proverbs 24:3,4

Leadership qualities make a pastor acquire a church building for his church. Buying buses or instruments for your church is different from building a church facility. A wise manager would acquire properties for his company. I can assure you that it takes the strength of leadership to build a nation. Weak leaders cannot build anything! Decide today to be a builder. A husband who builds a house for his wife and children is a true leader.[1]

The first president of Ghana, Kwame Nkrumah, is often hailed as a great leader. One of the things he did was to build many things for the nation. For instance, he built the Akosombo Dam, which has the largest man-made lake in the world. The things he built testify to the fact that Ghana once had a great leader. *Leadership is manifested by the presence of buildings*. A good leader leaves something behind.[2]

Western countries have well-developed infrastructure that testify of the kind of leadership they have enjoyed. African countries that have been ruled by illiterate dictators and vampire-style despots, have very little infrastructure. Truly, buildings and development are a sign of good leadership. Solomon was a wise leader.

> **I made me great works; I builded me houses; I planted me vineyards: I made me gardens and orchards, and I planted trees in them of all kind of fruits: I made me pools of water, to water therewith the wood that bringeth forth trees:**
>
> **Ecclesiastes 2:4-6**

Because I have been involved in building, I can understand why most people shy away from it. But I believe that God has called leaders to build. Nehemiah, one of the great leaders of the Bible, motivated the people of God to rise up and build. His famous sermon was simple—arise and build!

> **…The God of heaven, he will prosper us; therefore we his servants will arise and build…**
>
> **Nehemiah 2:20**

Chapter 60

Be Constantly Aware of Your Life's Vision

Pilate therefore said unto him, Art thou a king then? Jesus answered, Thou sayest that I am a king. To this end was I born, and for this cause came I into the world, that I should bear witness unto the truth. Every one that is of the truth heareth my voice.

John 18:37

Jesus knew why he was in this world. Even in times of great stress, he explained his life's purpose. A leader is someone who is constantly aware of his purpose. I am constantly aware of what God has called me to do. Everyday of my life is spent trying to fulfil the calling of God on my life. When you are aware of what you are supposed to do, you are guided aright into spending your time appropriately.[1]

If you only remember that you are a pastor when you arrive in church, then you are probably not a real pastor. When I was a lay person working in the hospital, I was constantly aware of my calling into the ministry. Even when Jesus was a child, He said, "I must be about my Father's business."

And he said unto them, How is it that ye sought me? wist ye not that I must be about my Father's business?

Luke 2:49

Dear leader, what is your life's purpose? Are you a businessman trying to make money? Then why does your business run like a charity? Why do you not cut your expenses and begin to make profits? Are you a minister of the gospel? Then don't be taken up with the love of money. God did not call you to acquire great wealth. He called you to serve in the ministry. Do the ministry even if you have to live in poverty.

God gave me a dream. In the dream, I saw myself walking on a long road. Along this road were many heaps of gold. As I walked on the path, I would pass by these heaps of gold. The Lord specifically told me, "Do not stop at any of these heaps. There are many heaps of gold on this road. There will be no need for you to stop by any of them."

You see, God was showing me that I should stick with my vision. He was telling me not to deviate into business or the search for money. Are you a leader? Then let your vision fill your heart and mind so that you will not deviate from your original calling. If you are a minister, remember that it is souls, souls and more souls. Not money, money and more money!

Chapter 61

Always Stay One Step Ahead

A leader is someone who is ahead of his followers. That is what makes him a leader. You've got to be seen to be at least one step ahead of the people you are leading. Jesus was a good leader. He was definitely one step ahead when it came to prayer. He prayed more than his disciples did. He preached more than his disciples did. He sacrificed more than his disciples did.

A Christian leader has invisible areas in which he must stay ahead. It is his leadership in these invisible areas that make him a true leader.

Ten Areas for Every Christian Leader to Stay Ahead in

1. Stay ahead in prayer.
2. Stay ahead in Bible reading.
3. Stay ahead in reading Christian books.
4. Stay ahead in listening to tapes.
5. Stay ahead in sacrificing to God.
6. Stay ahead in the area of giving.
7. Stay ahead in waiting on God.
8. Stay ahead in holiness.
9. Stay ahead in the love of God.
10. Stay ahead in your relationship with God.

Are you a leader? If you are, then you must be at least one step ahead! You must not only be a step ahead in public, but you must be a step ahead in private. If you are prayerful in secret, your followers will recognize it and do likewise.

Some years ago, somebody gave me some advice on my way to church. He told me, "Listen to all that the priest says. Do what he says, but don't do what he himself does." A true leader must be able to say like Paul did, "Follow me as I follow Christ."

Be ye followers of me, even as I also am of Christ.
1 Corinthians 11:1

If you are not prepared to straighten out your life so that people can see the good thing and follow it, then you are not prepared to be a leader.

Chapter 62

Avoid Distraction

Then he said unto him, Come home with me, and eat bread. And he said, I may not return with thee, nor go in with thee: neither will I eat bread nor drink water with thee in this place: For it was said to me by the word of the Lord, Thou shalt eat no bread nor drink water there, nor turn again to go by the way that thou camest. He said unto him, I am a prophet also as thou art; and an angel spake unto me by the word of the Lord, saying, Bring him back with thee into thine house, that he may eat bread and drink water. But he lied unto him. So he went back with him, and did eat bread in his house, and drank water. And it came to pass, as they sat at the table, that the word of the Lord came unto the prophet that brought him back: And he cried unto the man of God that came from Judah, saying, Thus saith the Lord, Forasmuch as thou hast disobeyed the mouth of the Lord, and hast not kept the commandment which the

Lord thy God commanded thee, But camest back, and hast eaten bread and drunk water in the place, of the which the Lord did say to thee, Eat no bread, and drink no water; thy carcase shall not come unto the sepulchre of thy fathers. And it came to pass, after he had eaten bread, and after he had drunk, that he saddled for him the ass, *to wit*, for the prophet whom he had brought back. And when he was gone, a lion met him by the way, and slew him: and his carcase was cast in the way, and the ass stood by it, the lion also stood by the carcase.

1 Kings 13:15-24

Seven Distractions a Minister Should Avoid

1. **Avoid the distractions that come from people who have not heard from God the way you have.**

Although many other people are ministers, like myself, I realize that we are not on the same level. I do not do things just because others are doing them. Once I told a pastor friend about how we were reaching out to certain villages. He smirked and remarked that he had no interest in such ventures. I was discouraged, wondering whether I was doing the right thing. But I strengthened myself in the Lord and persisted in the calling God gave to me. I'm glad I did.

2. **Avoid the distraction that comes by trying to compete.**

This will drag you into all sorts of activities in which you are trying to outdo another minister.[1]

3. The distraction of phone calls.

The telephone is a modern day distraction that will take you away from the presence of God. Any minister who has not learnt to put the telephone in its right place in his life will constantly be distracted from prayer and Bible study.

4. The distraction of false brethren.

False brethren are people who are sent by the enemy to take up your time. The time that should have been spent with real sheep is spent on these false sheep that have sucked up all your time and energy. These are the very people who will turn around one day to accuse you and be ungrateful. They do not remember the hours you spent investing in their lives.

5. The distraction of carnal leaders and people who are not as committed as you are.

When I relate with ministers who have my level of commitment, they sharpen me and I also sharpen them. Relating with people who do not care about the things of God as much as you do will make you wonder if you are normal. If you are supposed to be a full-time minister and you talk to some lay ministers you may wonder if you are doing the right thing.

6. Avoid the distraction of unproductive arguments and quarrels.

But foolish and unlearned questions avoid, knowing that they do gender strifes.

2 Timothy 2:23

I hate arguments and rarely have time to debate an issue. I love the Scripture that says you cannot do anything against the truth.

> For we can do nothing against the truth, but for the truth.
>
> **2 Corinthians 13:8**

This means that arguments, shouting and proving your point do not affect the truth of the matter. The truth will outlive every lie! Every true minister will be derided, scorned and accused. As you go higher in ministry, more and more lies will be spread about you.

> **The lip of truth shall be established for ever: but a lying tongue is but for a moment.**
>
> **Proverbs 12:19**

7. Avoid doing other people's jobs.

This is one of the greatest distractions of leaders. If I employ someone to look after my security and I have to go around checking the doors myself, then I am doing someone else's job in addition to mine. Many leaders are distracted into doing unnecessary things to compensate for non-performing or irresponsible workers.

Pastors who are called to spiritual things must avoid doing secular and administrative jobs that others can do. I am a pastor so I don't see why I should become an accountant, secretary, banker, security man or protocol officer. This is exactly what Peter did when he ran away from the job of serving tables in order to prevent distraction from holy things.

> **Then the twelve called the multitude of the disciples unto them, and said, It is not reason that we should leave the word of God, and serve tables. But we will give ourselves continually to prayer, and to the ministry of the word.**
>
> **Acts 6:2,4**

Chapter 63

Make People Obey You When You Are Not Present

But it is good to be zealously affected always in a good thing, and not only when I am present with you.

Galatians 4:18

To be able to make people carry out your wishes even when you are not present with them is an art every leader must master. Without this ability, you cannot lead many people. After all, how many people are going to remain in your presence all the time?

Four Keys to Make People Obey You When You Are Not Present

1.   Teach loyalty.

When people are loyal to you they love you and try to do what you want, even when you are away from them.

2.   Teach people that they are dealing with God and not with man.

God is everywhere and he sees everything we do. When people are aware of this, they will try to live in the right way. When a person has a faithful heart, he will obey you because he understands that he is actually dealing with God. It is when people think they are dealing with human beings that they tend to mess around.

> **Servants, be obedient to them that are your masters according to the flesh, with fear and trembling, in singleness of your heart, as unto Christ; Not with eyeservice, as menpleasers; but as the servants of Christ, doing the will of God from the heart;**
>
> **Ephesians 6:5,6**

3.   Teach people that they will be promoted directly by God and not by man.

When they understand that God is the one who will bless them, their attitude will be the same whether you are in or out of their presence. You must train your staff to understand that promotion does not come from the east or the west but that it comes from God. They will not need to see you to be motivated. They know that the eyes of the Lord are everywhere.

> **For promotion cometh neither from the east, nor from the west, nor from the south.**
>
> **Psalm 75:6**

I learnt long ago that the one I have to deal with is God and not man. God is the one who has promoted me in ministry. Men have rather discouraged and attacked me. As soon as you get a revelation of the fact that you are dealing with God, your life will change forever. If you want people to follow you and obey you, even when you cannot see them, teach them this great principle—it is God you are dealing with.

> **…all things are naked and opened unto the eyes of him with whom we have to do.**
>
> **Hebrews 4:13**

When Jesus left the earth he gave commandment concerning the Great Commission. He left us with this great command. Many have obeyed and are still obeying it even though we cannot see Jesus. Become a leader who is obeyed whether seen or not seen.

4. Look for signs and symptoms.

A symptom is a revelation of hidden things. Whenever you do not see something directly you must develop a system of looking for warning signs and indicators. When people do the right thing there are usually some indicators of this. I look for symptoms all the time. I don't have to see everything—I know I won't anyway.

Chapter 64

Hide and Flourish Like a Snake

Behold, I send you forth as sheep in the midst of wolves: be ye therefore wise as serpents, and harmless as doves.

Matthew 10:16

Jesus said, "Be wise as serpents." What is the wisdom of a serpent? *The wisdom of a serpent is the ability to function without unduly attracting your enemy's attention.* Snakes are everywhere. All of us would kill the next snake we see! Such is the enmity between human beings and serpents! Yet snakes flourish and are abundant all around us. How do they do this? By wisdom!

Three Reasons Why a Leader Should Hide and Flourish Like a Snake

1. **Because Christians are hated by the world.**

A Christian leader should *never underestimate* the amount of hatred that Satan and his agents have for the man of God. When you see the Press mercilessly destroying a man of God you will understand that there is an instinctive and inherent hatred for the kingdom of God.

And ye shall be hated of all men for my name's sake...

Matthew 10:22

2. **To avoid being attacked too early in ministry.**

Your leadership will not survive some attacks at a certain stage of your ministry. If you kick a newborn Doberman pinscher or Alsatian dog, it will probably die. But if that same Alsatian or Doberman was allowed to develop and grow, it could probably kill you. There are certain attacks you do not need at a certain stage of your ministry.

When our church used to meet in the canteen of the medical school, we never placed a signboard or banner outside the church. I did not want to attract attention. I knew that if we attracted attention unduly, hateful people would drive us away. Through wisdom we were able to run a large Charismatic church in the middle of a teaching hospital for almost four years. That was the wisdom of a serpent in action — the wisdom to hide and to flourish. When the attacks began, we were a bigger and stronger church.

Some medical students had committed suicide and the Dean of the medical school had come to appreciate the presence of our church in the middle of the hospital. He felt we were meeting a need for the medical community. This made him sympathetic to our presence. He refused to move against us.

Later on, we faced stronger attacks to get rid of us from the hospital. But our church had flourished and we had a member of the board of the medical school in our church. I told the board member that we were being driven out of the medical school canteen. She promptly called the authorities and asked them why they were harassing her church.

"Which church?" they asked in surprise.

"My church," she answered. "The church in the canteen is my church! That is where I go to church! Why are you harassing us?"

They were shocked. "We never knew you went to church there! We will have to look into this."

This slowed down the pressure that was building up against us. That allowed us enough time to acquire our own church building and move out.

After we left the canteen, another church decided to meet in that same place. I soon noticed their big banners displayed outside. After a short while, the hospital community took note of this church's activities. Satan's hatred is not for one particular church, but for all churches. Unfortunately, after a few months they were kicked out of the hospital canteen before they had the chance to flourish. Learn the wisdom of the serpent: the wisdom to hide and to flourish!

3. To avoid attracting an enemy you cannot handle.

Snakes know that they cannot survive in the presence of human beings. I would personally kill every snake I see, whether it was poisonous or non-poisonous, and so would you. This is the reason why snakes live in grass and under rocks where they cannot be seen. The snakes have a good time, do all that they want to do and multiply in their protected environment. They do not attract human beings who are enemies they cannot handle.

I once stopped my national TV program because I thought we were attracting big enemies who hated our success. Upon analysis, I felt that the sight of our growth and ministry was stirring up too many potential enemies, like the government and the Press. I knew that my ministry did not need television *per se* to be fulfilled. So I cut it off! The wisdom of a snake is the wisdom to hide and to flourish. I don't need enemies I cannot handle.

Chapter 65

Overcome the Effect of Rumours, Questions and Controversies about Your Person

When Peter began his ministry there were rumours flying about that he was a gravedigger and that he had stolen the body of Jesus. Many people believed this story, even up till today.

And when they were assembled with the elders, and had taken counsel, they gave large money unto the soldiers, Saying, Say ye, His disciples came by night, and stole him away while we slept. And if this come to the governor's ears, we will persuade him, and secure you.

So they took the money, and did as they were taught: and this saying is commonly reported among the Jews until this day.

Matthew 28:12-15

But Peter had to minister in spite of the controversies and rumours that were whirling around him. Every successful minister must learn to overcome the rumours, stories, questions and controversies that he may face.

Seven Ways to Overcome Rumours, Controversies and Questions

1. Never mention the controversial subject.
2. Stop talking about your past mistakes.
3. Do not repeat the bad things people say about you.
4. Recognize that everyone is limited in one way or the other.
5. Do not magnify a question or rumour about your life or ministry.

There is no need to even speak about it.

6. Do not advertise the rumours manufactured by your enemies.
7. Leave it to God.

He will fight for you.

The Lord shall fight for you, and ye shall hold your peace.

Exodus 14:14

Learn from Jesus

But while he thought on these things, behold, the angel of the Lord appeared unto him in a dream, saying, Joseph, thou son of David, fear not to take unto thee Mary thy wife: for that which is conceived in her is of the Holy Ghost.

Matthew 1:20

1. Jesus was born of a virgin.

   Behold, a virgin shall be with child, and shall bring forth a son, and they shall call his name Emmanuel, which being interpreted is, God with us.

   Matthew 1:23

2. Hundreds of people probably laughed at Joseph for marrying Mary.

3. Jesus was probably thought of as the son of an unfaithful woman or perhaps the son of an unknown man.

4. Some people called him the son of Mary.

   Is not this the carpenter, the son of Mary, the brother of James, and Joses, and of Juda, and Simon? and are not his sisters here with us? And they were offended at him.

   Mark 6:3

5. They probably mocked him and said, "The fatherless self-proclaimed son of God."

6. But Jesus never discussed the issue! Jesus never spoke about Joseph.

7. No Scripture ever brought up the question of his background or his parentage.

8. The question of his father and his mother was never once discussed in any of Jesus' teachings.

Chapter 66

Take That Decision! Most Decisions Will Involve Choosing Between Two Bad Options Anyway!

It is important to realize that things are not perfect. Most decisions that a leader will have to make are not decisions between the obviously good and obviously bad. Most things are not a clear-cut choice between black and white or light and darkness. A good leader must recognize the need to decide when he is faced with such choices. A good leader knows how to choose the lesser of two bad options. Often, life presents us with two bad choices. *Many leaders are paralysed into inaction because of the imperfect choices presented to them.* They refuse to take that important step because they cannot see two very contrasting alternatives.

Marriage is one such decision. God did not create bad women and good women. Men are not choosing between the good and the bad. God did not create the charming and the ugly.

The choice is not between a princess and a frog. Every woman has something attractive about her. Unfortunately, every beautiful woman also has some unattractive aspects. Some men are paralysed into indefinite bachelorhood because they are looking for the perfect female. There is no such thing. Some of the so-called beauties come with horrible flaws.

The same thing applies to women deciding on husbands. There is no such thing as the perfect male. Dear sister, you are going to have to choose between two imperfect options. The "tall and handsome" may come with quarrels and beatings. The "short and stocky" may come along with lifelong financial hardships. The scar-faced man may come with peace and spirituality. Life is like that! You do not have to be paralysed into inaction because you do not see two obviously different things. You have to take a decision! Choose the better of the two. When you fail to choose, you have chosen to have nothing. Perhaps that is why you have nothing today.[1]

Jesus Taught This

Jesus told us clearly that it was better to go to Heaven with one arm than to go to Hell with two arms.

And if thy right eye offend thee, pluck it out, and cast it from thee: for it is profitable for thee that one of thy members should perish, and not that thy whole body should be cast into hell.

Matthew 5:29

To go to Heaven with one arm is not a good thing! When everyone is raising his or her hands in worship, you will have only one arm! When the saints are clapping, you will have to beat your chest! That is truly a tragedy!

However, to go to Hell is even worse. Having two arms or two legs will not mean anything to you in the fires of Hell. Jesus taught us to take the better of these two options. Jesus taught us to choose Heaven with one arm rather than Hell with two arms! Some people have not prospered because they have not understood this important principle. They do not understand that if they do not choose the lesser evil they will have only one other worse option.

Years ago, our church was being thrown out of the medical school canteen. We were under pressure from the authorities to leave the Korle-Bu Teaching Hospital. We located an old, decrepit roofless cinema hall situated next to a rubbish dump and an exploding toilet. I took friends there and asked, "What do you think about this place?" "Horrible!" was the general response of everyone. However, as the leader I was faced with two bad choices. Acquire this nasty, rundown structure and move in or stay in the canteen and face the possible collapse of the church. I chose the decaying building by the rubbish dump. That was one of the best decisions of my ministry.

Do you want to be a good leader? Then you must realize that there are often only two bad options. Be analytical! You must realize quickly that you do not have much choice in this imperfect world.

I once advised a pastor who had a problem to relocate to a different city. This brother could not see that he had two difficult options. I told him, "This is your chance of continuing your ministry." It is not easy to relocate. It is not easy to move into a new city. I explained to him, "You will be more accepted in the new place because your reputation is tarnished here." I told him, "You must move out and make a fresh start.. God is giving you a second chance!" Unfortunately, this pastor could not see that relocation was a better option than the total loss of his ministry. He did not listen and his ministry deteriorated until he became a proverb and a byword.

Examples of Seven Decisions That Are Between Two Imperfect Options

1. Whom to marry.

Every marriage partner comes with peculiar blessings and difficulties. You are not choosing between a prince and a frog.

2. Where to live.

Every country has its advantages and disadvantages. Europe is developed but a more stressful place to live and a godless society. Africa has more God-fearing people and less stressful lifestyle, but is also less developed.

3. What job to do.

Being a lawyer may make you rich, but you may become a cantankerous individual. Being a doctor may make you prosperous but you may spend most of your life in the hospital, overseeing misery and death.

4. What to study in school.

It may be quicker and shorter to study carpentry. But in the end it may be more profitable to study medicine which is more difficult, and requires many years of study.

5.   Which church to attend.

Every church has its strengths. You may be in a church that is strong in the anointing but weak in teaching. Some churches have no miracles but teach the Word.

6.   Whom to vote for.

Each political party has its good and bad sides. Do not be deceived into thinking that you are choosing between the good and the bad. Most elections are between two bad options.

7.   Which car to drive.

A Korean car may be cheaper but not as strong as a German car. Japanese cars are not as strong as German cars but they are easier to handle and cheaper to maintain.

Chapter 67

Don't Destroy Your Ministry by Saying the Wrong Things in Public

Thou art snared with the words of thy mouth, thou art taken with the words of thy mouth.

Proverbs 6:2

A leader must be careful about the things he says. By your words, you are snared and by your words, you will be judged. Be careful of the things you say.[1]

And Nabal answered David's servants, and said, Who is David? and who is the son of Jesse? there be many servants now a days that break away every man from his master. Shall I then take my bread, and my water, and my flesh that I have killed for my shearers, and give it unto men, whom I know not whence they be?

1 Samuel 25:10,11

This statement almost cost Nabal his life.

Now David had said, Surely in vain have I kept all that this fellow hath in the wilderness, so that nothing was missed of all that pertained unto him: and he hath requited me evil for good. So and more also do God unto the enemies of David, if I leave of all that pertain to him by the morning light any that pisseth against the wall.

1 Samuel 25:21,22

If you are a leader, pick your words very carefully. If you do not know what to say or how to say it, then say nothing. People are looking for an opportunity to take you up on your words. They want to write an article about you and make you out to be something that you are not.[2]

There is no need to tell everyone what class you travel on an airline. There is no need to tell people the cost of your clothes. There is no need to tell the congregation what you bought for your wife. Not everyone appreciates these things. Some people hate you because they feel that you are having a good time with their money. Your closest friends may appreciate God's blessings on your life, but most people feel that ministers should be poor.

I am a very frank person. I often say exactly what I think. Because of this I totally avoid interviews and journalists. I do not want to be provoked into giving foolish answers to foolish questions. Even Apostle Paul had to do that sometimes because he was so aggravated by the foolishness of certain people.

Would to God ye could bear with me a little in my folly: and indeed bear with me.

2 Corinthians 11:1

I see no reason why I should go for an interview only to be asked where I live, what car I drive and what I eat for breakfast. I have heard ministers being asked these questions repeatedly and I consider these questions frivolous. Learn the art of saying the right thing in public or saying nothing at all! A leader is someone who says the right things. Build your ministry by saying the right things in public.

Chapter 68

Avoid Becoming an Artificial Leader. Develop Natural Leadership Skills

Eighteen Signs of a Natural Leader

1. A natural leader inspires.
2. A natural leader speaks off the cuff.
3. A natural leader acts out his belief.
4. A natural leader is practical.[1]
5. A natural leader is emotional.
6. A natural leader leads by example.
7. A natural leader makes great sacrifices for his beliefs.[2]

8. A natural leader uses himself as an example because he is a good one.[3]
9. A natural leader is God-made and God-appointed.
10. A natural leader says what he believes.
11. A natural leader is often criticized.
12. A natural leader is often controversial.
13. A natural leader has a genuine concern.
14. A natural leader is concerned about the real thing.
15. A natural leader is not keen on much debate and analysis. He wants to get to the job.
16. A natural leader is not interested in what title he is given. He is more interested in the job.
17. A natural leader is not motivated by money.
18. A natural leader loves people.[4]

Fifteen Signs of an Artificial Leader.

1. An artificial leader is boring.
2. An artificial leader often reads his speeches.
3. An artificial leader holds seminars and conferences but takes no action.
4. An artificial leader is theoretical.
5. An artificial leader shows no emotion.
6. An artificial leader prepares ideal speeches, says the right things but does nothing.
7. An artificial leader never uses himself as an example (as he is not a good example).
8. An artificial leader is man-made and man-appointed.
9. An artificial leader says what people want him to say.

10. An artificial leader is often not criticized.
11. An artificial leader fits the accepted mode.
12. An artificial leader is concerned in an official capacity but not in a real way. He does not love the people.
13. An artificial leader is concerned about the ceremony and not the job.
14. An artificial leader is very concerned about titles.
15. An artificial leader is most concerned about salaries and benefits.

How to Induce Natural Leadership Qualities

1. Form an opinion and develop a conviction.

It is your conviction that makes you stand out.

2. Observe natural leaders.

Observe and admire natural leaders. Notice what they do and do not do. Watch the artificial appointed leaders and don't do what they do.

3. Fellowship with natural leaders.

Do not miss an opportunity to spend a few moments with great leaders.

4. Study the lives of different natural leaders.

5. Fellowship with great leaders through their books and tapes.

6. Listen to great natural leaders.

Chapter 69

Do Not Allow Tiredness to Be an Excuse

Someone said, "The world is run by tired people." If you are not a true leader, you will not give up your life for anything. A non-leader is not prepared to work because he is tired. Do not allow tiredness to be an excuse. If tiredness is an excuse then you cannot be a leader. If I used the excuse of tiredness, I would not have accomplished seventy per cent of what I have accomplished.[1]

Jesus said, "I am the good shepherd: the good shepherd giveth his life for the sheep" (John 10:11). Tiredness is part of giving your life for the sheep.[2]

As soon as you begin to give up your life, it tells on you. I am not saying that every leader should be exhausted. What I am saying is that leadership is very exacting. Sometimes I see non-leaders murmuring about being tired. All they want to do is to go away.

It is a known fact that many workers have no interest in their places of employment except in their salaries.

Such people (who are usually not leaders) are not prepared to become unduly tired.

For which cause we faint not; but though our outward man perish, yet the inward man is renewed day by day.

2 Corinthians 4:16

As I write this book, I can assure you that I am exhausted. But I know that I have to do it. A good leader often does much hard work in secret. It is these hidden jobs and unseen pressures that make our leaders tired. If you want a life of relaxation and ease, you are probably not a leader.[3]

Heads of State, Chief Executives and prominent leaders are often viewed as glamorous jet-setters who have many privileges at their disposal. I can assure you that these privileges are a very small compensation for the genuine leader who gives his life for a great cause.

Are you a leader? If you are living a life of constant ease and pleasures, perhaps you are on leave from true leadership.[4]

Chapter 70

Gain Control over Your Domestic Life

One of the first qualifications that Paul gave for leadership was to have a wife and disciplined children. It is interesting that the qualifications for ministry were basic and domestic.[1]

A bishop then must be blameless, the husband of one wife, vigilant, sober, of good behaviour, given to hospitality, apt to teach; One that ruleth well his own house, having his children in subjection with all gravity;

1 Timothy 3:2,4

Six Signs That You Are in Control of Your Domestic Situation

1. The sign of having acquired a wife or husband.
2. The sign of a stable home.[2]
3. The sign of a marriage that is working.
4. The sign of a student who does well in school.
5. The sign of financial stability and being debt- free.
6. The sign of a stable job.

Have you been able to instil peace and order in your own home? Is your marriage working? If you are a student, have you been able to get your academic life under control?[3]

I was a pastor when I was a medical student. I made sure that I did well in all my exams. I made sure that I had no problems with school. Leadership begins by bringing your domestic affairs under control. Look at your domestic affairs: your school, your job, your home and your marriage. If these are in order then you are well on the road to leadership.[4]

Chapter 71

Be Sincere, Not a Hypocrite

When Jesus was alive, there was a group of people he did not get along with. They were the hypocritical Pharisees and Sadducees.[1]

Woe unto you, scribes and Pharisees, hypocrites! for ye are like unto whited sepulchres, which indeed appear beautiful outward, but are within full of dead men's bones, and of all uncleanness.

Matthew 23:27

Sooner or later, people will see the different standards that you maintain. They will see beauty on the outside, but ugliness inside. This has the potential to drive away every follower. A leader wants to have followers. Hypocrisy is an offensive vice. It has the power to scatter all your followers in a short period. Make sure that what you do outside is what you are inside.[2]

The reason why so many children do not obey their parents is because they resent what they see at home. They see hypocrisy. They hear their parents talking about ideal values in public but there is only ugliness at home. This makes many children decide within themselves: *I will never be like daddy, and I will never be like mommy.* They turn away from all the high standards and expectations of their parents. Do you consider yourself a leader? Remove all skeletons from your wardrobe. Be as pure inside as you are outside and you will have a good following.[3]

A good leader is able to sustain trust over a long period. Unfortunately, as time goes by, much trust is eroded. *But God is raising up a new breed of leaders who do what they say and say what they do.*[4]

Chapter 72

Know Your Limitations

Every leader has limitations. God did not make us into supermen. Even Jesus knew when his time was up. He knew when it was time for the Comforter to take over. He began to speak of the Comforter, which is the Holy Spirit. He promised that the Comforter would make a great difference in their lives. Unfortunately, the disciples could not believe that there could be a better substitute for Jesus.[1]

Nevertheless I tell you the truth; It is expedient for you that I go away: for if I go not away, the Comforter will not come unto you; but if I depart, I will send him unto you.

John 16:7

How many leaders realize when it is time for them to leave the scene? How many leaders are prepared to accept that other leaders with different talents are needed? You will be rewarded for fulfilling your calling. You will not receive a heavenly award for impressing human beings.

And he said unto them, Ye are they which justify yourselves before men; but God knoweth your hearts: for that which is highly esteemed among men is abomination in the sight of God.

Luke 16:15

The admiring smiles of people around you have no influence on the opinions of your Heavenly Father. That is why I do not really care what others think about me. Because I am human, it occurs to me that people may find me weird. I often think that many of my medical colleagues see me as strange. But what does it matter?

Do not try to please people anymore! Try to please the Lord. When it is time for others to play their role allow them to. Do not stifle others. See yourself as building the Kingdom of God and enhancing the Body of Christ.

Recognize that you cannot do everything. Allow others to play a role. They will be blessed and so will you!

Moses allowed seventy other men to help him in the ministry. That decision certainly prolonged his life.

When Jesus called the services of the Comforter, he was not acknowledging defeat. There are some pastors who lack administrative and management skills. If you do not employ the services of the appropriate people, your ministry may crumble.

Do you consider yourself to be a great leader? Recognize your limitations.

Chapter 73

Be Courageous

Do you want to lead people? You are going to need a lot of courage.

In Joshua 1, God exhorted Joshua three times to be courageous.

> **Be strong and of a good courage: for unto this people shalt thou divide for an inheritance the land, which I sware unto their fathers to give them. Only be thou strong and very courageous... Have not I commanded thee? Be strong and of a good courage; be not afraid...**
>
> **Joshua 1:6,7,9**

This was the beginning of Joshua's life as a leader. Obviously, courage was very important for the ministry of Joshua to succeed. It takes a courageous person to advance into fearful and frightening circumstances. It takes courage to advance when the outcome is uncertain. You need a lot of courage when failure looks like a real option.

When defeat is rallying around to welcome you, you need to be bold to press on to victory. We all know that the bystanders are waiting for our downfall. It takes courage to continue on a certain course of action. Without courage, you cannot call yourself a leader. It takes courage to start a church or a business. What about if it fails? What about if it doesn't? It takes courage to follow a new idea.[1]

It is only courageous people who can be leaders. Success or failure depends on being courageous. It takes courage to stand up for the truth. The reason why many people do not try new aspects of ministry is because they lack courage. It takes courage to pray for the sick. It takes courage to minister the Spirit. It takes courage to launch out! What if no one is healed?

Ask God for the Spirit of Joshua. You will find yourself advancing on to higher heights when you are very courageous!

Chapter 74

Get People to Follow You Somewhere

Jesus was able to get people to follow Him. If you are a leader in the Body of Christ, you must be able to make people follow you. How do you do this?[1]

And Jesus said unto them, Come ye after me, and I will make you to become fishers of men.

Mark 1:17

Three Steps to Make People Follow You

1.   Be yourself.

When a young man proposes marriage to a young lady he is trying to get her to follow him. The proposal must come from the bottom of your heart. I did not read a speech to my wife when I proposed to her. The most successful leaders are those who are "real". People love to hear leaders speaking naturally from their hearts rather than reading boring speeches that say all the right things. No one wants to follow a pretender![2]

2.   Believe totally in where you are going.

You must believe in the future your leadership is creating. If you propose marriage to someone, you must believe that you are going to give yourself and the young lady a good future.[3]

3.   Go yourself where you are trying to get people to follow you.

You cannot get people to pray if you do not pray yourself. I have found it easier to make people pray by just leading them in a prayer meeting. When my people see me praying they are highly motivated to pray. Pastors who tell their members to do one thing when they do something else, often do not get good results.[4]

Chapter 75

Mix Truth with Grace to Gain More Followers

And the Word was made flesh, and dwelt among us, (and we beheld his glory, the glory as of the only begotten of the Father,) full of grace and truth.

John 1:14

The glory of Jesus Christ is in his presentation of truth with grace. Truth without grace is dangerous. Truth without grace will eliminate most of the followers of Christ. Most Christians would not make the mark if God dealt with us based on only the truth. Let's face it, how many Christians really do what the pastor tells them to do? How many Christians walk in love and forgive one another? If the church were to wipe out its mistake-laden members, most churches would be empty. King David described it well in Psalm 130:3.[1]

If thou, LORD, shouldest mark iniquities, O Lord, who shall stand?

Psalm 130:3

A good leader always combines a mixture of truth and grace when dealing with his followers. A mixture of truth and grace will allow some of your followers to straighten out and become great ministers. However, with some people, even the grace of God does not change them. I have many sons and daughters in the ministry who have turned out well after a mixture of grace and truth had been applied to their lives. Truth without grace would have eliminated many of the wonderful ministers and leaders who work with me today.

Four Examples on How to Use a Mixture of Grace and Truth

1. **Jesus knew the truth about Judas but he mixed it with grace.**

Jesus could have moved on Judas because he knew the truth, that Judas was a betrayer! Jesus allowed Judas to benefit from the grace of God. He mixed truth with grace to give Judas a chance but Judas ended up destroying himself.

I allow people to destroy themselves if that is their destiny. I am not in a hurry to prove anything. I believe that people will either straighten out or destroy themselves eventually. When people come to me with accusations against pastors I tell them, "If I confront this person, he will deny the accusation. I will just leave him to the grace of God and to time. If he is destined to destroy himself he will. If he is destined to straighten himself out, he will!"

2. Jesus knew the truth about Peter but he mixed it with grace.

Jesus knew that Peter was open to satanic and worldly influences but he still worked with him. Jesus did not disconnect from Peter.

> **But he turned, and said unto Peter, Get thee behind me, Satan: thou art an offence unto me: for thou savourest not the things that be of God, but those that be of men.**
>
> **Matthew 16:23**

Jesus knew the truth about Peter—that he slept at prayer meetings. But the grace of God allowed Jesus to continue to work with Peter. Jesus overlooked Peter's frailties.

> **And he cometh unto the disciples, and findeth them asleep, and saith unto Peter, What, could ye not watch with me one hour?**
>
> **Matthew 26:40**

Jesus knew the truth about Peter. Jesus knew Peter would let him down but he still worked with him. Jesus did not disconnect himself from Peter. He forgave him.

> **Jesus answered him, Wilt thou lay down thy life for my sake? Verily, verily, I say unto thee, The cock shall not crow, till thou hast denied me thrice.**
>
> **John 13:38**

Jesus knew the truth about Peter, that he would leave the ministry and backslide into secular work. After all the training that Peter had received, he abandoned the ministry and went back to fishing. Jesus did not change the plans he had for Peter.

There were together Simon Peter, and Thomas called Didymus, and Nathanael of Cana in Galilee, and the sons of Zebedee, and two other of his disciples. Simon Peter saith unto them, I go a fishing. They say unto him, We also go with thee. They went forth, and entered into a ship immediately; and that night they caught nothing.

John 21:2,3

All these bad things about Peter were true, but the glory of Christ is in the glory of truth presented with grace. *And we beheld his glory, the glory as of the only begotten of the father, full of grace and truth.* In the end, Peter turned out to be a great leader of the church. That is what truth mixed with grace can do.

3. Jesus knew the truth about Thomas but he mixed it with grace.

Thomas did not believe that Christ could rise from the dead. And Jesus knew it. The truth about this great apostle was that he did not believe in the resurrection. The grace of God gave Thomas another opportunity to become a believer. And he did. A mixture of grace and truth gave birth to another ardent follower.

And after eight days again his disciples were within, and Thomas with them: then came Jesus, the doors being shut, and stood in the midst, and said, Peace be unto you. Then saith he to Thomas, Reach hither thy finger, and behold my hands; and reach hither thy hand, and thrust it into my side: and be not faithless, but believing. And Thomas answered and said unto him, My Lord and my God. Jesus saith unto him, Thomas, because thou hast seen me, thou hast believed: blessed are they that have not seen, and yet have believed.

John 20:26-29

4. Jesus knew the truth about the ten disciples but he mixed it with grace.

Jesus knew the truth about his disciples. He knew that his disciples would desert him when he needed them the most.

> …Then all the disciples forsook him, and fled.
>
> Matthew 26:56

Many of Jesus' disciples went back to their secular jobs after Jesus left.

> **There were together Simon Peter, and Thomas called Didymus, and Nathanael of Cana in Galilee, and the sons of Zebedee, and two other of his disciples. Simon Peter saith unto them, I go a fishing. They say unto him, We also go with thee. They went forth, and entered into a ship immediately; and that night they caught nothing.**
>
> John 21:2,3

The grace of God made Jesus ignore the frailties, weaknesses and mistakes of his followers. He overlooked their faults and allowed his men to become mighty apostles. If you overlook the faults of your followers, work with them, and pray for them, you will bear more fruit.

Leadership Is the Art of Overlooking Faults

Leadership can also be described as the art of overlooking faults. It is almost impossible to effectively lead without intentionally overlooking faults, mistakes, and shortcomings of others. This is because God has called you to lead human beings and not angels. If God had called you to lead a group of angels you would not need to overlook any faults. I sometimes wonder why human beings find it so difficult to overlook the mistakes of others.[2]

I thank the Lord for people who have accommodated and still accommodate my shortcomings. Many of the nice people I work with have faults. It is not that I don't see their shortcomings, but I realize that I must give them many opportunities to grow out of that stage. If you cut off the hands of your child because he touched something you asked him not to, would he ever grow up to become a responsible citizen? By the time he is an adult, he would have neither arms nor legs because you would have amputated all his limbs for his numerous mistakes during childhood! A leader is someone who intentionally overlooks glaring faults and gives people the opportunity to become great.

Do not give up on the people you are investing in. See into the future and know that whatever you have sown will definitely be reaped. If you have spent time teaching and training people, they will grow up to be responsible leaders. If you have invested in the lives of people, it will definitely yield something. Do not be overwhelmed by the shortcomings of those you trust. Give it some time. A leader is a father. And every father believes that one day his son will become somebody great.

Chapter 76

The Eight Greatest Decisions of a Leader

1.   To be born again.

The beginning of wisdom is to fear God. The very first decision of your life is to take Jesus as your Saviour. Every other decision is foolishness.

2.   To be a committed Christian.

You have several choices. You can be committed to education, politics or sports. A person who chooses to be committed to Christ by giving his time and energy will discover that he has made one of the greatest decisions of his life.

3. To choose the Bible as your most important book.

Put all the books you know about on the left, but put the Bible on the right on its own. The Bible is different from any other book on this earth.

F.F. Bruce said on page 15 of *The New Testament Documents*, "The evidence for our New Testament writings is ever so much greater than the evidence for many writings of classical authors, the authenticity of which no one dreams of questioning. And if the New Testament were a collection of secular writings, their authenticity would generally be regarded as beyond all doubt. It is a curious fact that historians have often been much readier to trust the New Testament than have many theologians."

4. To marry the right person.

The person you marry will prove to be a challenge to you. That decision is one of the most important you will ever make.

5. To choose the right church.

The church you belong to makes a world of difference.

6. To follow the right person.

Whether you believe it or not, everyone follows someone else. We all have spoken or unspoken heroes or mentors we look up to. The one you choose will make all the difference in your life. Paul advised his church members to follow him.

> **Be ye followers of me, even as I also am of Christ.**
>
> **1 Corinthians 11:1**

> That ye be not slothful, but followers of them who through faith and patience inherit the promises.
>
> **Hebrews 6:12**

7.   To choose the right city, country and people to live amongst.

Since your success is connected to a place, your choice of where to live is very important. Make this decision very early in your life and you will experience great success as a leader.

8.   To choose your friends.

Your choice of friends is one of the most important decisions of your life. Whether you like it or not, your friendships help to carve your future. Show me your friends and I will predict your future.

Chapter 77

Carefully Choose Your Mentors

A mentor is someone who is an advisor, guide, counsellor, teacher, and tutor to you. Your mentor is a picture of your future. There are several ways to predict the future. One of the ways is to simply look at someone's mentor. If you look at Joshua you could predict his future by looking at his mentor, Moses. You could predict the future of Peter, James and John by looking at their mentor, Jesus. You could predict the future of Elisha by looking at his mentor, Elijah.[1]

There are several people who have mentored me. There are some things I would not like to have in my life. I see them in some of the people who are ahead of me. Because of this, I carefully choose who mentors me. Someone who has lived long, achieved a lot, worked faithfully for the Lord, and stayed successfully married would be a good mentor.[2]

Eight Things a Leader Should Know about Mentoring

1. **Not every successful person can be your mentor.**

   Not everyone in the world can be your mentor. God has chosen certain people to mentor you.

2. **You can be mentored from afar.**

   Someone who does not even know you can mentor you. Most of the mentors I have do not know me personally. They have mentored me through their books and tapes.

3. **Your future can be predicted by looking at your mentor.**

   You could predict the future of Peter, James and John by looking at their mentor, Jesus.

4. **You can be mentored to a greater or lesser extent depending on how close you become to your mentor.**

   Jesus did not affect everyone in the same way. He had five hundred people whom he appeared to after he rose from the dead. He had one hundred and twenty people who waited for the Holy Ghost in the upper room. And he had twelve disciples who followed him everywhere. He also had a whole lot of women who ministered to him of their substance.

> And it came to pass afterward, that he went throughout every city and village, preaching and shewing the glad tidings of the kingdom of God: and the twelve were with him, And certain women, which had been healed of evil spirits and infirmities, Mary called Magdalene, out of whom went seven devils, And Joanna the wife of Chuza Herod's steward, and Susanna, and many others, which ministered unto him of their substance.
>
> Luke 8:1-3

Then he had Mary, his mother, and Mary Magdalene who stood by the cross during his last moments on earth. He had the inner core made out of Peter, James and John. Then he had Peter who was the head of his team. He also had John whom he loved specially.

5. **Almost every successful Bible character had a mentor.**

   a. Jesus' mentor was the Father.

   b. Jesus was the mentor of Peter, James and John.

   c. Joshua's mentor was Moses.

   d. Elisha's mentor was Elijah.

6. **You cannot mentor a proud person.**

You cannot be mentored if you are too proud to learn from another.[3]

7. There are natural and spiritual mentors.

Moses had a natural mentor in Pharaoh. He learnt about leadership and government from Pharaoh. David also studied leadership and government in the courts of his mentor, the demonised King Saul. These were natural mentors given by God to train his servants in natural things. After this natural training, spiritual training takes place. I received my natural training from my parents and from my formal education.

My medical training has provided me with an essential part of my preparation for ministry.[4]

8. Your mentor is a human being.

Pick the good things and leave the bad ones. When you are served with a meal, and you do not like something on the plate, you eat what you like and leave the rest!

Chapter 78

Inspire People

I have coveted no man's silver, or gold, or apparel. Yea, ye yourselves know, that these hands have ministered unto my necessities, and to them that were with me. I have shewed you all things, how that so labouring ye ought to support the weak, and to remember the words of the Lord Jesus, how he said, It is more blessed to give than to receive. And when he had thus spoken, he kneeled down, and prayed with them all. And they all wept sore, and fell on Paul's neck, and kissed him,

Acts 20:33-37

A leader is somebody who inspires the people around him. Human beings are emotional! Study closely the results of almost any election and you will discover that people vote by their emotions. Some regions in the country vote en bloc for certain individuals.[1]

A true leader must recognize the emotional nature of human beings and must lead people with that in mind. You must be able to speak in a way that inspires people to follow you. How would you be able to lead people to give their lives to the Lord if your speeches are lifeless and emotionless? Notice how people wept after Paul finished preaching.[2]

And they all wept sore, and fell on Paul's neck...

Acts 20:37

Decide to be an inspiring and motivational leader. Put away your lifeless speeches and speak from your heart. Practise this until you find yourself doing it naturally and easily. Once again, to do this you need to operate from the bottom of your heart. Peter said,

...such as I have give I thee...

Acts 3:6

You cannot motivate people if you yourself are not motivated. You cannot affect the emotions of anyone unless you yourself are emotional about what you are doing.[3]

Chapter 79

Find Solutions and Solve Problems

Finding solutions and solving problems will distinguish you from other people. One of the last instructions I give my staff when I'm travelling is: "Solve problems, I'll be back." I am happy to have people who can solve problems. Every assignment you will ever give has problems associated with it. The man who can solve problems as they come up, is the one who is truly valuable and truly a leader!

When I give someone an assignment, I expect him to return to me having accomplished it. Unfortunately, many employees only come back with more problems. Sometimes I look at them with amazement as they tell me about all the problems that they have encountered. Most of the time, I just tell them to solve those problems, and come back with results.

The greatness of an employee is in his ability to find the solutions to all the problems that arise on the job.

Moses' assignment was to take the people out of Egypt and into the Promised Land. Surely, he ran into all sorts of problems. First, there was the Red Sea, then there was no water, then there was no food. Then they found water but it was bitter. After this, Moses began to have management problems. People began to complain and murmur. Then he had problems of insubordination with his employees and relatives. As you can see, for Moses to lead his people out of Egypt he had to be able to solve all sorts of problems.

The world is also full of unsolvable problems. There are problems everywhere; there are difficulties at every turn. Everyone is looking for someone who will be able to take them forward.

Moses stood by the Red Sea and faced a crisis. The advancing Egyptian army was breathing down his neck. How could there be a way forward? But Moses found a solution.

And Moses stretched out his hand over the sea; and the Lord caused the sea to go back by a strong east wind all that night, and made the sea dry land, and the waters were divided. And the children of Israel went into the midst of the sea upon the dry ground...

Exodus 14:21,22

If you are a pastor, one of the difficult problems that will face you is how to make your church grow. You must strive to lead the people into growth and prosperity. It is not easy, but that is the job of the leader. A successful pastor is someone who has solved the problem of making the church grow.

If you are a businessperson, you will be faced with the difficulty of making profits in the face of stiff competition. Your job is to lead your company into success. If you are a political leader you will be faced with corruption, industrial action and betrayal at all levels. How can you make something good out of a desperate situation? Remember that it is the leader's job to find solutions and solve problems.[1]

The Master Key to Finding Solutions and Solving Problems

The master key is wisdom. The Bible teaches that Solomon was a very wise man and he became the richest man that ever lived. He became a stable political leader. He had peace and stability in his reign. These things came by the wisdom of God.[2]

Can wisdom solve problems? The Bible teaches about a city that was in crisis. Enemy forces surrounded it and there was no hope for anyone. However, deliverance came to the city through a poor but wise man. Solutions for impossible situations come through wisdom.[3]

> **There was a little city, and few men within it; and there came a great king against it, and besieged it, and built great bulwarks against it: Now there was found in it a poor wise man, and he by his wisdom delivered the city; yet no man remembered that same poor man.**
>
> **Ecclesiastes 9:14,15**

Two Ways to Receive Wisdom

1. Wisdom comes through reading.

Read the books of Proverbs and Ecclesiastes everyday and ask God to give you wisdom for the affairs of this life. Take it from me. Life is full of impossible situations. Life is full of problems with no solutions. That is why God raises up leaders, to help bring answers to questions that have no answers.[4]

2. Wisdom comes through prayer.

The most important prayer for a leader is the prayer for wisdom. A leader must constantly ask God for wisdom.[5]

If any of you lack wisdom, let him ask of God, that giveth to all men liberally, and upbraideth not; and it shall be given him.

James 1:5

Chapter 80

Be a Thinker

    Every good doctor must be able to diagnose the problem of his patient. Making a diagnosis is eighty per cent of the solution. Your job as a leader is to think about the problem, listen to the story, examine the situation and come up with an analysis of what is going on. When you do not think about the work you are doing, you often cannot do it well. You must be consumed with your work, and you must think about it all the time. Anyone who does not think about his work will not do well. As someone said, "You will only be remembered for your obsession." I notice that some of my employees hardly think of the jobs that they do. Their minds are not on it. They are not obsessed, and it shows.[1]

Six Advantages of Being a Leader Who Thinks about His Work

1.   A great thinker always comes up with solutions to intractable problems.

    So I returned, and considered all the oppressions that are done under the sun: and behold the tears of such as were oppressed, and they had no comforter; and on the side of their oppressors there was power; but they had no comforter.

    Ecclesiastes 4:1

2.   A leader who thinks about his work constantly comes up with improvement.

    Again, I considered all travail, and every right work, that for this a man is envied of his neighbour. This is also vanity and vexation of spirit.

    Ecclesiastes 4:4

3.   A leader who thinks a lot about his work will hear the Spirit of God whispering direction.

    Then I saw, and considered it well: I looked upon it, and received instruction.

    Proverbs 24:32

4.   A leader who thinks will be open to brilliant and life-changing ideas.

This wisdom have I seen also under the sun, and it seemed great unto me: Then said I, Wisdom is better than strength: nevertheless the poor man's wisdom is despised, and his words are not heard.

Ecclesiastes 9:13,16

5. A leader who thinks a lot will come up with new goals and visions.[2]

I communed with mine own heart, saying, Lo, I am come to great estate, and have gotten more wisdom than all they that have been before me in Jerusalem: yea, my heart had great experience of wisdom and knowledge.

Ecclesiastes 1:16

6. A leader who thinks a lot will receive wisdom.

And I gave my heart to seek and search out by wisdom concerning all things that are done under heaven: this sore travail hath God given to the sons of man to be exercised therewith.

Ecclesiastes 1:13

Three Keys to Becoming a Great Thinker

1. Wait on God.

2. Read books which expand your imagination and frontiers of knowledge.

3. Think more deeply about whatever you see or hear.

Allow your mind to consider issues when they come up. Do not just take things at the surface level.

I have seen the travail, which God hath given to the sons of men to be exercised in it.

Ecclesiastes 3:10

There is a sore evil which I have seen under the sun, namely, riches kept for the owners thereof to their hurt.

Ecclesiastes 5:13

Then I looked on all the works that my hands had wrought, and on the labour that I had laboured to do: and, behold, all was vanity and vexation of spirit, and there was no profit under the sun.

Ecclesiastes 2:11

I have often had to think about the state of affairs of my church. I am constantly analysing what is going on, therefore, I am constantly taking decisions. Once, I was having a discussion with one of my contractors and I told him, "I am the most important person you need to talk to about this project."

I continued, "I think about this project more than the architects do."

A good leader analyses his work and it's related problems all the time. Perhaps the reason why you are ineffective as a leader is that your heart and your mind are not constantly on your assignment.

King Solomon analysed the problem of poverty around him. He concluded (diagnosis) that much of the problem was caused by lack of hard work. He figured out that if he could deal with sleep and folding of arms there would be more prosperity.

Then I saw, and considered it well: I looked upon it, and received instruction. Yet a little sleep, a little slumber, a little folding of the hands to sleep: So shall thy poverty come as one that travelleth; and thy want as an armed man.

Proverbs 24:32-34

Chapter 81

Reproduce Yourself in Others

Thou therefore, my son, be strong in the grace that is in Christ Jesus.

2 Timothy 2:1

Being a good leader involves reproducing yourself in others. God made us in his image. He reproduced images of himself in us. When he sees us walking, he can see himself.

If you have a forty-year-old son who depends on you for everything, you have failed as a leader. But if you have a forty-year-old son who does not need you anymore to survive, then you have successfully trained up your child. Leadership is not the art of making a whole lot of people dependent on one person.[1]

Jesus, the perfect leader, was constantly preparing his disciples for the time when he would no longer be with them. A good leader is someone who is reproducing himself in others so that he is no longer essential. Jesus used phrases like, "When the time shall come", "In a little while" and "In that day". What day was he referring to—the day when he would no longer be around. Every leader must prepare himself for that day.[2]

But these things have I told you, that when the time shall come, ye may remember that I told you of them. And these things I said unto you at the beginning, because I was with you. But now I go my way to him that sent me...

John 16:4,5

A little while, and ye shall not see me...

John 16:16

And in that day ye shall ask me nothing...

John 16:23

The better your leadership, the more sons and daughters you will have. Your absence will not matter because you have reproduced yourself in so many others.[3]

Five Ways to Reproduce Yourself in Others

1. Be a father.

When you have the heart of a father, those that relate with you will naturally relate to you as sons.

2. Be a teacher.

Do not assume that people will learn things by osmosis. You must actually teach them what you want them to know.[4]

3. Be a friend.

Through friendship you will informally pass on many lessons.

4. Expose them to the challenges of ministry.

Experience teaches you what a hundred years of schooling cannot.

5. Send them into the ministry.

There are certain things people will never learn until they are sent.

> **To Titus, mine own son after the common faith... For this cause left I thee in Crete, that thou shouldest set in order the things that are wanting, and ordain elders in every city, as I had appointed thee:**
>
> **Titus 1:4,5**

Chapter 82

Be a Can-Do Leader

Twenty Five Statements of a Can-Do Man

1.	All things are possible.[1]

For with God nothing shall be impossible.

Luke 1:37

2.	Let us work hard.

3.	Let us try it. Let us give it a chance.

4.	We have nothing to lose.

Then Elisha said, Hear ye the word of the LORD; Thus saith the Lord, To morrow about this time shall a measure of fine flour be sold for a shekel, and two measures of barley for a shekel, in the gate of Samaria. Then a lord on whose hand the king leaned answered the man of God, and said, Behold, if the LORD would make windows in heaven, might this

thing be? And he said, Behold, thou shalt see it with thine eyes, but shalt not eat thereof. And there were four leprous men at the entering in of the gate: and they said one to another, Why sit we here until we die?

2 Kings 7:1-3

5. Let us copy the one who has done it successfully.

That ye be not slothful, but followers of them who through faith and patience inherit the promises.

Hebrews 6:12

6. I will do it even if no one helps me.
7. We are as good as those who have done it.
8. It is not too late to learn something new.
9. Let us make the change now.[2]
10. It is not too late to start.
11. Let us start right now.
12. Let us work until it is finished.
13. Let us not go home till we have accomplished it.
14. I will never give up.
15. I have no time for the opposition.
16. God is the same; he will help us in the same way.

Jesus Christ the same yesterday, and to day, and for ever.

Hebrews 13:8

17. Why not?
18. I will survive.
19. I will shine.

20.   I will not stay down forever.

Rejoice not against me, O mine enemy: when I fall, I shall arise; when I sit in darkness, the Lord shall be a light unto me.

Micah 7:8

21.   My enemies will be disappointed.

22.   I want your opinion.

When Jesus came into the coasts of Caesarea Philippi, he asked his disciples, saying, Whom do men say that I the Son of man am?

Matthew 16:13

23.   Though my beginning is small, my end shall be great.

24.   Let us go.

25.   Let us try the new plan.

Secrets of the Can-Do Leader

1.   A can-do leader does not mind being in the minority.

But the men that went up with him said, We be not able to go up against the people; for they are stronger than we.

Numbers 13:31

2.   A can-do leader has an independent opinion about what to do.

And Caleb stilled the people before Moses, and said, Let us go up at once, and possess it; for we are well able to overcome it.

Numbers 13:30

3.   A can-do leader sees good and positive things.³

And they spake unto all the company of the children of Israel, saying, The land, which we passed through to search it, is an exceeding good land.

Numbers 14:7

4.   A can-do leader goes into action at once.

And Caleb stilled the people before Moses, and said, Let us go up at once, and possess it; for we are well able to overcome it.

Numbers 13:30

5.   A can-do leader knows that every project can, and should start immediately if it is to succeed.

And Caleb stilled the people before Moses, and said, Let us go up at once, and possess it; for we are well able to overcome it.

Numbers 13:30

He knows that visions often die when they are delayed.⁴

6.   A can-do leader is loyal to his father.

Joshua was faithful to Moses.

And Joshua the son of Nun, and Caleb the son of Jephunneh, which were of them that searched the land, rent their clothes:

Numbers 14:6

7.   A can-do leader does not allow negative people to influence him, but he rather influences them.

> And Joshua the son of Nun, and Caleb the son of Jephunneh, which were of them that searched the land, rent their clothes:
>
> **Numbers 14:6**

8. A can-do leader has faith in God.[5]

> If the Lord delight in us, then he will bring us into this land, and give it us; a land which floweth with milk and honey.
>
> **Numbers 14:8**

9. A can-do leader is ready to fight.

10. A can-do leader is ready to die.

11. A can-do leader is ready to take a risk.

12. A can-do leader does not see himself as a grasshopper.

> And there we saw the giants, the sons of Anak, which come of the giants: and we were in our own sight as grasshoppers, and so we were in their sight.
>
> **Numbers 13:33**

13. A can-do leader is unpopular when he is in a backward and unprogressive community.

> But all the congregation bade stone them with stones. And the glory of the Lord appeared in the tabernacle of the congregation before all the children of Israel.
>
> **Numbers 14:10**

14. A can-do leader is not intimidated by the enemy.

> Only rebel not ye against the Lord, neither fear ye the people of the land; for they are bread for us: their defence is departed from them, and the Lord is with us: fear them not.
>
> **Numbers 14:9**

The Art of Leadership

15. A can-do leader has a spirit of boldness.

16. A can-do leader has a spirit of adventure and discovery that leads to development.

17. A can-do leader will be vindicated in the long run.

But all the congregation bade stone them with stones. And the glory of the Lord appeared in the tabernacle of the congregation before all the children of Israel.

Numbers 14:10

Chapter 83

Accept the Reality of Loneliness

At my first answer no man stood with me, but all men forsook me: I pray God that it may not be laid to their charge.

2 Timothy 4:16

The very nature of leadership makes you a lonely person. To be a leader means to be ahead of the crowd. Leaders are lonely people. Many decisions are left to them. They have no one to help them when it comes to certain things.[1]

Loneliness is the way of all leaders. They often have no one to share their problems with. They cannot voice their fears openly. Many followers feel that their leaders are fearless but any honest leader will tell you about real fears that ravage his mind on a daily basis.

Many followers think that their leaders will live forever. But the leader often fears that he could die suddenly. Who can the leader speak to about his marital problems? Who would understand that the pastor also has a problem? No one! This is what makes leaders lonely. Leaders must fellowship with other leaders. All they have is each other.

When a leader comes up with a new vision, old friends often back off. Once again, the leader is left all alone. When the Lord was sending a message to the churches in Asia, the message was sent to the leaders of the churches. Leaders are often alone when they hear God speaking to them. The Bible tells us how Moses went up into the mountain and waited on God for forty days and forty nights.

The word "consecration" means "to be set apart". If you have been consecrated as a leader, it means that you have been set apart in many ways. That is the responsibility of a leader. This is the reason why leaders are often paid much more than followers. It is an attempt to compensate them for the cost of leadership.

Eight Leaders Who Experienced Loneliness

1. Jesus prayed alone in the garden of Gethsemane whilst everyone else slept.

> **And he went a little farther, and fell on his face, and prayed, saying, O my Father, if it be possible, let this cup pass from me: nevertheless not as I will, but as thou wilt. And he came and found them asleep again: for their eyes were heavy. And he left them, and went away again, and prayed the third time, saying the same words.**
>
> Matthew 26:39,43,44

Accept the Reality of Loneliness

He went to the cross alone whilst everyone ran away.

Then all the disciples forsook him, and fled.

Matthew 26:56b

2. Elijah was alone in the wilderness when he was fed by ravens.

That is where he heard the call of God.

But he himself went a day's journey into the wilderness, and came and sat down under a juniper tree: and he requested for himself that he might die; and said, It is enough; now, O Lord, take away my life; for I am not better than my fathers. And as he lay and slept under a juniper tree, behold, then an angel touched him, and said unto him, Arise and eat.

1 Kings 19:4,5

3. John the Baptist lived a lonely life in the wilderness.

He was described as a voice crying in the wilderness.

As it is written in the book of the words of Esaias the prophet, saying, The voice of one crying in the wilderness, Prepare ye the way of the Lord, make his paths straight.

Luke 3:4

Do not be depressed if you seem to be a lonely voice in a wilderness. It is part of the call to leadership.

4. David spent many lonely years running away from King Saul.

Even outsiders noticed that he was alone.

Then came David to Nob to Ahimelech the priest: and Ahimelech was afraid at the meeting of David, and said unto him, Why art thou alone, and no man with thee?

1 Samuel 21:1

5. Jonah was the only person cast out of the ship.

He went alone into the belly of the fish. He prayed out of that dark hole and God heard him.

Then Jonah prayed unto the Lord his God out of the fish's belly,

Jonah 2:1

6. Noah was the only one who went into the ark.

The whole world was full of wickedness. Not even one other human family went along with him.

And the Lord said unto Noah, Come thou and all thy house into the ark; for thee have I seen righteous before me in this generation.

Genesis 7:1

7. Abraham was selected out of his family.

God separated him into a life of loneliness away from the country and the family that he knew.

Now the Lord had said unto Abram, Get thee out of thy country, and from thy kindred, and from thy father's house, unto a land that I will show thee:

Genesis 12:1

8. Moses was alone when he met the Lord in a burning bush.

He was also alone when he went up onto the mountain.

And Moses alone shall come near the Lord: but they shall not come nigh; neither shall the people go up with him.

Exodus 24:2

Chapter 84

Don't Forget Those Who Helped You

And thou shalt remember all the way which the LORD thy God led thee these forty years in the wilderness, to humble thee, and to prove thee, to know what was in thine heart, whether thou wouldest keep his commandments, or no.

Deuteronomy 8:2

The Lord took the Israelites out of Egypt and warned them about forgetting all that he had done for them.

In the natural world, it is important to remember whose seed you are. It is important to remember your mother and your father. Remember the provision they made for you. You must remember who helped you to go to school and who put food on your plate for many years. Unfortunately, with the passage of time many people forget where they came from. They also forget how they came to have the blessings they have. Others want people to think that they are self-made and have had no input from anywhere.[1]

> **When thou hast eaten and art full, then thou shalt bless the Lord thy God for the good land which he hath given thee. Beware that thou forget not the Lord thy God, in not keeping his commandments, and his judgments, and his statutes, which I command thee this day: Lest when thou hast eaten and art full, and hast built goodly houses, and dwelt therein; And when thy herds and thy flocks multiply, and thy silver and thy gold is multiplied, and all that thou hast is multiplied; Then thine heart be lifted up, and thou forget the Lord thy God…**
>
> **Deuteronomy 8:10-14**

A good leader is someone who remembers who inspired, motivated and influenced him. A good leader is someone who remembers his teachers. One of the first tenets of the physician's oath speaks of doctors remembering their teachers. Remembrance is important in every sphere of life. A good leader remembers the one who believed in him when he was nothing. A good leader remembers the one who helped him financially, and advised him.[2]

When leaders forget, they often become rebellious. Pastors who have bad memories often do not preach well because they cannot give testimonies of what God has done. My preaching is full of testimonies of what the Lord has brought me through. A leader who has a bad memory lacks true compassion. He cannot remember where he came from. When he sees someone in the same state he had been in a few years before, he cannot relate with the person. This is unfortunate! The Bible teaches us that God brings us through situations so that we will be able to help others one day.

> **And whether we be afflicted, it is for your consolation and salvation… or whether we be comforted, it is for your consolation and salvation.**
>
> 2 Corinthians 1:6

Paul said very clearly, that the experiences that he had had were for the benefit of others. A dangerous feature of a leader with a bad memory is that he may mock those who once helped him. He may even despise those below him.[3]

All these traits have dangerous consequences. This is why I am teaching that a good leader must have a good memory. I try to remember the difficult times I have had in ministry. I try to remember the mistakes I have made in ministry. It gives me a lot of compassion for those coming after me. I remember the days I was ridiculed and criticized by all and sundry because I had begun a new church. That is why I am very sympathetic towards up and coming pastors.

Chapter 85

Translate Your Vision into Reality

What dreams do you have? If you are a leader, you will be able to make those dreams a reality. Everyone has dreams. But when a leader dreams it becomes a reality. I have a dream of many souls being saved. I have a dream of many churches being established. I have a dream of fulfilling my ministry. I believe I can see these dreams come to pass.[1]

What are you doing about your dreams? If there is a leader in you, rise up and pay the price to have your dreams come true. What is the key to realizing your visions and dreams? You must be determined and ready to make great sacrifices.[2]

Chapter 86

Go in First and People Will Follow You Anywhere

Then said Jesus unto his disciples, If any man will come after me, let him deny himself, and take up his cross, and follow me.

Matthew 16:24

If you go anywhere yourself, people will be prepared to follow you there. In 1990 I left my medical profession and followed the road of ministry. Today there are several other doctors who have followed me on the same road. Whether they would prosper or not in the ministry did not matter. They were led to take up their crosses and go anywhere it would lead. Why have other doctors and professionals followed me on this road? Because I went in first and called for them to come after me!

The master key to leading people anywhere is to walk the road yourself. Jesus never told his disciples to do things that he himself did not do.[1]

When a young lady decides to follow a young man for the rest of her life, she is actually following him anywhere. Do you remember the marriage vows? "For better or for worse, in prosperity and adversity." Marriage is convincing someone to follow you anywhere. The thing about marriage is that you go in together.

Today, I want you to ask yourself whether you are really a leader. Are people prepared to follow you into prosperity or adversity? Have you wondered why your followers do not do certain things? Perhaps you haven't set the example. They fear to go where no man has tread. They think to themselves, "If you won't go, why should I go?"[2]

Jesus was such a good leader that he got his disciples to follow him to the cross. He actually told them, "Take up your cross and follow me." In other words, "let's go to the morgue and lay down together". He had the authority to say this because he himself had taken up the cross. Convince people to go anywhere by going first.

Develop the art of naturally convincing people to follow you anywhere that it is necessary to go to.[3]

Peter said unto him, Though I should die with thee, yet will I not deny thee. Likewise also said all the disciples.

Matthew 26:35

Jesus was a good leader. He was able to get his disciples to the point where they were able to follow him even unto death.

Chapter 87

Make Your Followers Love You. Make Sure They Don't Resent You.

   A good leader is surrounded by willing servants. A good leader is surrounded by people who are glad to carry out his wishes. If you are a leader, look into the eyes of those who follow you. Are those eyes gleaming with eagerness or do they radiate resentment and bitterness? King David was surrounded by many mighty men. Many of them would have laid down their lives for him if he had asked them to.[1]

And they came and besieged him in Abel of Beth-maachah, and they cast up a bank against the city, and it stood in the trench: and all the people that were with Joab battered the wall, to throw it down. Then cried a wise woman out of the city, Hear, hear; say, I pray you, unto Joab, Come near hither, that I may speak with thee.

2 Samuel 20:15,16

What made David's men so ready to give up their lives so that he could have a drink of water? Look into the eyes of the people you want to lead. Do they love you? Are they genuinely happy to be with you and to follow you? What can you do to make the people who are following you genuinely willing to obey and to flow with you? All human beings have the unspoken desire to feel important, loved and respected.[2]

How to Make Your Followers Love You and Not Resent You

1. Make people feel that they are generally respected by you.

Once a feeling of self-worth and genuine respect is there, you have gone a long way in making your followers love you. People naturally love those who respect them.[3]

2. Transform the people who follow you into eminent, distinguished, celebrated and impressive men.

Jesus transformed his followers into the great apostles that we know them to be. He promised them mansions in Heaven as well as many other rewards. That's how Jesus treated his followers. No wonder they died for him.[4]

A true leader wants the people he is leading to become great. When the people you lead feel that in following you they will become great in this life, they will be very willing to stay close. Ask yourself this question: Are the people who are following you going to amount to anything? Will they become great? Can they prosper in the system you have created? Can they become mighty men in the ministry you are leading? Is it the case that you are the only one who will ever experience a certain level of significance in ministry?[5]

3. Sacrifice for your followers.

A true leader has willing followers. Decide from today to make the people around you enthusiastic about their jobs and their association with you. In order to do this you will have to sacrifice to make them happy. You must give them a future and a hope. When a congregation sees a pastor constructing a church building for them they become far more enthusiastic about the church. But if they only see the pastor acquiring nice things for himself, their readiness to flow with him will be severely compromised. *Pay good salaries and make sure that everyone who works for you has a home, cars and enough money.*[6]

Chapter 88

Watch out for Discontentment and Deal with it Decisively

Discontentment will scatter your followers. Anyone who loses an election loses it because people are no longer content with his leadership. "To be content", means "to be *satisfied, gratified, appeased* and *delighted"*, with something. It also means "to be *thrilled, tickled, bewitched, captivated, charmed* and *enraptured"*, with what you have. Monitor the level of contentment of your followers at all times. I want to work with people who are thrilled, captivated, charmed and enraptured by their job with me in the ministry.

Discontentment is an evil spirit that needs to be dealt with. You cannot lead people who are not thrilled, satisfied and delighted to be with you. No circumstance is perfect. Contentment is a product of the heart and not a product of one's circumstances. I know people who do not have much but are very happy.

The Single Greatest Manifestation of Discontentment

The single greatest manifestation of discontentment is *comparison*.

> **...but they measuring themselves by themselves, and comparing themselves among themselves, are not wise.**
>
> **2 Corinthians 10:12**

Whenever people focus on what others have, they become discontented. In the story below, the master had promised good wages to his workers. Initially, they did not complain about the salary because they thought it was fair. At the end of the day, however, new workers were employed who were given the same wages.

> **For the kingdom of heaven is like unto a man that is an householder, which went out early in the morning to hire labourers into his vineyard. And when he had agreed with the labourers for a penny a day, he sent them into his vineyard. And he went out about the third hour, and saw others standing idle in the marketplace, And said unto them; Go ye also into the vineyard, and whatsoever is right I will give you. And they went their way.**

Again he went out about the sixth and ninth hour, and did likewise. And about the eleventh hour he went out, and found others standing idle, and saith unto them, Why stand ye here all the day idle? They say unto him, Because no man hath hired us. He saith unto them, Go ye also into the vineyard; and whatsoever is right, that shall ye receive.

So when even was come, the lord of the vineyard saith unto his steward, Call the labourers, and give them their hire, beginning from the last unto the first. And when they came that were hired about the eleventh hour, they received every man a penny. But when the first came, they supposed that they should have received more; and they likewise received every man a penny.

And when they had received it, they murmured against the goodman of the house, Saying, These last have wrought but one hour, and thou hast made them equal unto us, which have borne the burden and heat of the day. But he answered one of them, and said, Friend, I do thee no wrong: didst not thou agree with me for a penny? Take that thine is, and go thy way: I will give unto this last, even as unto thee. Is it not lawful for me to do what I will with mine own? Is thine eye evil, because I am good?

Matthew 20:1-15

Suddenly, discontentment reared its ugly head. The original team of workers were no longer happy with their wages. Many people are content with what they have until they look next door to see what someone else has. I am happy with what God has given me. I may not have what Benny Hinn, Oral Roberts or T.D. Jakes have, but I am content with what God has given me. If I start to compare myself with some of these people I may begin to think that I am inadequate. If you start to compare yourself with someone else, you will degenerate into discontentment. You become a complainer, a doubter and an ungrateful person.

Be a wise leader and detect this canker as soon as it shows up. Your followers are not equal and it is not possible to reward everyone with the same package. As soon as your followers begin to grumble and complain, like Moses, you may lose control and your mission may fail.

Three Ways to Deal with Discontentment

1. Give good salaries and wages and be confident that people are getting something good.

If people are generally not receiving enough remuneration, they have a genuine cause to be discontented. Within the limits of your context, give people a good remuneration. Those who follow you must not only be hopeful for the future, they must be satisfied now. If you are the manager of a company, ask yourself whether your workers are happy in the now. It is nice to have flowery promises for the future but what about now? Jesus not only promised blessings for the future; He offered contentment and satisfaction for the now!

Then Peter began to say unto him, Lo, we have left all, and followed thee. And Jesus answered and said, Verily I say unto you, there is no man that have left house, or brethren, or sisters, or father, or mother, or wife, or children, or lands, for my sake, and the gospels, But he shall receive an hundredfold now in this time, houses, brethren, and sisters, and mothers, and children, and lands, with persecutions; and in the world to come eternal life.

Mark 10:28

There were houses and prosperity for the now and there was eternal life for the future. If you want to be a successful manager, offer something now and have a promise for the future. That was the strategy of Jesus. Thank God for the promises of the future. But people want something now as well![1]

2. Teach about contentment.

Teaching the Word of God fights the deception that comes from Satan. Teaching will always heal the curable traces of discontentment in your organization.[2]

> **And having food and raiment let us be therewith content.**
>
> **1 Timothy 6:8**

> **Let your conversation be without covetousness; and be content with such things as ye have: for he hath said, I will never leave thee, nor forsake thee.**
>
> **Hebrews 13:5**

3. Recognize incurable discontentment and dismiss those affected.

> **Blessed is the man that walketh not in the counsel of the ungodly, nor standeth in the way of sinners, nor sitteth in the seat of the scornful.**
>
> **Psalm 1:1**

There are some people who love money so much that nothing you do for them will ever be satisfactory.

> **He that loveth silver shall not be satisfied with silver; nor he that loveth abundance with increase...**
>
> **Ecclesiastes 5:10**

Such people receive high salaries and more benefits but do not show any gratitude. When they receive an extra bonus or gift, they just make some unintelligible remark such as, "I'll take it like that!" In other words, "It's not good enough but I'll manage!"[3]

I once had some employees who were constantly grumbling about their salaries. I discerned that they were suffering from incurable discontentment. One day I called them up and said to them, "I think you people are not happy with your salaries."

I asked my administrator to sort out a nice settlement package for them and sent them off. After some months of being in the secular labour market, one of them came back to me and said, "I now realize that when I was with you, I had one of the best jobs in the country." I was glad that this revelation had finally come. Some people are cured of their discontentment only after experiencing the realities of life.[4]

Chapter 89

Waste No Time on Critical People

Twenty Things Every Leader Should Know about Criticism and Critical People

1. **A critical person is someone who sees nothing good in what you do.**

   How could those who criticized Jesus not have heard or seen his powerful teaching and miracles? A critical person sees nothing good in whatever you do. That is how political parties in the opposition behave. No matter what, they see nothing good in the ruling party.

2. Critical people are often frustrated people who have failed in life.

Frustration creates bitterness. Bitterness is made manifest by criticism.

3. Critical people are often disappointed and disillusioned in their personal lives.

Do not forget to ask a few questions about the one who is criticizing you most. You will be amazed to find that he or she is an immoral, lying and stealing individual.

4. Critical people are often people who build their lives by destroying others.

These people have not succeeded at anything. All they try to do is to pull down everyone to their level of non-achievement.

5. Critical people do not often live long.

The Bible is very clear on this principle. If you love life, keep your mouth from saying the wrong things.

> **For he that will love life, and see good days, let him refrain his tongue from evil, and his lips that they speak no guile:**
>
> **1 Peter 3:10**

6. Critical people often have psycho-social problems.

Such people are often rejected and unloved people who have not had the love of a father or mother. Their criticism is often a cry for attention.

7. Jesus did not answer his critics.

Jesus responded to the hunger and thirst of the multitudes and not to the hatred of his enemies.[1]

> **And as soon as he knew that he belonged unto Herod's jurisdiction, he sent him to Herod, who himself also was at Jerusalem at that time. And when Herod saw Jesus, he was exceeding glad: for he was desirous to see him of a long season, because he had heard many things of him; and he hoped to have seen some miracle done by him. Then he questioned with him in many words; but he answered him nothing. And the chief priests and scribes stood and vehemently accused him.**
>
>

Luke 23:7-10

8. Criticism is part of the ministry.

There is nothing like ministry without criticism. Jesus was perfect. If he was criticized, accused and murdered what do you think will happen to someone like you who is not perfect?[2]

9. It is not possible to minister without accusation.

It is part of the package. Jesus promised rewards with persecution.

> **But he shall receive an hundredfold now in this time, houses, and brethren, and sisters, and mothers, and children, and lands, with persecutions; and in the world to come eternal life.**
>
>

Mark 10:30

10. Someone said, "Criticism is the death gargle of a non-achiever."

Think about that!³

11. I am yet to meet a critical individual who is a good person.

Criticism seems to be a symptom of many other evils stored within an individual. It is people who are defiled and unbelieving who see impurities in everything. "Unto the pure all things are pure: but unto them that are defiled and unbelieving is nothing pure; but even their mind and conscience is defiled" (Titus 1:15).

12. Critical people are often trying to lure you into an argument or a debate.

Do not be deceived. Satan wants your emotions to be worked up because of unbelievable accusations and criticisms.

13. Critical people are often trying to trap you through your words.

Critics are full of suspicion. They suspect you of all sorts of evils. They want further evidence to justify their suspicions.

14. You can learn something from your critics.

Your friends are not likely to point out your mistakes. Your enemies are more likely to magnify your shortcomings in an attempt to bring you down. It is worth taking note of what they say, so that you can make the necessary adjustments.

15. Enemies do not give "constructive" criticism.

Your enemy is not trying to build up (construct) your life. How can he give you anything "constructive"? It is not wrong to label everything that comes from your enemy as destructive. Decide to pick wisdom and direction from this dangerous criticism without being contaminated.[4]

16. Refuse to listen to certain criticisms because they are arrows of accusation intended to injure your heart.

Keep your heart with all diligence for out of it are the issues of life.[5]

17. Critical people are often ignorant.

Much criticism is based on incomplete information. Many critical people are ignoramuses.

18. Critical people are often inexperienced.

Much criticism comes from the mouths of men of straw. These are men of no substance. They have neither knowledge nor experience.

19. Critical people minister poison which spreads to those who hear it.

The people who criticize you, often hate you deeply. They want others to hate you as well.

20. Your response to every criticism should be, "Full stop and back to you!"

This is what my children advise!

Chapter 90

Familiarity Is a Leadership Emergency. Deal with it Urgently

Twenty Things Every Leader Should Know about Familiarity

1. Familiarity is the disease that kills the ministry of a prophet.

    But Jesus said unto them, A prophet is not without honour, but in his own country, and among his own kin, and in his own house.

    Mark 6:4

2. **It was the most powerful antagonist to the anointing on Jesus' ministry.**

   And he could there do no mighty work, save that he laid his hands upon a few sick folk, and healed them.

   Mark 6:5

3. **Familiarity is a product of frequent interaction with a leader.**

   ...From whence hath this man these things? and what wisdom is this which is given unto him, that even such mighty works are wrought by his hands? Is not this the carpenter, the son of Mary, the brother of James, and Joses, and of Juda, and Simon? and are not his sisters here with us? And they were offended at him.

   Mark 6:2,3

4. **Familiarity is a product of much knowledge of a leader.**

   This is why every leader should maintain some degree of privacy and mystique.

   And he could there do no mighty work, save that he laid his hands upon a few sick folk, and healed them.

   Mark 6:5

5. **Familiarity incubates contempt and disrespect.**

   The inhabitants of Jesus' hometown were angered at his preaching. They were not neutral. They were outraged and thought that Jesus should be silenced.

> And all they in the synagogue, when they heard these things, were filled with wrath, And rose up, and thrust him out of the city, and led him unto the brow of the hill whereon their city was built, that they might cast him down headlong.
>
> Luke 4:28,29

6. Friendship incubates familiarity.

Jesus' friendship with Peter created a problem of familiarity. This showed up when Jesus asked Peter his opinion about his ministry.

> He saith unto them, But whom say ye that I am? And Simon Peter answered and said, Thou art the Christ, the Son of the living God. And Jesus answered and said unto him, Blessed art thou, Simon Barjona: for flesh and blood hath not revealed it unto thee, but my Father which is in heaven.
>
> Matthew 16:15-17

Peter thought he had the right to say things he did not even understand.

7. Promotion incubates familiarity.

Jesus promoted Peter to be the head of the church.

> And I say also unto thee, That thou art Peter, and upon this rock I will build my church; and the gates of hell shall not prevail against it.
>
> Matthew 16:18

Sometimes when people are elevated a little they feel that they are equal to their seniors and teachers. This is unfortunate.

8. Familiarity is detected when subordinates make comments about certain things.

This is presumptuous. The fact that your leader has discussed personal things with you does not mean that you should step out of order.

9. Familiarity is detected when a subordinate attempts to correct his leader.

Peter began to feel "extra free". He thought that he could now correct Jesus.

> **Then Peter took him, and began to rebuke him, saying, Be it far from thee, Lord: this shall not be unto thee.**
>
> **Matthew 16:22**

Although a leader needs his fair share of correction, the subordinate is not qualified to do this.

10. Familiarity is detected when a follower attempts to direct his leader.

Peter began to make pronouncements about the ministry of Jesus. Peter thought that his friendship with Christ gave him the authority to direct and to correct Jesus. He thought that his conversation about people's opinions of Christ made him an opinion-holder. Perhaps he thought that Jesus needed his input.

11. Be quick to detect subtle indications of familiarity.

Jesus was very quick to notice that Peter was out of order.

I once entered my office and there was a junior pastor holding a meeting with some other pastors. He was sitting in my chair behind my desk and everyone else was sitting around him. He was teaching them something just as if I was conducting the meeting. As soon as I saw him, I knew that something was wrong. I immediately said to him, "Never sit on that chair again. Never sit behind that desk again!" Then I told everyone, "If I am not here, no one should ever sit behind my desk or on my chair."[1]

12. In unambiguous terms, bring down to size every follower who is too familiar.

Suddenly, Jesus was transformed from a kind and gentle Jesus into a Jesus of steel. He rebuked His close friend and associate in the harshest possible way. He called Peter "Satan"! Think about that! Peter was brought down to size instantaneously.[2]

13. Address and confront familiarity anywhere you find it.

There are times I sense familiarity when I am preaching. I address it and make everyone aware of that evil spirit.

14. Yawning is a distinctive sign of familiarity.

Preachers and teachers must watch out for yawning, especially when the yawns come at the beginning of the message. Watch out for "early yawners", they are usually suffering from familiarity.

15. Like Jesus, every leader should avoid the places where familiarity has taken root.

After Jesus detected a spirit of familiarity in Nazareth, he moved his headquarters to Capernaum.

> **And came down to Capernaum, a city of Galilee, and taught them on the sabbath days.**
>
> **Luke 4:31**

16. Every leader should spend more time where he is celebrated and welcomed with joy and excitement.

Like Jesus, every leader should avoid the places where familiarity has taken root.

17. Make clear distinctions between the leaders and the followers to prevent familiarity.

Jesus slept in the boat whilst his disciples rowed and worked hard.

> Now it came to pass on a certain day, that he went into a ship with his disciples: and he said unto them, Let us go over unto the other side of the lake. And they launched forth. But as they sailed he fell asleep: and there came down a storm of wind on the lake; and they were filled with water, and were in jeopardy.
>
> **Luke 8:22,23**

Jesus rode on a donkey whilst his disciples walked. Jesus did not hire twelve donkeys so that they could all ride.

18. Draw boundaries so that you will ensure some level of privacy.

Privacy drives away familiarity. If everyone knows everything about you, do not be surprised that they will be so familiar.

19. Break the monotony. Introduce new ideas. Monotony incubates familiarity.

Repetitiveness, dullness and uniformity are the perfect context for familiarity. The same sermons in the same way from the same person at the same time have a way of incubating familiarity. When the people wanted Jesus to come and preach in the same way, he refused to enter their monotonous pattern and decided to go to the next city. He knew that they would soon be yawning at him so he decided to travel. It is good to have annual programs for instance, but at times it is necessary to break the monotony.[3]

> **And when they had found him, they said unto him, All men seek for thee. And he said unto them, Let us go into the next towns, that I may preach there also: for therefore came I forth. And he preached in their synagogues throughout all Galilee, and cast out devils.**
>
> **Mark 1:37-39**

20. Don't always do what people are expecting you to do.

The same people who impress upon you to do what you have been doing all the time are those who become familiar. It is because people know what you are going to do that they become familiar. Remember: too much knowledge incubates familiarity. Sometimes a prayer meeting or a worship session instead of the expected sermon will help to break the familiarity.

Chapter 91

Fight Only Battles You Can Win

And David arose, and fled that day for fear of Saul, and went to Achish the king of Gath. And the servants of Achish said unto him, Is not this David the king of the land? did they not sing one to another of him in dances, saying, Saul hath slain his thousands, and David his ten thousands?

And David laid up these words in his heart, and was sore afraid of Achish the king of Gath. And he changed his behaviour before them, and feigned himself mad in their hands, and scrabbled on the doors of the gate, and let his spittle fall down upon his beard.

Then said Achish unto his servants, Lo, ye see the man is mad: wherefore then have ye brought him to me? Have I need of mad men, that ye have brought this fellow to play the mad man in my presence? shall this fellow come into my house?

1 Samuel 21:10-15

In this story, David realized that he was not in the position to fight the king. He changed his behaviour and pretended to be mad. He even pretended to join the side of the Philistines. A real leader does not engage in battles he cannot win. Jesus himself taught that you must count the cost before you go to war. I have observed pastors engage in building projects that they can never finish. All they are doing is fighting a battle they cannot win.

Failure breeds failure. Success breeds success. Each failure you chalk, demoralizes your followers. You must avoid getting into a "failure" situation as much as you would avoid a snake.

A real leader needs to know which case should go to court. You should not bother fighting certain things in court. I personally know people who have committed crimes against my church and me. I even have evidence to that effect, but I have decided not to fight them legally. Why is this? I know when I will not win a fight!

Why waste your time playing a match in which the referee is a player against you? Every wise leader should avoid a match in which the referee and the linesmen are openly for the other team! Whenever *you* are about to score, they will whistle, "off-side"! Whenever *they* are about to score, the whistle will be blown for a penalty against you. The fact is that you lost the match before it even started. You may even be scored a record 100-0 and enter the Guinness Book of Records for your efforts.

When the seed of disloyalty enters the heart of a betrayer, it is often a waste of time trying to change his mind. Have you ever wondered why Jesus never counselled Judas Iscariot? It was not worth the time![1]

Whenever somebody hands in a resignation, I often ask no questions. Why waste your time trying to change someone who has made up his mind? I do not want the person to stay on longer than is necessary. Sometimes they want to leave in a month's time, but I help them to leave immediately.[2]

Are you a leader? Pick your battles carefully and win every time!

Chapter 92

Use Symptoms and Signs to Guide You

Behold that which I have seen: it is good and comely for one to eat and to drink, and to enjoy the good of all his labour that he taketh under the sun all the days of his life, which God giveth him: for it is his portion. Every man also to whom God hath given riches and wealth, and hath given him power to eat thereof, and to take his portion, and to rejoice in his labour; this is the gift of God.

Ecclesiastes 5:18,19

You will notice the phrase "behold that which I have seen". King Solomon often spoke about things that he noticed.

Perhaps my medical background has made me sensitive to the concept of symptoms and signs. Symptoms and signs reveal hidden things. They tell you about what is not obvious.

Seven Things You Can Use Symptoms and Signs to Detect

1. Use symptoms and signs to detect disloyalty.

In my book, *Loyalty and Disloyalty*, I share about several signs of disloyalty. Betrayal is something that does not announce itself. You must look for the signs. If you fail to see the signs that leaders are supposed to notice, you will be at the mercy of traitors.

2. Use symptoms and signs to detect familiarity.

You can detect familiarity by noticing little changes in people's attitudes. Their comments, disinterest and yawning at meetings are all important indicators.

3. Use symptoms and signs to detect backsliding.

In my book, *Backsliding*, I share about twenty-five symptoms of backsliding. If you use these symptoms, you will be able to detect backsliding in its early stages.

4. Use symptoms and signs to detect unforgiveness.

Many people claim to have forgiven others. In reality, they are full of bitterness. In my book, *Forgiveness Made Easy*, I outline the signs of lingering unforgiveness.

5. Use symptoms and signs to supervise employees.

You will not always be present to see if people are working well or not. I use certain indicators to supervise the people who work for me. Accomplishing targets within a deadline is the most important indicator for me.[1]

6. Use symptoms and signs to uncover future leaders.

Paul did this. In 1 Timothy 3, he outlined the signs that Timothy was to look for in potential leaders.[2]

7. Use symptoms and signs to detect the call of God on people's lives.

I think that the greatest sign of the call of God is the desire for ministry. I always look out for people who have a desire to work for God.[3]

Dear leader, keep your eyes open and see the things that others do not. Often when I see my church members, I know when something is wrong. Why is that? Because I am a leader. I use symptoms and signs.

Chapter 93

Be a Loyal Leader

Five People You Must Be Loyal To

Moreover it is required in stewards, that a man be found faithful.

1 Corinthians 4:2

One of the cardinal qualifications for a leader is loyalty. You must be loyal to your God, your church, your spouse and your friends. A leader must also learn to be loyal to the people who follow him. When it is time for your followers to be rewarded, be faithful and let the rewards be given to the deserving persons.[1]

1. Be loyal to the people who have laboured for you.

Do not withhold the blessings of those who have laboured with you. When one of your followers is in trouble, show your loyalty. Your followers are watching you closely. They will do what they see. If you do not betray them in their time of difficulty, they will not betray you in your time of difficulty.

2. Be loyal to your superiors.

A leader must be loyal to his superiors. When David had the opportunity to kill Saul, he did not! He was loyal to the king. He did not execute his own father.

> **Then said Abishai to David, God hath delivered thine enemy into thine hand this day: now therefore let me smite him, I pray thee, with the spear even to the earth at once, and I will not smite him the second time. And David said to Abishai, Destroy him not: for who can stretch forth his hand against the Lord's anointed, and be guiltless? David said furthermore, As the Lord liveth, the Lord shall smite him; or his day shall come to die; or he shall descend into battle, and perish. The Lord forbid that I should stretch forth mine hand against the Lord's anointed: but, I pray thee, take thou now the spear that is at his bolster, and the cruse of water, and let us go.**
>
> **1 Samuel 26:8-11**

Many years later, David himself made a mistake. He murdered one of his soldiers called Uriah. David could have lost his life through that mistake. Many of his leaders could have revolted. However, this did not happen. His men were loyal to the king's authority. They refused to kill the Lord's anointed because they had learnt it by example.

3.   Be loyal to your friends.

A leader must be loyal to his friends. When David became the king, he realized that his position was a privileged one. When he was established, he asked for a way to show kindness to an old friend.

> **And David said, Is there yet any that is left of the house of Saul, that I may shew him kindness for Jonathan's sake?**
>
> **2 Samuel 9:1**

These acts of loyalty to friends teach others about the true character of their leader. A good character is attractive. People are more inclined to follow someone with a good heart.[2]

4.   Be loyal to your spouse.

A leader must be loyal to his spouse. Because marriage is such a difficult thing for many people, anyone whose marriage works is hailed as a natural leader. You become a natural leader in society because your domestic affairs are under control. Loyalty to your spouse involves self-control and Christian love. Everyone would like to have a leader with self-control and love.

> **A bishop then must be blameless, the husband of one wife…**
>
> **1 Timothy 3:2**

5. Be loyal to your vision.

A leader must be loyal to his vision. Nobody wants to follow someone who is unpredictable. Many years ago, I declared my interest in soul-winning and establishing people in Christ. I am still moving with the same vision. Much water has passed under the bridge but the vision is still the same— a soul is a soul and is precious to God. He may be a beggar, a lawyer or a doctor—a soul is a soul and is precious to God. She may be a groundnut seller, a prostitute or a nurse —a soul is a soul and is precious to God.[3]

Keep the same vision. The Bible teaches that you should not associate with people who are prone to sudden mutations and sharp turns. It is dangerous to sit in a car when the driver constantly makes sudden turns.[4]

My son, fear thou the Lord and the king: and meddle not with them that are given to change:

Proverbs 24:21

Are you a leader? Be a faithful, stable, constant and loyal person. You will have a large following.

Chapter 94

Overcome Hatred and Opposition

Six Things Every Christian Should Know about Opposition

1. **If you cannot handle opposition, you cannot be a leader.**

Every time I have embarked on the road of leadership, it has been met with stiff opposition. If you cannot handle the enemies who are destined to oppose you, you cannot be a great leader. Every great leader has many enemies!

2. **The greater the leader, the greater the hatred and opposition.**

Consider the life of Elijah. He was hated by the king and by the king's wife. There was a death warrant out for his life. Elijah was hated and hunted because of his ministry.

And he said, What have I sinned, that thou wouldest deliver thy servant into the hand of Ahab, to slay me? As the Lord thy God liveth, there is no nation or kingdom, whither my lord hath not sent to seek thee: and when they said, He is not there; he took an oath of the kingdom and nation, that they found thee not. And now thou sayest, Go, tell thy lord, Behold, Elijah is here.

1 Kings 18:9-11

We all know that Elijah was one of the greatest prophets. The greater you are in leadership, the more you will be hated and hunted. Human nature cannot stand the success of another colleague. If you are not prepared for hatred and opposition, please resign from your leadership position immediately. If everybody speaks well of you, you are probably a hypocrite.[1]

Woe unto you, when all men shall speak well of you! for so did their fathers to the false prophets.

Luke 6:26

3. **Every new step of leadership results in fresh arrows of hatred and opposition.**

Every step of strong leadership encounters real antagonism. When I began my church, I was called every name you can think of. Since Jesus himself was accused of using the power of Beelzebub, I consider it a privilege to be called anything derogatory for his sake. If you do not want to be criticized, then you cannot be a leader. When Nehemiah ventured out to rebuild the walls of Jerusalem, you would have thought that everyone would have been happy. But Sanballat and Tobiah rose up to oppose him.[2]

> **But when Sanballat the Horonite, and Tobiah the servant, the Ammonite, and Geshem the Arabian, heard it, they laughed us to scorn, and despised us, and said, What is this thing that ye do? will ye rebel against the king?**
>
> **Nehemiah 2:19**

4. Opposition often comes in the form of plausible accusations.

When David spoke of killing Goliath, his brothers reacted angrily and accused him of pride and naughtiness. Isn't it amazing that good people are often given the most wicked labels?[3]

> **And Eliab his eldest brother heard when he spake unto the men; and Eliab's anger was kindled against David, and he said, Why camest thou down hither? and with whom has thou left those few sheep in the wilderness? I know thy pride, and the naughtiness of thine heart; for thou art come down that thou mightest see the battle.**
>
> **1 Samuel 17:28**

David had to handle the hatred of his own brothers and then the hatred of his father Saul. Hatred and opposition are part of leadership.[4]

5.   Develop a hard forehead for opposition.

> **Be not afraid of their faces: for I am with thee to deliver thee, saith the LORD.**
>
> **Jeremiah 1:8**

Do not be distracted or deterred by opposition. If the least opposition is able to stop you, then you are a poor leader.

> **Behold, I have made thy face strong against their faces, and thy forehead strong against their foreheads. As an adamant harder than flint have I made thy forehead: fear them not, neither be dismayed at their looks, though they be a rebellious house.**
>
> **Ezekiel 3:8,9**

6.   Opposition is often a sign that you are in the will of God.

Rejoice, there is good news. Satan would not attack a dead piece of wood. You are now a threat to Satan, that is why he is attacking you.

> **Yea, and all that will live godly in Christ Jesus shall suffer persecution.**
>
> **2 Timothy 3:12**

Chapter 95

Relate with All Kinds of People Including People Who Are Not Your "Type"

A leader is someone who is trying to get people to follow him. It seems to me that leaders sometimes forget that they are supposed to have followers. If you are a leader, you must make sure that you have people following you. Otherwise, you are not a leader. You must realize that your "type" of person is a limited species upon this earth. You are not likely to find many people in your age group, with your background, colour or accent. If you want to succeed as a leader you must realize very early that you need to be able to relate with all kinds of people, especially people who are not like you.[1]

> **And he said unto them, Ye know how that it is an unlawful thing for a man that is a Jew to keep company, or come unto one of another nation; but God hath showed me that I should not call any man common or unclean.**
>
> **Acts 10:28**

Peter was so rigid in his understanding of leadership that he restricted his ministry to a small group of Jews. But God had a bigger plan for him. God wanted him to reach many other people. As you read this book, I sense that God wants to give you a wider scope of ministry. Do not be myopic. There are more people different from you than there are like you.

My father is from Ghana and my mother is from Switzerland. I was born in England but I have lived in Ghana all my life. My colour is neither black nor white. When I was growing up, most of my friends had European parents or a mixture of white and black. This was because my mother is Swiss and therefore had many European friends.

My father was an unusual man. He loved classical music and played bridge and owned racehorses. Because of this, many of his friends were not Ghanaian. Many of his friends were British, Indians or Lebanese. As I grew up, my hobbies were table tennis, squash, horse riding and swimming. I can assure you that there are very few people in the world who have the same background that I have. Not because I am special, but because this is an unusual combination of culture and circumstances.

If I have been raised up to be a leader, you tell me how many people will have a similar background to what I have just shared with you? Not many! To become a leader of many people I must relate with people who do not have my background. Many of my friends have had a very different background. But I relate with them naturally and easily.

If you are a pastor and you have a poor educational background, rise up and relate with all kinds of people, including rich people. You will definitely need some rich people in your church. Do not drive away all the educated people because of your lack of education. You can educate yourself![2]

Do you consider yourself to be a leader? Ask yourself, "What type of person am I? What type of person am I not? Make a decision to relate with every type of person.[3]

To the weak became I as weak, that I might gain the weak: I am made all things to all men, that I might by all means save some. And this I do for the gospel's sake, that I might be partaker thereof with you.

1 Corinthians 9:22,23

Chapter 96

Don't Be Surprised by Ingratitude

Every leader comes face to face with ingratitude. People are not grateful for the services you render them. It will not take you long to discover this. Many years ago, I found out that people whom I loved could turn around and hurt me. Men that I had trained did not remember that they had been helped. However, I have continued to believe in people and to trust people. I have no choice. If I begin to retaliate because of ingratitude, I will lose my position.[1]

Jesus answered them, Many good works have I showed you from my Father; for which of those works do ye stone me?

John 10:32

Jesus experienced ingratitude. He was killed by an ungrateful mob of Jews. After ministering for twenty years, I have seen pastors being run out of town. That is why the constitution of my church does not give anyone the right to throw me out under any circumstances. I have seen it before and I know that if human nature is allowed to run its course, my end will be no better than my Lord's. Jesus was murdered for His good deeds. He was exchanged for an armed robber. But he never responded to the evil spirit of ingratitude.

Do not look to people for gratitude. A leader looks to God for rewards.

Knowing that whatsoever good thing any man doeth, the same shall he receive of the Lord, whether he be bond or free.

Ephesians 6:8

The Scripture teaches that your rewards depend on God and not on the people you helped. God is the only one who can reward you adequately. Do not expect much from people, expect your rewards from God.

Many years ago, I stopped expecting people to commend me after I had finished preaching. I do not care whether people commend me or not! I am not expecting appreciation from men. My duty is to preach from the Bible. I have done my duty. When I decided not to look for man's approval, I felt a sense of liberty. I was free from men and accountable to the Lord.[2]

Chapter 97

Allow People to Know You So They Can Trust You and Follow You

That which was from the beginning, which we have heard, which we have seen with our eyes, which we have looked upon, and our hands have handled, of the Word of life; (For the life was manifested, and we have seen it, and bear witness, and show unto you that eternal life, which was with the Father, and was manifested unto us;)

1 John 1:1,2

Let the people know that you are real! Everybody will readily follow a genuine leader.

Why did Jesus come into this world? He came so that we would know Him and trust Him. That's why He allowed us to hear Him, see Him and touch Him. Does anyone have the chance to hear you, see you or handle you? Are you a mysterious superman who has no faults? Openness produces a great following.

Are you a leader? Then you must allow people to know you as you really are. Nobody wants to follow a mystery. A mystery speaks of the unknown. A mysterious person smacks of something foreboding.[1]

Who wants to follow a mysterious person into a dark valley where something bad may happen to him? Let me tell you an important secret about leadership. *The more open you are, the more readily people will follow your leadership.* I did not say that the more perfect you are the more people will follow you. Everyone knows that his neighbour is not perfect. It is no secret that there is no perfect person on the earth. Someone who is open and honest about his weaknesses is more likely to have a following. If you are a pastor, let the people know that you are real! Everybody will readily follow a genuine leader.[2]

Chapter 98

Influence People by Example

Who in the days of his flesh, when he had offered up prayers and supplications with strong crying and tears unto him that was able to save him from death, and was heard in that he feared;

Hebrews 5:7

But we will give ourselves continually to prayer, and to the ministry of the word.

Acts 6:4

You may wonder why I have quoted the above Scriptures. What is the correlation between them? The first one speaks about Jesus' prayer life whilst he was on Earth. The second one speaks of Peter's prayer life after Jesus left. Jesus taught His disciples to pray by example. Peter was influenced by Jesus' prayer life.[1]

Listen to What They Say But Don't Do What They Do

Many years ago, I heard a man advising me to listen to what the priest said but not to follow his example. How strange! It is very difficult to follow somebody's words and not his example. There was an old Chinese proverb printed in the physiology laboratory in my former medical school.

It said, *"I hear and I forget, I see and I remember, I do and I understand."* This proverb tells us all about the power of influencing people through what they see. You never forget what you see. Did you know that you only retain about eleven per cent of what you hear?[2]

Jesus did not only teach about prayer. He acted prayer. He lived prayer. That is why Peter was so determined not to be distracted from his prayer life. Many ministers today do not know the importance of prayer. They have never lived with someone who prayed. They have never seen it acted out. Remember that your example is more important than your words.

Dear friend, do you want to be a leader? Please remember that your example is more important than your words![3]

Chapter 99

Recognize Your Desire As a Symptom of Your Call to Leadership

Are you a leader? Can you become a leader? The answer is yes! In this chapter, I will be showing you certain symptoms that reveal the leader within. Paul wrote to Timothy and told him to look for people with leadership qualities.

A Desire

...If a man desire the office...

1 Timothy 3:1

It is interesting to note that Paul wanted people who had the desire for the office. Timothy was instructed to look for certain qualities in people who had the desire for the office. A desire to lead is a symptom of a leader within. A desire to help other people is a great symptom that God has given you the gift of leadership. A desire to serve others with the good things you have, is a great sign of leadership.[1]

Brethren, my heart's desire and prayer to God for Israel is, that they might be saved.

Romans 10:1

Paul had a desire to help the Jews. He was constantly burdened by this desire. All true leadership stems from the burden to help people whom you love. The greatest sign of leadership is the burden and desire which compels the leader into action. That overwhelming burden/desire is the common feature in every great leader.[2]

I say the truth in Christ, I lie not, my conscience also bearing me witness in the Holy Ghost, That I have great heaviness and continual sorrow in my heart. For I could wish that myself were accursed from Christ for my brethren, my kinsmen according to the flesh:

Romans 9:1-3

Some people go through difficulties in life. After they have recovered from their pain, they have a strong desire to help others avoid the pain and suffering they went through. A true father wants his children to have what he couldn't have. A true leader wants his followers to be better than himself. Jesus said,

Verily, verily, I say unto you, He that believeth on me, the works that I do shall he do also; and greater works than these shall he do...

John 14: 12

Jesus wanted his followers to do greater things than he had done. If you do not have a desire to help people to become great, perhaps you are not a leader. If you just have a desire to help yourself, that is not leadership! Leadership is a desire to help other people achieve great things for themselves. A man who has a desire to win the lost at any cost is a leader for the cause of the gospel.

In the earlier days of my ministry, I did not even know what the office of a pastor, evangelist or apostle was. I thought these were far-fetched positions which I could never occupy. All I wanted to do was to help people to meet Jesus. All I wanted to do was to help people to grow in Christ. I felt that once people grew up in the Lord, many of their problems would go away. A desire to help people is a symptom of the call of God.[3]

Misuse of Leadership

There are some people who have a desire for money, power and fame. Without knowing it, they intend to use the position of leadership to gain these things. That is not leadership! That is what I call the art of vampirism. A vampire is a bloodsucking bat or in human terms, someone who preys ruthlessly on others.[4]

Africa, and many nations of the world, have been well endowed with vampire-like leaders who have sucked the wealth of their nations. Unfortunately, some churches have also had leaders, who like vampires, have sucked away the wealth and the life of the church. *A vampire is not a leader and a leader is not a vampire!* Peter warned against this in his letter to the church.

The elders which are among you I exhort, who am also an elder, and a witness of the sufferings of Christ, and also a partaker of the glory that shall be revealed: Feed the flock of God which is among you, taking the oversight thereof, not by constraint, but willingly; not for filthy lucre, but of a ready mind; Neither as being lords over God's heritage, but being ensamples to the flock.

1 Peter 5:1-3

Obviously, leaders with wrong motives were not uncommon in Peter's time. They are certainly not uncommon in our time. God is looking out for men and women who will agree to take up the mantle of leadership and pay the price thereof. That desire within you to help others is the sign of a call of God upon your life. It is time to help. God wants to raise you up to do just that. As you read this book, may the anointing to lead be upon you in the name of Jesus.[5]

Chapter 100

Do Not Rush around from One Emergency to Another

Two Types of Leadership

1. **Emergency style leadership.**

   This involves running around from one crisis to another. It is not an effective style of leadership. The solving of a crisis gives a false feeling of security to the emergency style leader. After settling one crisis, he feels he has accomplished something great. But he does not know that the next crisis is brewing. Pastors solving leadership crises, financial crises, crises over rebellion, crises over debts, crises over breakaways are fully engaged all the time. But there is a better way!

2. Preventive leadership.

Preventive leadership involves a style of leadership, which prevents the occurrence of all these crises. There are fewer crises under this style of leadership. People involved with the preventive style of leadership often hold training conferences, shepherds camps, teaching seminars, etc. Such leaders are more relaxed and more in control of their churches or organizations.

Seven Steps to Preventive Leadership

1. Teach your people what you want them to know.

I have discovered that almost everything can be taught. It is possible to get whatever you desire from your subordinates by teaching them. Every subject on Earth is taught by someone. Learn to teach in order to achieve your desired result.

2. Train people to be loyal.

Disloyalty is one of the causes of crises in organizations. Rebels and traitors have a way of destabilizing entire churches. You can minimize your crises by emphasizing loyalty.

3. Hold regular conferences, retreats and camps.

These are opportunities for teaching and discussion.

4. Do not borrow money.

Debts create uncertainty! The possibility that your whole world could come crashing down on you because of debt is disturbing. I hate debt. I do not borrow. And I would not advise you to borrow money. It is possible to live without debt.

Owe no man any thing, but to love one another: for he that loveth another hath fulfilled the law.

Romans 13:8

5. Distinguish between unimportant but urgent requests and important but non-urgent duties.

Jesus was summoned urgently to attend to Lazarus but it was more important for him to do other things. He did not rush around to unplanned activities unless it was absolutely necessary. *It is important for a leader to be able to distinguish between requests that require abandonment of scheduled activities and ones that do not.* A wise leader will not rush around to unplanned activities unless it is absolutely necessary.

Now a certain man was sick, named Lazarus, of Bethany, the town of Mary and her sister Martha. (It was that Mary which anointed the Lord with ointment, and wiped his feet with her hair, whose brother Lazarus was sick.) Therefore his sisters sent unto him, saying, Lord, behold, he whom thou lovest is sick. When Jesus heard that, he said, This sickness is not unto death, but for the glory of God, that the Son of God might be glorified thereby. Now Jesus loved Martha, and her sister, and Lazarus. When he had heard therefore that he was sick, he abode two days still in the same place where he was.

John 11:1-6

A pastor has many important non-urgent duties. A pastor must spend time in prayer and in the Word. Praying and studying the Word do not sound as urgent as someone dying in the hospital. Waiting on God does not sound as urgent as having to write cheques or sort out administrative issues. Yet, a leader who attends to his non-urgent but important duties will achieve more.

6. Do not overextend yourself.

You can only do so much with your life. Overextending yourself means you take up things that God has not sent you to do. This creates stress and crises. Evangelists who become pastors have one leadership crises after another. They are incapable of extending themselves into an area God has not ordained for them. God does not expect us to do everything. We are not as essential as we may think. If we were that important, no young pastor would ever die! If we were that important in the scheme of things, James, the brother of John, would not have died in the middle of his ministry. Do your part and leave the rest to God. Have you never read where God says you must rest?

> **There remaineth therefore a rest to the people of God. For he that is entered into his rest, he also hath ceased from his own works, as God did from his. Let us labour therefore to enter into that rest, lest any man fall after the same example of unbelief.**
>
> **Hebrews 4:9-11**

7. Delegate whenever you can.

Jesus ministered for three years and delegated the rest of the work to his disciples. He had no delusions about what he could accomplish on his own. He did not even attempt to go beyond the borders of Israel to minister. He delegated that aspect of his ministry to his disciples.

Do you remember that Jesus sent his disciples to the uttermost part of the Earth? Did you notice that Jesus did not attempt to go to the uttermost parts of the Earth? He delegated the work of going to the uttermost parts of the Earth to the disciples. He did not try to prove to anyone that He could go to the uttermost parts of the Earth himself.

His role was to minister to the Jews and to die on the cross. Jesus' job was defined in Matthew 15:24. He intended to stick to his assignment. He delegated the rest to us.

> **But he answered and said, I am not sent but unto the lost sheep of the house of Israel.**
>
> **Matthew 15:24**

Chapter 101

Always Remember: "Nobody Wins until We All Win!"

When I was in medical school this truth was very real to me. Our end-of-year exams were very stressful. One of the most tense moments of my life was when I waited for my final results. By the grace of God I passed every exam. However, there was always a friend or other who did not make it. I came to discover that unless we all passed, our joy was never really complete. How can you rejoice when your best friend has to repeat the year? How can you rejoice when six people are becoming doctors and one has to repeat the year?

Every leader must remember that nobody wins unless we all win. If your marriage is working, you will never be fully happy unless your friend's marriage is also working.[1]

Five Lessons That Teach Us That "No One Wins unless We All Win"

1. Jacob had twelve sons and lost Joseph to slavery.

Even though after Joseph was lost, he still had eleven sons left, he could not rejoice. Jacob was a wise man. He knew that no one wins unless we all win.

> **And he knew it, and said, It is my son's coat; an evil beast hath devoured him; Joseph is without doubt rent in pieces. And Jacob rent his clothes, and put sackcloth upon his loins, and mourned for his son many days. And all his sons and all his daughters rose up to comfort him; but he refused to be comforted; and he said, For I will go down into the grave unto my son mourning. Thus his father wept for him. And the Midianites sold him into Egypt unto Potiphar, an officer of Pharaoh's, and captain of the guard.**
>
> **Genesis 37:33-36**

2. Jesus taught about the shepherd who left the ninety-nine sheep to seek for the lost one.

> **How think ye? if a man have an hundred sheep, and one of them be gone astray, doth he not leave the ninety and nine, and goeth into the mountains, and seeketh that which is gone astray? And if so be that he find it, verily I say unto you, he rejoiceth more of that sheep, than of the ninety and nine which went not astray.**
>
> **Matthew 18:12,13**

3. Jesus taught about the woman who swept the entire house to find one lost coin.

Either what woman having ten pieces of silver, if she lose one piece, doth not light a candle, and sweep the house, and seek diligently till she find it?

Luke 15:8

4. Jesus taught about the prodigal son's father who had one son but waited hopefully for the prodigal son to return.

For this my son was dead, and is alive again; he was lost, and is found. And they began to be merry.

Luke 15:24

5. Jesus taught about the banquet that did not begin until all of the seats were taken.

…Then the master of the house being angry said to his servant, Go out quickly into the streets and lanes of the city, and bring in hither the poor, and the maimed, and the halt, and the blind. And the servant said, Lord, it is done as thou hast commanded, and yet there is room. And the lord said unto the servant, Go out into the highways and hedges, and compel them to come in, that my house may be filled.

Luke 14:21-23

Chapter 102

Know the Names of Many People

...and the sheep hear his voice: and he calleth his own sheep by name, and leadeth them out.

John 10:3

People will follow someone who knows their names! It is very important that a leader knows the names of the people he works with. No one is a number or an object. If you want to lead people, try to remember their names and call them by name.

Five Reasons Why You Should Know the Names of Many People

1. **Every successful leader knows the names of many people.**

2. **People feel special when you know their names.**

Everyone gravitates towards where he feels special. People do not feel disregarded or despised when you call them by name.

3. **When you know the names of people they feel that you are friendly and human.**

People are attracted to someone who is friendly and warm.[1]

4. **Knowing people by their names connects you to them in a personal way.**

This creates the bond of leader and follower.

5. **Knowing the names of people makes you closer to them.**

I sometimes wonder at pastors who may have only sixty members and cannot remember all their names. If you cannot remember people's names, they will not like to follow you. When you know somebody's name, they feel you are real and they feel you are near enough. People are less inclined to follow a distant figurehead.

King David was a great leader. One of the reasons he was loved is because he was near enough to the people he led.[2]

> **But all Israel and Judah loved David, because he went out and came in before them.**
>
> 1 Samuel 18:16

Chapter 103

Invest in Yourself

Take heed unto thyself, and unto the doctrine; continue in them: for in doing this thou shalt both save thyself, and them that hear thee.

1 Timothy 4:16

Every leader who invests in himself will ensure that he remains the leader.

Three Reasons Why Every Leader Must Invest in Himself

1. Because of the law of deterioration.

This law says that everything is decaying naturally. Nothing on earth stays in a healthy original condition for long. This is why the Bible warns that the crown (your leadership position) is not guaranteed forever.

> **Be thou diligent to know the state of thy flocks, and look well to thy herds. For riches are not for ever: and doth the crown endure to every generation?**
>
> **Proverbs 27:23,24**

2. Because of the law of staying one step ahead.

There is no leadership unless you are a step ahead. I am constantly investing in myself in order to stay at least one step ahead of my followers. Without doing this, I would actually fall out of my position.[1]

3. Because of the law of taking care of yourself before you can take care of someone else.

Whenever there is any problem on a plane, adults are instructed to take care of themselves before taking care of their children. Paul said the same thing. There is no way you can save others unless you save yourself. A doctor cannot attend to others if he is sick. The blind cannot lead the blind.

> **Take heed unto thyself, and unto the doctrine; continue in them: for in doing this thou shalt both save thyself, and them that hear thee.**
>
> **1 Timothy 4:16**

Seven Ways Every Leader Can Invest in Himself

1. Read the Bible everyday.

In 1986 I travelled to London as a student. I bought one thing for myself--a special reference Bible. I used up all my meagre student's allowance to invest in myself. I have never regretted that investment.

> ...but he that soweth to the Spirit shall of the Spirit reap...
>
> **Galatians 6:8**

2. **Read Christian books everyday.**

   Read books about things you do not know.

3. **Listen to audio tapes.**

   When added up, the hours spent listening to tapes are equivalent to several semesters of lectures at the university.

4. **Attend seminars, conferences and church services.**

   These will make you a better person.

5. **Spend more money on your books than you do on your clothes and your hair.**

6. **Watch video tapes of anointed men of God teaching wisdom.**

7. **Build up a personal library of books and tapes.**

Chapter 104

Value Time and Manage Time

Six Ways to Manage Your Time

1. **Distinguish between important and urgent things.**

Many people claim they cannot do certain things because they have no time. However, the reality is that they are unable to manage their time. Do you call yourself a leader? If you are a leader, you must be able to distinguish between the important things and the urgent things. *Many things that are urgent are not important and many important things are not urgent.* A real leader is someone who cuts away the unimportant things and ensures that he does what he is supposed to do.[1]

2. Do not get involved with things that are not on your schedule.

If you are a leader, you will know that many good things are not necessarily the things you must do. I have decided that I will spend my time in prayer and in the ministry of the Word. Even as I write this book, I am under pressure to do many other things. I have decided that to write this book is the most important thing for me to do at this time.[2]

Redeeming the time, because the days are evil.

Ephesians 5:16

3. Surround yourself with competent helpers who will do certain essential jobs for you.

A responsible employee who takes care of important things for you is a valuable asset. There are things that must be done for me so that I can have time for the things that only I can do.

I am a pastor overseeing over two hundred churches; you can imagine the number of problems that arise everyday. I have to decide what to do: counselling people, praying for people, sorting out financial problems, solving managerial issues, and the list goes on. With the help of intelligent administrators and problem-solvers I will have time for my work.

4. Get rid of people who fail to do jobs that are delegated to them.

These people will create problems for you and drag you into areas which should have been taken care of.

5. Stay in your calling.

How can you develop the art of using your time wisely? I want to share with you a secret which I believe is a key to managing your time effectively. It is also a key to fulfilling the will of God. Did you know that you have only seventy years to live (more or less)? This means that you have only a limited time to serve the Lord. God is expecting you to do certain things. A true leader discovers what he is supposed to do and sticks to it.

Stay in your calling. Don't branch out into other people's territory. If you a teacher, teach the Word. If you are a pastor, give yourself to pastoring, don't try to become a prophet.

6. Avoid useless socializing.

Chatting around and being friendly is often time you could have spent fellowshipping with your Heavenly Father. People may say that you are not very friendly but you know what you are doing. Avoid wasting your time on useless television programs. It is not that I cannot afford a television. I just will not have the time to waste on silly TV programmes![3]

Chapter 105

Great Achievements Require Great Discipline

"To be disciplined", means "to be controlled, restrained, well-organized, regular, orderly, and regimented".

Then was Jesus led up of the Spirit into the wilderness to be tempted of the devil. And when he had fasted forty days and forty nights, he was afterward an hungered.

Matthew 4:1,2

Jesus subjected Himself to the strict discipline of fasting for forty days and nights. That is no mean achievement! Anyone who has fasted without eating for even three days and nights will discover the terrible strain it puts on your self-control.

To be a great leader you must discipline yourself in prayer, fasting and reading the Bible. There are times I stay in one room for eight hours, praying to the Lord. I can stay alone for hours in the presence of the Holy Spirit. You cannot do this without self-discipline.[1]

Do you want to be a great leader? It is time to discipline yourself in every way. To write this book, involves great self-discipline. For hours and hours, I transmit unto the paper the words that you are reading. It has not been an easy task! But I know that there will be no great achievement without great discipline.

Five Things Every Leader Should Be Disciplined About

1. A daily quiet time
2. To spend several hours in prayer[2]
3. To read the Bible everyday
4. To fast regularly
5. To read books

Chapter 106

Have a Vision

The greatest secret about vision is this: Your vision will make you into what you desire to become. Every great leader moves towards the vision and goal that he has set.

Where there is no vision, the people perish: but he that keepeth the law, happy is he.

Proverbs 29:18

The vision a man has makes him a leader. Your vision is what drives you and propels you out. If you are a leader and there is no vision before you, I really question whether you are a leader or not.[1]

It is what I see ahead that keeps me going. In my mind's eye, I see a megachurch! I see thousands of people being brought to Christ. I see many miracles taking place in my life and ministry. That is what keeps me going. You do not make your vision, it is your vision that makes you![2]

What is the key to having a great vision? I'll give you a good secret. Look around you and see anyone doing the things you like to do. Make it your vision to achieve what that person has achieved and more. Without such a vision, you will flounder in the sea of aimlessness.[3]

Chapter 107

Value Every Moment in the Presence of a Great Leader

Three People Who Valued Their Fellowship with Great Leaders

1. **John the disciple spoke of his interaction with Jesus.**

He shared how he had actually touched the Lord and heard Him speak.

> That which was from the beginning, which we have heard, which we have seen with our eyes, which we have looked upon, and our hands have handled, of the Word of life; (For the life was manifested, and we have seen it, and bear witness, and show unto you

that eternal life, which was with the Father, and was manifested unto us;)

1 John 1:1,2

This was the greatest experience of his life. A few moments in the presence of a great leader will teach you many things.

2. Elisha refused to go away from the presence of Elijah.

He knew how important it was for him to stay close. On four different occasions, he refused to go away.

And Elijah said unto Elisha, Tarry here, I pray thee; for the Lord hath sent me to Bethel. And Elisha said unto him, As the Lord liveth, and as thy soul liveth, I will not leave thee. So they went down to Bethel.

2 Kings 2:2

3. Joshua was also greatly affected by his close interaction with Moses.

Remember that Joshua was the only one who went up the mountain with Moses.

And the Lord said unto Moses, Come up to me into the mount, and be there: and I will give thee tables of stone, and a law, and commandments which I have written; that thou mayest teach them. And Moses rose up, and his minister Joshua: and Moses went up into the mount of God.

Exodus 24:12,13

All the members of Moses' original team became "someway" as time elapsed. Aaron moved into idol worship. Miriam became disloyal and critical. But Joshua was full of wisdom because of his closeness to Moses.

And Joshua the son of Nun was full of the spirit of wisdom; for Moses had laid his hands upon him: and the children of Israel hearkened unto him, and did as the Lord commanded Moses.

Deuteronomy 34:9

Seven Things to Notice in the Presence of Great Leaders

1.   Notice their vision.

You will be inspired to have a greater vision.[1]

2.   Notice their achievements.

It will show you what is possible.

3.   Notice their focus.

You will see the secret of concentration at work.

4.   Notice their relationship with God.

It will inspire you to be closer to God.

5.   Notice their appearance and their language.

You will feel the atmosphere of greatness.

6.   Notice how they handle situations.

You will receive wisdom for your own situation.

7.   Notice their weaknesses.

When you see their great achievements in spite of their weaknesses, you will be encouraged.

Chapter 108

Take Charge!

And when he was entered into a ship, his disciples followed him. And, behold, there arose a great tempest in the sea, insomuch that the ship was covered with the waves: but he was asleep. And his disciples came to him, and awoke him, saying, Lord, save us: we perish. And he saith unto them, Why are ye fearful, O ye of little faith? Then he arose, and rebuked the winds and the sea; and there was a great calm. But the men marvelled, saying, What manner of man is this, that even the winds and the sea obey him!

Matthew 8:23-27

Jesus was called up when there was a problem. It was raining and everyone was drowning. When Jesus was called, he took charge. I remember my first night alone as the doctor-in-charge of the Korle-Bu Hospital emergency room. It was a frightening experience for me. I was a new doctor and I was expected to lead the way and to know what to do in each case. Throughout the night, people were brought in unconscious, sick and some even dead. But I rose to the occasion and became the leader in the emergency room. How did I do it? I just did what I thought was right from the training that I had received. As time went by it became easier.

When Saul became a new leader, Samuel gave him this very instruction, "Do what you think is right and the Lord will be with you."

And let it be, when these signs are come unto thee, that thou do as occasion serve thee; for God is with thee.

1 Samuel 10:7

What is the key to taking charge as a leader? *The key to taking charge is to simply take charge.* Just rise up and speak confidently! Do what you think is best and God will be with you.

Chapter 109

Master the Art of Raising Money

Every leader is going to need some money to accomplish his mission. If you do not know how to raise money, you will not be a successful leader.

Elisha the prophet was a bold fundraiser. He met with a widow who was about to eat her last meal. Elisha convinced this woman to give up her last meal for his ministry. When the woman did that, she was led into a great financial miracle. It took a bold man of God to raise money for the work of ministry.

Five Keys to Successful Fundraising

1. Trust.

I have come to accept the fact that part of my job as a leader is to raise money. I am often raising money for different projects. What is the key to successful fundraising? People must trust you! Trust is something that builds up over the years. The more people trust you, the more they will be prepared to release their wealth. There are people who would give me thousands of dollars if I were to ask. They trust me because they have been with me for many years.[1]

Dear leader, the key to your fundraising ability is integrity. Whenever money is raised for a specific purpose, use the money for that specific purpose. As time goes by people will trust you.[2]

2. Be careful about projects which will take a long time to complete.

If you start something that does not conclude, people will think that you deceived them. They will think that you collected the money and used it for something else.

3. Do not raise money for inappropriate projects.

Do not raise money to meet the personal needs of pastors. I would advise you not to raise money to buy clothes, cars or to finance a holiday for the pastor and his wife. The congregation will not be happy to pay for luxuries that they themselves do not have. People prefer to give money to missionary work, evangelism and building projects.[3]

4. Do not raise funds too often.

Donor fatigue sets in when fundraising is too frequent. Depend on regular tithes and offerings for most things.

5. Be conscious of the 80-20 rule when you are raising funds.

Most people can give very little. However, a few people can give much more. The 80-20 Rule tells us that 80% of our income comes from 20% of the people. Raise funds from the eighty per cent but expect much more from the wealthy twenty per cent.

Never forget this fact. A leader will always need money to fulfil God's vision. Pray for financiers. Be a man of integrity. God will help you and you will never lack![4]

Chapter 110

Be Merciful

Blessed are the merciful: for they shall obtain mercy.

Matthew 5:7

    A leader is someone who knows the importance of showing mercy. Certain political leaders came on the scene spitting fire and brimstone. They passed judgements on others for minor crimes and sentenced them to death. Years later, they discovered that members of their own government were doing worse things. If they were to apply the same measuring rod to these individuals, they would probably have to execute their entire government. Blessed is the merciful for he shall obtain mercy. A wise leader knows that he may need mercy himself one day. That is why a true leader is merciful to his followers.[1]

Are You Spiritual?

Brethren, if a man be overtaken in a fault, ye which are spiritual, restore such an one in the spirit of meekness; considering thyself, lest thou also be tempted.

Galatians 6:1

This Scripture says that people who are spiritual must be careful to be merciful. Have you caught a thief today? Please show mercy! I know that you find it difficult to appreciate the circumstances under which you could be accused of being a thief one day.[2]

I am not predicting that every man of God will fall. All I am saying is that it is wise to be merciful rather than judgemental. Mercy triumphs over judgement. Surely you will need the mercy of God in your life. God looks at how much mercy you show to others.[3]

The blessing of merciful people is that they will also receive mercy. A leader is a humble person who also knows that he is capable of falling one day.[4]

Years ago, I met a pastor who was so judgemental about Kenneth Hagin. He spoke at length and described the faults of Kenneth Hagin to me. He then gave me a book full of criticisms about Kenneth Hagin. As this pastor spoke, I marvelled at the critical spirit he possessed. Some years later, this critical pastor divorced his wife and lost his ministry. The next I heard of him, he was in prison. There is no need to be judgemental. Are you a leader? Be merciful; you may need it one day.[5]

Chapter 111

Have Genuine Friends

One of the first things a real leader does is to make friends. It is these same friends who will help you. The people who support you will become your followers. Are you a person who makes friends, or scatters people? Your friendships form a basis for acts of loyalty, support and even sacrifice.

What is the secret to having genuine friends? Be a genuine friend yourself.[1]

A man that hath friends must show himself friendly: and there is a friend that sticketh closer than a brother.

Proverbs 18:24

Never forget that you reap what you sow. If you are a traitor, traitors and rebels will surround you. If you are a loyal person, loyal people will surround you. No matter how loyal you are, you will still have some traitors. Betrayal is a part of real life. Jesus was a loyal friend and leader, but he had Judas.

In spite of this, decide to be a real friend so that you will gather genuine people around you. If you are honest, dishonest people will not flow with you. If you are holy, unholy people will not be at ease to become your friends. As they say, "Birds of a feather flock together."[2]

Chapter 112

Work Harder Than All Those around You

To succeed as a leader you will have to work harder than all those around you. If you think that being a leader means enjoying more and more nice things, you are in for a rude shock. If you think being a leader means to relax as a "potbellied" ruler, you will discover that it is not so![1]

A true leader is someone who works harder than everyone around him. Although I am the head of a large church, and I have many people under me, I often work much harder than all those I lead. Leadership is hard work. Prepare your mind for hard work! A pastor must pray more than his followers. He must be more diligent than anyone else. He often puts in more hours than his followers. Notice how Jesus worked harder than his followers.[2]

> **And he went a little farther, and fell on his face, and prayed, saying, O my Father, if it be possible, let this cup pass from me: nevertheless not as I will, but as thou wilt. And he cometh unto the disciples, and findeth them asleep, and saith unto Peter, What, could ye not watch with me one hour? Watch and pray, that ye enter not into temptation: the spirit indeed is willing, but the flesh is weak. And he came and found them asleep again: for their eyes were heavy. And he left them, and went away again, and prayed the third time, saying the same words. Then cometh he to his disciples, and saith unto them, Sleep on now, and take your rest: behold, the hour is at hand, and the Son of man is betrayed into the hands of sinners.**
>
> **Matthew 26:39-41,43,45**

Notice how Jesus prayed whilst his disciples slept. He was working harder than his followers. Being the leader, he understood what was at stake. That night he put in more than everyone else. True leaders are often left alone by their followers and workers as they plod on through the night, putting in more and more effort.

There are many people who do not understand why top leaders are paid far more than their subordinates. Many unlearned people rebel against this reality. They do not know that successful leaders are actually working harder than everyone else. There are even certain diseases like ulcers, heart attacks, heart illness, high blood pressure that are associated with top executives. Their work schedules actually give rise to many stress-related illnesses. Often, the privileges of top leaders just cushion the effect of their stressful work lives. Dear leader, welcome to the world of hard work.

Chapter 113

Start Humble and End Humble

Many leaders start out humble and end up proud, full of themselves and of their achievements.

Pride goeth before a fall and it is this self-destructive button that becomes prominent in the lives of many leaders. Two of the greatest leaders that ever lived started humble and ended humble. Learn from their example.

Jesus Began and Ended His Ministry in Humility

1. Jesus Christ started his ministry in a manger.

And she brought forth her firstborn son, and wrapped him in swaddling clothes, and laid him in a manger; because there was no room for them in the inn.

Luke 2:7

2. Jesus Christ ended his ministry on a cross.

And when Jesus had cried with a loud voice, he said, Father, into thy hands I commend my spirit: and having said thus, he gave up the ghost.

Luke 23:46

Four Stages of Paul's Humility

Paul went through four stages of progressive humility.

1. He declared that he was not behind any of the apostles.

…for in nothing am I behind the very chiefest apostles…

2 Corinthians 12:11

2. As he progressed he felt that he was the least of the apostles.

For I am the least of the apostles, that am not meet to be called an apostle, because I persecuted the church of God.

1 Corinthians 15:9

3. After some more time, Paul thought that he was the least of all saints.

> **Unto me, who am less than the least of all saints…**
>
> **Ephesians 3:8**

As you can see, Paul's estimation of himself kept diminishing as he became more experienced in ministry. The higher you go in the Lord, the more you realize how dispensable you are. You discover that it is God's grace that is at work and not your own efforts.

4. At the end of his ministry, Paul decided he was the chief of sinners.

> **…Christ Jesus came into the world to save sinners; of whom I am chief.**
>
> **1 Timothy 1:15**

This was not because Paul had committed some grievous sin. With maturity came the consciousness of his sinful nature and indeed, that of all men.

Don't Let Your Achievements Make You Proud

Do not let your achievements change your opinion of yourself. Nebuchadnezzar made an awful mistake when he walked on the rooftop of his castle. He thought that he had achieved great things by *his own* strength.

> **At the end of twelve months he walked in the palace of the kingdom of Babylon. The king spake, and said, Is not this great Babylon, that I have built for the house of the kingdom by the might of my power, and for the honour of my majesty? While the word was in the king's mouth, there fell a voice from heaven, saying, O king Nebuchadnezzar, to thee it is spoken; The kingdom is departed from thee.**
>
> **Daniel 4:29-31**

When Nebuchadnezzar developed an elevated opinion of himself, God punished him. If you are a leader, do not make foolish statements about your achievements. I have heard political leaders make very foolish statements after being in power for some time. Some leaders even think they will live forever. But you can be very easily removed. Ask your fathers and ancestors whether they lived forever.

Your fathers, where are they? and the prophets, do they live for ever?

Zechariah 1:5

Do Not Laugh at Other Leaders

Maintain a humble opinion of yourself because you are mere flesh. Do not laugh at another leader who is in difficulty. History has taught us that judgmental leaders are prone to fall. Do not mock when other leaders fall into sin. What was David's reaction when Saul was killed in battle? Did he say, "It serves him right?" No, he did not! Mourn with those that mourn and pray for them. Notice the words of a great leader as he lamented over the fall of another great leader.

Thy beauty of Israel is slain upon thy high places: how are the mighty fallen! Tell it not in Gath, publish it not in the streets of Askelon; lest the daughters of the Philistines rejoice, lest the daughters of the uncircumcised triumph. Ye mountains of Gilboa, let there be no dew, neither let there be rain, upon you, nor fields of offerings: for there the shield of the mighty is vilely cast away, the shield of Saul, as though he had not been anointed with oil.

2 Samuel 1:19-21

Chapter 114

Convince People to Believe in You

Jesus saw Nathanael coming to him, and saith of him, Behold an Israelite indeed, in whom is no guile! Nathanael saith unto him, Whence knowest thou me? Jesus answered and said unto him, Before that Philip called thee, when thou wast under the fig tree, I saw thee. Nathanael answered and saith unto him, Rabbi, thou art the Son of God; thou art the King of Israel.

John 1:47-49

Jesus got Nathaniel to believe in Him. Nathaniel had a personal conviction that Jesus was a good person and that he should follow him. No one can truly follow your ideas unless he believes in you personally. The two go together. One of the reasons why leaders must be open is so that people get the chance to know them personally. I sometimes wonder as I watch preachers who say nothing about their personal lives. Could it be that they have no example to give or no testimony to share? Dear friend, the people you lead need to have faith in you as a person. How can this happen except you open up to them. People get to know what is in your heart by your words.

...for out of the abundance of the heart the mouth speaketh.
Matthew 12:34

When people can relate with the things that are in your heart, they will more readily go anywhere you want them to. They will be ready to do anything you tell them to do. I am not impressed with people who read speeches that have been written for them. I cannot know much about the person until I hear him speaking from his heart. It is the heart that really matters. When people can feel your passion, drive and vision, leadership will become natural. If you don't have a passion for anything or a drive to accomplish something, you are not a leader.

Pray for a passion and a conviction. Learning some rules about delegation, authority and management does not make anyone a real leader. That can only augment true leadership, which is from the heart. The reason why there are so many schools and books on leadership and yet we have such few leaders is because leadership is from the heart. *People will not follow you with their hearts until they believe in you with their hearts.*

Seven Ways to Make People Believe in You

1. Be open about your private life.

When there are many mysteries surrounding your life people will not naturally gravitate towards you.

2. Be honest about your problems.

Everyone has problems, including leaders. People rally around leaders whom they perceive to be real. A real leader is someone who has the same challenges as everyone else but overcomes them. If you have marital challenges, admit them openly and share how God helps you and your spouse to overcome them.

3. Preach from your heart.

Never read a sermon out to people. I once heard a secular head of state complain about his priest. He said, "I make speeches and I speak from my heart. Why should a priest who hears from God read his message to me?" When you read sermons your hearers may doubt your sincerity. Everything that is written is carefully thought out. What we want to hear is what is in your heart.

> **But I say unto you, That every idle word that men shall speak, they shall give account thereof in the day of judgment.**
>
> **Matthew 12:36**

4. Share your personal experiences with God.

Having a personal experience with God gives credibility and authority to the leader. After all, your Christian leadership is based on your having a relationship with God. If you have had a visitation by an angel or Jesus, share it and it will bring down the awesome presence of God.

5. Tell people what God told you.

If God spoke to you, share it. Being able to tell people that God told you something is a mighty step of faith. It shows that you have a personal commission from the Lord. People want to follow God, so if you have heard from God then they will want to follow you.

6. Sacrifice towards your vision.

People can see the sacrifices you are making towards what you believe. Your sacrifice will speak louder than a hundred sermons. I have sacrificed my medical profession for the ministry. That one act has given me more credibility than anything else. People will believe in you when they see your sacrifice.

7. Be prayerful. prayer generates spiritual authority. Authority is that "not-easily-defined, invisible, magnetic aura that surrounds a man of God."

Authority emanates from your closeness to God. The closer you are to a person, the more confidently you will speak about him. People will believe in you because of your prayer life. This is a secret that many prayer-less people do not know. People do not follow prayer-less leaders. Your private prayer will make people believe in you.

Chapter 115

Say a Lot or Say Nothing, Depending on Who You Are Talking to

A leader must learn to speak more or less, depending on who he is speaking to. Jesus Christ spoke for hours when he was surrounded by eager listeners. People came from miles around to hear and to be healed. He would preach for hours until people could not go back home.

And straightway many were gathered together, insomuch that there was no room to receive them, no, not so much as about the door: and he preached the word unto them.

Mark 2:2

And it came to pass, that, as the people pressed upon him to hear the word of God, he stood by the lake of Gennesaret...

Luke 5:1

When Jesus was in the presence of people who hated and scorned him, he said nothing. He knew that time would tell it all.

Three People Jesus Refused to Speak to

1. Jesus had nothing to say to the religious leaders.

    And the high priest stood up in the midst, and asked Jesus, saying, Answerest thou nothing? what is it which these witness against thee? But he held his peace, and answered nothing...

    Mark 14:60-61

2. Jesus had nothing to say to the governor, Pontius Pilate.

    And Pilate asked him, Art thou the King of the Jews? And he answering said unto him, Thou sayest it. And the chief priests accused him of many things: but he answered nothing. And Pilate asked him again, saying, Answerest thou nothing? Behold how many things they witness against thee. But Jesus yet answered nothing; so that Pilate marvelled.

    Mark 15:2-5

3. Jesus had nothing to say to Herod.

    And as soon as he knew that he belonged unto Herod's jurisdiction, he sent him to Herod, who himself also was at Jerusalem at that time. And when Herod saw Jesus, he was exceeding glad: for he was desirous to see him of a long season, because he had heard many things of him; and he hoped to have seen some miracle done by him. Then he questioned with

him in many words; but he answered him nothing. And the chief priests and scribes stood and vehemently accused him.

Luke 23:7-10

These were people who hated Jesus and he knew it. He knew that nothing he said would change their minds. I would rather follow the example of Jesus than to follow the guidance of a communications expert. I have left many matters to God and to time. He can best answer every accusation. You will notice that Jesus was accused vehemently, but refused to comment or respond to these accusations. It was not that Jesus could not speak. We see how he preached the Sermon on the Mount. We see how he taught at the seaside. We see how he preached so long that he had to feed the people afterwards.

Many pastors and leaders feel the need to attend interviews and discussions. They feel that they are obligated to clear their name and to improve their image. Mind you, I am not saying that it is wrong for pastors to speak to the press or to be interviewed. What I am saying is that Jesus did not bother to speak to hostile, disapproving interviewers who would never change their minds anyway. I would advise every minister to follow the example of Jesus Christ.

Three Reasons Why Pastors Are Not Obliged to Speak to the Press

1. The media has no power to make or destroy a minister of the gospel.

I know that many media men think that they have that power. Pilate also thought that he had power to destroy or establish Jesus.

Then saith Pilate unto him, Speakest thou not unto me? knowest thou not that I have power to crucify thee, and have power to release thee?

John 19:10

But Jesus corrected him.

Jesus answered, Thou couldest have no power at all against me, except it were given thee from above: therefore he that delivered me unto thee hath the greater sin.

John 19:11

In the same way, many press men feel that they have the power to destroy a man of God or a church if they want to. No one has the power to do anything unless God allows it. If Jesus had thought his ministry was being destroyed by those unanswered accusations, he would have spoken out. Learn this secret; no human being can destroy what God has built. Those accusations only serve as a basis for the future judgement of those liars. It may seem as though they have destroyed something, but in reality no one can destroy God's handiwork.

2.   Pastors must reserve their words for their congregations who will truly appreciate them.

Pastors must know that the appropriate forum for ministering is in the church and not to scoffing, scornful talk show hosts who despise your very existence. When hostile interviewers who were already biased questioned Jesus, he explained to them that He had nothing new to say. He had said all he had to say in church already.

The high priest then asked Jesus of his disciples and of his doctrine. Jesus answered him, I spake openly to the world; I ever taught in the synagogue, and in the temple, whither the Jews always result; and in secret have I said nothing. Why askest thou me? ask them which heard me, what I have said unto them: behold they know what I said.

John 18:19-21

Such an answer would annoy most reporters. Indeed, it irritated the men of that day.

And when he had thus spoken, one of the officers which stood by struck Jesus with the palm of his hand, saying, Answerest thou the high priest so? Jesus answered him, If I have spoken evil, bear witness of the evil: but if well, why smitest thou me?

John 18:22,23

3. There is no need for a pastor to justify himself to men.

If you are acceptable to God there is no need to appear pleasing to human society. Efforts to make yourself more acceptable to human beings may actually incur the displeasure of God.

And he said unto them, Ye are they which justify yourselves before men; but God knoweth your hearts: for that which is highly esteemed among men is abomination in the sight of God

Luke 16:15

Chapter 116

Accept the Principle of Ranking

They shall run like mighty men; they shall climb the wall like men of war; and they shall march every one on his ways, and they shall not break their ranks.

Joel 2:7

Ten Things Every Leader Should Know about Rank

1. **We are not created to be the same. Ranking is the acknowledgement of that reality.**

Some political ideologies have tried to make everybody the same. God did not create us to be equal. A leader is somebody who understands that he has a place in the scheme of things.

2.   Your rank defines your level of operation.

It tells you how high or low you are. Your rank may be designated by God or by your human superiors.

3.   Ranking eliminates confusion within an organization.

4.   Ranking shows you how much higher you can go.

I know of people who have more growth in their ministries than I do. I rejoice with them at what the Lord is doing. I know that I am not at the highest level that there is. I respect those who are ahead of me.

5.   Ranking shows you how low you can sink.

Understand that there are always people who are senior or junior to you.

6.   Ranks are changeable and very often they are changed.

Once you understand that your current rank is not necessarily your position for life, you will have hope for promotion in the future.

7.   Every rank has to be explored fully before you move on to the next.

If God places you at the level of a pastor, explore it fully and discover all that there is in the pastoral office.

8.   There are principles that determine promotion from rank to rank.

For instance, faithfulness and fruitfulness within your rank are very important for promotion.

9. A real change of rank occurs when God promotes you Himself.

I said unto the fools, Deal not foolishly: and to the wicked, Lift not up the horn:

Psalm 75:4

Promotion comes from the Lord. My position in the Lord is God-given and so is yours. Let us respect one another and God will move us to a higher rank.

10. Promotion to a higher rank often goes with new attacks. New levels bring new devils.

David's problems began when he killed Goliath. By killing Goliath he moved from the ranks of an unknown youth to the ranks of a famous warrior. It was then that Saul began to "eye" him and persecute him.

Promotion from God comes with persecution. You must know the implications of a higher rank. I never knew that God would raise me to where I am in ministry. I also never expected that I would encounter such persecution.

But he shall receive an hundredfold now in this time, houses, and brethren, and sisters, and mothers, and children, and lands, with persecutions...

Mark 10:30

Chapter 117

Turn the People around You into Better Human Beings

For I know that this shall turn to my salvation through your prayer, and the supply of the Spirit of Jesus Christ,

Philippians 1:19

    A good leader changes his followers. The people you influence will never forget you. They will be indebted to you forever. If God has told you to be a leader, you must see yourself working on the lives of the people you lead. Leadership is not just being called Chairman or President. Leadership is not a matter of sporting fancy titles. To lead is to work on people until they become better human beings.

By the time Jesus had led his disciples for three years, their lives had been completely transformed.[1]

Now when they saw the boldness of Peter and John, and perceived that they were unlearned and ignorant men, they marvelled; and they took knowledge of them, that they had been with Jesus.

Acts 4:13

Being with a good leader changes your life forever. A good leader changes the lives of his followers until he is unforgettable in their lives. A good leader affects the lives of his followers so much that his followers will be indebted to him. This is what happened between Paul and Philemon. Apostle Paul reminded Philemon how much he had affected his life. He told him that he owed him his very life![2]

...Albeit I do not say to thee how thou owest unto me even thine own self besides.

Philemon 19

8 Ways to Become an Unforgettable Leader

1.　Lead someone to Christ.

When you lead someone to Christ he will be forever indebted to you for bringing him to the Lord.

2.　Lead someone to be filled with the Holy Spirit.

They will forever be indebted to you for leading them to the greatest power and helper on the earth today.

3.　Establish someone in the Word of God.

They will forever be indebted to you for leading them to the greatest source of wisdom and direction for mankind. I am forever indebted to my mother in the Lord who taught me how to have a quiet time. My daily quiet time with the Word of God has become the greatest secret of my life. Most definitely I am indebted to the one who taught me this great secret.

4. Lead someone to the right church.

The right fellowship makes the difference between Christians. It is the most important factor that challenges a Christian to stay on the right path after salvation.

5. Help somebody find his way into the ministry.

The ministry is the highest calling on earth. It is the best vocation for a human being. It is the only job with eternal value. We will all find out that there is no higher privilege than to be called to serve in the ministry. It is just a matter of time.[3]

6. Help somebody to get married.

Finding a marriage partner is one of life's greatest decisions after choosing Christ. It will make or break you. If you help someone to get married to the right person at the right time he is indebted to you for life!

7. Help to save somebody's marriage.

Marriage is like glass, it is easily broken. Troubled marriages are very difficult to heal. If you successfully help to heal someone's marriage, he will remember you for life.

8. Help somebody to make the right decisions at the crossroads of his or her life.

Decisions make a great difference in a person's life. For instance, where you live, your job, school, etc. If you influence somebody in the right direction you will be an unforgettable person to him.

> ...Albeit I do not say to thee how thou owest unto me even thine own self besides.
>
> **Philemon 19**

Chapter 118

Move into High Gear by Moving to the Right Geographical Location

Many people waste precious years of their lives oscillating between one location and another. Where you live is very important for your success. This is because God has not called you everywhere but *somewhere!* No one is successful everywhere! Even Jesus did not succeed everywhere. He never stayed where he was not wanted. I used to think that Jesus did powerful miracles everywhere, but I found out that he didn't. The Bible says that he *could not* do miracles in his own country.

> **And he went out from thence, and came into his own country; and his disciples follow him. And he could there do no mighty work, save that he laid his hands upon a few sick folk, and healed them.**
>
> Mark 6:1,5

Even in the places where he had a good flow, Jesus had varying levels of success. He did many mighty works, but *most of these* were done in particular cities. There were physical locations where there was more success in Jesus' ministry. Be willing to go to places you have never been if God is calling you there. We all love our familiar surroundings and our comfort zones. God's promotion is waiting for you when you are prepared to obey and relocate for his purpose.

> **Then began he to upbraid the cities wherein most of his mighty works were done... Chorazin... Bethsaida... ...Capernaum...**
>
> Matthew 11:20,21,23

Seven People Who Became Successful When They Moved

1. Jesus' ministry blossomed when He moved away from His birthplace and set up His headquarters in Capernaum.

   The people in his hometown were angry when he preached.

   > **And he came to Nazareth, where he had been brought up: and, as his custom was, he went into the synagogue on the sabbath day, and stood up for to read. And all they in the synagogue, when they heard these things, were filled with wrath,**
   >
   > Luke 4:16, 28

However, the people of Capernaum loved his ministry. In Capernaum, Jesus taught, preached and did many of his mighty works.

And came down to Capernaum, a city of Galilee, and taught them on the sabbath days. And they were astonished at his doctrine: for his word was with power.

Luke 4:31,32

I have seen the greatest miracles of my ministry in certain places. I know that God has specific places where he will do great things.

2. Joseph became successful when he moved to live in Egypt.

Sometimes we are unwilling to go where God wants us to be. Like Joseph, we sometimes have to go there as prisoners.

And Joseph was brought down to Egypt; and Potiphar, an officer of Pharaoh, captain of the guard, an Egyptian, bought him of the hands of the Ishmeelites, which had brought him down thither.

Genesis 39:1

3. Ruth became successful when she moved out of Moab to live in Jerusalem.

And Ruth said, Entreat me not to leave thee, or to return from following after thee: for whither thou goest, I will go; and where thou lodgest, I will lodge: thy people shall be my people, and thy God my God:

Ruth 1:16

Sometimes circumstances make people change location. Ruth had become a widow. Her life had taken a sour turn. It was these very circumstances that would lead her to the place where she was destined to become famous. Ruth is important because she became the great grandmother of King David, Israel's greatest king. Ruth is also famous because she was the great-great grandmother of Solomon, the richest man who ever lived.

4.   Daniel became successful when he was displaced from Jerusalem to Babylon.

He was destined to be a prime minister for three different regimes. Daniel served in the highest office of Nebuchadnezzar's government, Belshazzar's government and Darius the Persian. Many economic refugees from Africa are being used by God to do his work in atheistic Europe.

5.   Abraham's life changed when he moved out of his own country and into Canaan.

Now the LORD had said unto Abram, Get thee out of thy country, and from thy kindred, and from thy father's house, unto a land that I will show thee:

Genesis 12:1

God wanted to separate Abraham from his idol-worshipping relatives. It was necessary for Abraham to move away. It may be necessary to relocate before God's will for your life can materialize.

6. Jacob's business flourished when he moved to live with his uncle Laban.

And Laban said unto him, I pray thee, if I have found favour in thine eyes, tarry: for I have learned by experience that the Lord hath blessed me for thy sake. And the man increased exceedingly, and had much cattle, and maidservants, and menservants, and camels, and asses.

Genesis 30:27,43

7. Paul lived among the Gentiles after God called him.

His ministry was to the Gentiles and not to the Jews, and he knew it. As a wise leader he knew that he would only succeed when he was physically located at the right place. From the very beginning Paul avoided staying in Jerusalem. The remainder of his life was among the Gentiles. This was one of the keys of Paul's success as a leader.

To reveal his Son in me, that I might preach him among the heathen; immediately I conferred not with flesh and blood: Neither went I up to Jerusalem to them which were apostles before me; but I went into Arabia, and returned again unto Damascus.

Galatians 1:16,17

Chapter 119

Control Your Carnal Instincts

God is not working through angels, he is working through men and women who have what I call "carnal instincts".

But we have this treasure in earthen vessels, that the excellency of the power may be of God, and not of us.

2 Corinthians 4:7

The earthen vessels in this Scripture are referring to the flesh. You must first control yourself before you try to control others. A leader must learn to control and direct his natural desire for carnal things. If this carnal instinct is unchecked, a person will discover that he can lead no one. Certain people are unable to fast. They cannot control their stomachs. You cannot be a good leader if your natural instincts lie unchecked.

Some women have the natural instinct to be jealous or quarrelsome. If you do not check these carnal instincts then you can lead no one. I remember a church where the pastor kept having children with his church members (other than his wife). Naturally, the members of the church dwindled until there was almost no one left. The pastor did not have control over his carnal instincts.

Jesus Overcame His Carnal Instincts

For we have not an high priest which cannot be touched with the feeling of our infirmities; but was in all points tempted like as we are, yet without sin.

Hebrews 4:15

When Jesus was in the Garden of Gethsemane, his natural instincts made him recoil from the thought of the cross. However, he prayed earnestly about it and was able to gain control of it himself. He walked to the cross for you and I. Even on the cross, his natural instincts made him think of calling on angels to deliver him. But once again, he held himself in check.

It is gaining control of these natural instincts that separates leaders from followers. Do not think that leaders are people who have no feelings, temptations or fleshly desires. They have as many of these lower instincts as anyone else. The key to leadership is gaining control of your lower instincts. If we were to follow our natural instincts, we would never pray, fast or read our Bibles.

The Apostle Paul spoke about how he kept his natural lower instincts in check. If Paul could do it then so can we.

But I keep under my body, and bring it into subjection: lest that by any means, when I have preached to others, I myself should be a castaway.

1 Corinthians 9:27

Chapter 120

Understand the Difference between the Ideal and the Real

An experienced person is someone who knows the difference between the ideal and the real. The "ideal" is like the stars of the sky. It tells us where we want to go. The real is what is "on the ground". It tells us where we really are. Theoretical knowledge will tell you the ideal but experience will tell you what is real.

Young and inexperienced politicians have often come on the political scene with all sorts of idealistic philosophies. Many of such people have communist and socialist leanings. With time and experience, they often realize that things are not as straightforward as they thought. You will often find such people switching to capitalist ideologies.

The ideal and the real are also seen in the ministry. You may think that if you do certain things you will get certain results. As you mature you will discover that it is not as simple as that. Church growth principles may be applied, but the church will still not grow. This is because the ideal is different from the real. Experience will teach you that.

It is ideal to live up to seventy years, but I have watched as young pastors have died in the midst of their years. It is ideal for everyone to be healed, but the real is not so. Even Jesus did not try to heal everyone. Experience will make you mature and make you a more capable and able leader.

Do not despise the lessons of maturity that you are learning. Do not change your theologies because of your experiences. The Word of God is still true. The fact is that we don't know everything. There is a reason why the real is often different from the ideal. There are often other factors at work that we are not aware of. It is not everything that we know or understand. Paul did not understand everything. He described it as seeing through a dark glass.

For now we see through a glass, darkly; but then face to face: now I know in part; but then shall I know even as also I am known.

1 Corinthians 13:12

Idealism and Delusions

Leadership often requires maturity. Maturity comes from experience. Experiences in life will harden you. Maturity is required for leadership. Maturity drives away delusions and idealism.

Not a novice, lest being lifted up with pride he fall into the condemnation of the devil.

1 Timothy 3:6

Have you ever wondered why a presidential candidate must be at least forty years old? By the age of forty, experience would have driven delusions and idealism away. Walk on the road that will harden you and make you more experienced. Learn from each experience you have.

As I write this book, I am listening to music by Keith Green. I cannot understand why such a person's life should be cut short at the age of twenty-eight. The passion, zeal and anointing of his music can hardly compare with the watered down Christian music of today. Yet, Keith Green was removed in the midst of his years. He left behind a wife and little children. Do you have an explanation for this? I do not! The secret things belong to the Lord. Be mature!

The secret things belong unto the Lord our God: but those things which are revealed belong unto us and to our children for ever, that we may do all the words of this law.

Deuteronomy 29:29

Chapter 121

Identify the Different Types of Employees in Your Organization

There are different types of people who will work under a leader. It is important to identify the real differences that exist.

Five Types of Employees Every Leader Has to Deal with

1.   Employees Who Prefer Resting to Working.

God worked for six days and rested for one day. This means that it is better to work than to rest. Any employee who prefers resting to working, has not found his God-given task.

2. Employees Who Are Not Prepared to Do Anything Extra or New.

Such employees are not valuable, they want to do what they have always done. They don't want change.

3. Workers Who Are Prepared to Do Any Job.

Such people are valuable. They are prepared to learn. They want to advance. They want to please you.

4. Results-Producing Employees.

One of the most valuable things in an employee is his ability to produce results.

5. Workers Who Are Consumed and Obsessed with Their Work.

This is the highest kind of worker. Value them and pay them highly.

Seven Things Every Leader Should Teach His Employee

1. Teach every employee to write instructions down as you speak.
2. Teach your employees to repeat their instructions and ask questions about the instructions you have given them.
3. Teach them to call you, talk to you and consult you frequently.
4. Teach them to be ready to change jobs and accept new responsibilities.
5. Teach them to dress formally whilst at work.

Have you not noticed that the wealthiest organizations, such as banks, instruct their employees to dress very formally?

6. Teach them to solve problems they encounter in the course of their duties.

Instead of reporting problems, they should report how they solved those problems!

7. Teach them to think about their work whilst at home.

Someone who thinks about his work whilst at home is both consumed and obsessed by his job. Such people read books about their career. They spend their money and time in an effort to be better prepared for their task.

How to Be Consumed with Your Work

1. Know that you will only succeed with things that consume your whole being.
2. Find the job which does not make you conscious of time.

That is your God-given task.

3. Continue your work in your mind, even whilst at home.
4. Buy and read books about your work.
5. Have more of friends who are into your kind of work.

This will mean that even your leisure times relate to your work.

6. Spend money to be better trained and prepared for your work.

Chapter 122

Develop the Art of Keeping People Together

Five Keys to Keeping People Together

1. **Have a strong desire to keep everyone together. Fight to prevent the loss of even one person. Jesus' aim was to lose none of the people God had given Him.**

Pastoring a church is the art of keeping people together. At many points in the life of a church, there are situations that have the potential of dividing people. You must develop the art of keeping people together. What is the key to uniting people? You must believe that the people must be kept together. If you have a *"you can go to hell if you want to"* attitude, many people are going to drop out of your team.

Moses Kept People Together

Now the children of Reuben and the children of Gad had a very great multitude of cattle: and when they saw the land of Jazer, and the land of Gilead, that, behold, was a place for cattle; Wherefore, said they, If we have found grace in thy sight, let this land be given unto thy servants for a possession, and bring us not over Jordan. And Moses said unto them, If ye will do this thing, If ye will go armed before the Lord to war, And will go all of you armed over Jordan before the Lord, until he hath driven out his enemies from before him, …this land shall be your possession before the Lord.

Numbers 32:1,5,20-22

Moses came across a delicate situation. Some of the tribes of Israel did not want to cross the River Jordan. They wanted to stay where the grass was good for their cattle, meanwhile, there was a war to fight. They had been together up until this time and the nation Israel was about to split up into two parts. God gave Moses the wisdom to keep Israel united.

Moses could have cursed those tribes and could have told them to go to hell. He could have told them that they were damned. But he made it possible for them to have their dreamland and at the same time remain a part of Israel.

2. Love all the people God gives you.

Another key is to cherish and love people genuinely. When you love somebody genuinely, you do not easily want to part with the person. A leader must have real love for people. People will stay where they feel they are genuinely loved. Even if there is a reason for your followers to separate, your love for all the groups will make them stay together.[1]

3. **Use the wisdom of God to handle delicate situations.**

Then came there two women, that were harlots, unto the king, and stood before him.

And the one woman said, O my lord, I and this woman dwell in one house; and I was delivered of a child with her in the house. And it came to pass the third day after that I was delivered, that this woman was delivered also: and we were together; there was no stranger with us in the house, save we two in the house. And this woman's child died in the night; because she overlaid it. And she arose at midnight, and took my son from beside me, while thine handmaid slept, and laid it in her bosom, and laid her dead child in my bosom. And when I rose in the morning to give my child suck, behold, it was dead: but when I had considered it in the morning, behold, it was not my son, which I did bear.

And the other woman said, Nay; but the living is my son, and the dead is thy son. And this said, No; but the dead is thy son, and the living is my son. Thus they spake before the king. Then said the king, The one saith, This is my son that liveth, and thy son is the dead: and the other saith, Nay; but thy son is the dead, and my son is the living. And the king said, Bring me a sword. And they brought a sword before the king. And the king said, Divide the living child in two, and give half to the one, and half to the other.

Then spake the woman whose the living child was unto the king, for her bowels yearned upon her son, and she said, O my lord, give her the living child, and in no wise slay it. But the other said, Let it be neither mine nor thine, but divide it. Then the king

answered and said, Give her the living child, and in no wise slay it: she is the mother thereof. And all Israel heard of the judgment which the king had judged; and they feared the king: for they saw that the wisdom of God was in him, to do judgment.

1 Kings 3:16-28

King Solomon faced a delicate situation. Whose side was he on? Many times, people want to say that the leader supports this person or the other. In marriage counselling sessions, I have often been accused of being on either the side of the wives or the husbands. People want to say that you are on this side or the other. It takes the wisdom of God to handle delicate situations. Marriage is a delicate thing. Handle marital crises carefully and the couples in your church will stay together. A true leader is going to have his ability to handle delicate situations tested. If you fail, your people will not stay together.

4. Bring peace between people.

Most of the leaders of this world are engaged in settling conflicts. The reality is that human beings have so many conflicts and wars between each other that there is constantly no peace. Anyone who is a leader will need to learn the art of peace-making.

Follow peace will all men…

Hebrews 12:14

Have you not noticed that many presidents wish to be the ones who bring peace between warring factions? Successive American presidents have longed to be the ones to bring peace to the Middle East. They take famous photographs standing between sworn enemies. These pictures are important to them as they testify about their ability to lead. Anyone who is able to bring peace to this world has leadership abilities.

Are you a leader? Do you help to bring peace between enemies? Do you fuel hatred and strife? A leader does not bring more confusion; he brings peace.

5. Be at peace with others.

Some people are constantly at war. They pick quarrels with almost anyone they interact with. I know some pastors' wives who have driven away many people from their husbands' churches. You cannot lead people with whom you constantly fight. You may be wondering why nobody is following you. How can people follow someone who keeps stabbing them in the back? Would you follow someone who turns around every few minutes and throws a stone at you? Certainly not!

Do you desire to be a leader? Then develop the art of being at peace with those around you. Do not constantly threaten them. Do not frighten them with curses.

I was once invited to visit with a man of God. I did not want to go. I had seen that man curse people many times. I thought to myself, "Perhaps he will curse me today." I did not want to be around a man who effortlessly threw curses around.

The art of leadership is the art of being at peace with those around you. Do not be disturbed by other people's successes. Do not fight them because they have something you do not have. Be content with such things as you have. Accept other people's success and do not fight them.

What is the key to being at peace with others? Accept them as they are. Do not try to change everyone around you. We are only human and we have our mistakes.[2]

Chapter 123

Constantly Think about the Day of Accountability

Every leader will give account for what he or she is doing. Are you ready to account to God for the sheep he gave you? Jesus kept on saying that he had lost none of the sheep God had given him except the son of perdition. Paul kept saying that he would have to give account. These were leaders who were constantly thinking about the day of accountability.[1]

Obey them that have the rule over you, and submit yourselves: for they watch for your souls, as they that must give account, that they may do it with joy, and not with grief: for that is unprofitable for you.

Hebrews 13:17

Leadership is a great responsibility. I remember years ago, watching as several Ghanaian heads of state and ministers were executed by a firing squad. It was pathetic to see important people being humiliated and murdered. Most ordinary citizens did not receive such treatment. This is because most ordinary men had not taken up the responsibility of ruling the country. However, those who had taken up responsibility of leadership had to pay with their lives.

If you are constantly reminded that you will account for your leadership, you will become a better leader. Always remember that the day of accountability is coming. This will make you do the right thing. I am constantly aware that I will have to account to God for my ministry. I know that I will have to account for the members in my churches. This is why I make great efforts to look after them.[2]

Are you a leader? Are you constantly thinking of your day of accountability? Please do! It is the key to the greatest inner motivation.

Notes

Chapter 1

1. Leith Anderson, *Leadership that Works* (Minneapolis, Minnesota: Bethany House Publishers, 1999), 36.

Chapter 2

1. Bruce P. Powers, *Church Administration Handbook* (Nashville, Tennessee: Broadman and Holman Publishers, 1997), 57.

Chapter 3

1. Jerry White, *Honesty, Morality and Conscience* (Colorado Springs, Colorado: Navpress, 1978), 16; Aubrey Malphurs and Will Mancini, *Building Leaders* (Grand Rapids, Michigan: Baker Books, 2004), 136; Lee Ellis, *Leading Talents Leading Teams* (Chicago, Illinois: Northfield Publishing, 2003), 203.

2. Robert Lewis, *The Church of Irresistible Influence* (Grand Rapids, Michigan: Zondervan Publishing House, 2001), 60; J. Oswald Sanders, *Dynamic Spiritual Leadership* (Grand Rapids, Michigan, 1999), 75; Joseph M. Stowell, *Shepherding the Church* (Chicago, Illinois: Moody Press, 1997), 227-250; John C. Maxwell, *Be a People Person* (Colorado Springs, Colorado: Cook Communications, 2004), 83-88; Kenneth O. Gangel, *Team Leadership in Christian Ministry* (Chicago, Illinois: Moody Bible Institute, 1997), 266.

Chapter 4

1. Lee Ellis, *Leading Talents Leading Teams* (Chicago, Illinois: Northfield Publishing, 2003), 203.

2. Pat Williams, *The Paradox of Power* (U.S.A.: Warner Books, 2002), 50.

3. Bill Perkins, *Awaken the Leader Within* (Grand Rapids, Michigan: Zondervan Publishers, 2000), 108-112 and Leith Anderson, *Leadership that Works* (Minneapolis, Minnesota: Bethany House Publishers, 1999), 163.

Chapter 7

1. J. Oswald Sanders, *Dynamic Spiritual Leadership* (Grand Rapids, Michigan: Discovery House Publishers, 1999), 71.

2. Campbell McAlpine, *The Leadership of Jesus* (Kent, England: Clays Ltd., St. Ives Plc., n.d.), 39.

Chapter 8

1. Bill Perkins, *Awaken the Leader Within* (Grand Rapids, Michigan: Zondervan Publishers, 2000), 76-78.

2. Ibid., 105.

Chapter 9

1. Bill Perkins, *Awaken the Leader Within* (Grand Rapids, Michigan: Zondervan Publishers, 2000), 210.

2. Ibid., 176-178.

3. LeRoy Eims, *Be a Motivational Leader* (Colorado Springs, Colorado: Cook Communications, 1996), 37.

4. Ibid., 126.

5. Jennings F. Dake, *The Dake's Annotated Bible* (Lawrenceville, Georgia: Dake Bible Sales Inc., 1997), 282: 3 John:2, note d.

Chapter 10

1. Robert Lewis, *The Church of Irresistible Influence* (Grand Rapids, Michigan: Zondervan Publishing House, 2001), 45 and David Cape and Tommy Tenny, *God's Secret to Greatness* (Ventura, California: Regal Books, 2000), 104.

2. John C. Maxwell, *Be All You Can Be* (Colorado Springs, Colorado: Cook Communication Ministries, 2003), 107 and Kenneth O. Ga ngel, *Team Leadership in Christian Ministry* (Chicago, Illinois: Moody Bible Institute, 1997), 268.

3. LeRoy Eims, *Be a Motivational Leader* (Colorado Springs, Cook Communication Ministries, 1996), 29.

4. Ibid., 117.

5. Paul Winslow and Dorman Followwill, *Christ in Church*

Leadership (Grand Rapids, Michigan: Discovery House Publishers, 2001), 145 and Leith Anderson, *Leadership that Works* (Minneapolis, Minnesota: Bethany House Publishers, 1999), 75.

6. Bill Perkins, *Awaken the Leader Within* (Grand Rapids, Michigan: Zondervan Publishers, 2000), 29.

7. LeRoy Eims, *Be a Motivational Leader* (Colorado Springs, Cook Communication Ministries, 1996), 88.

8. John Foxe, *Foxe's Book of Martyrs* (Grand Rapids, Michigan, 1967), 212-215.

9. Ibid., 207-220.

10. Ibid., 210-213.

Chapter 11

1. David Cape and Tommy Tenny, *God's Secret to Greatness* (Ventura, California: Regal Books, 2000), 119 and Kenneth O. Gangel, *Team Leadership in Christian Ministry* (Chicago, Illinois: Moody Bible Institute, 1997), 98.

Chapter 13

1. Leroy Eims, *Be a Motivational Leader* (Colorado Springs, Colorado: Victor Publishers, 1981), 7.

2. Anderson Leith, *Leadership that Works* (Minneapolis, Minnesota: Bethany House Publishers, 1999), 154.

Chapter 14

1. John MacArthur, *The Master's Plan for the Church* (Chicago: Moody Press, 1991), 213.

2. John C. Maxwell and Jim Dornan, *Becoming a Person of Influence* (California: Maxwell Motivation Inc., 1997), 77.

3. Jay E. Adams, *Shepherding God's Flock* (Grand Rapids, Michigan: Zondervan Publishers, 1980), 332.

4. Ted Haggard, *The Life Giving Church* (Ventura, California: Regal Books, 2002), 87.

5. Anthony D'Souza, *Being a Leader* (Accra, Ghana: Africa Christian Press, 1990), 100.

6. Tom Marshall, *Understanding Leadership* (Tonbridge, Kent: Sovereign World Limited, 1991), 130.

Chapter 15

1. Emmanuel Kwabena Ansah, *Keys to Successful Succession* (Accra, Ghana: Scrolls Publishing House Ltd., 2002), 56.

Chapter 16

1. Leith Anderson, *A Church for the 21st Century* (Minneapolis, Minnesota: Bethany House Publishers, 1992), 63.

Chapter 17

1. Bob Briner and Ray Pritchard, *The Leadership Lessons of Jesus* (Nashville, Tennessee: Broadman & Holman Publishers, 1997), 27-28.

2. Max Depree, *Leadership Is an Art* (New York: Dell Publishers, 1989), 56.

Chapter 18

1. Oswald J. Sanders, *Spiritual Leadership* (Chicago: Moody, 1967), 97.

Chapter 19

1. Richard O. Lawrence and Hoeldtke Clyde, *Church Leadership Following the Example of Jesus Christ* (Grand Rapids, Michigan: Zondervan Publishers, 1996), 161.

2. Robert C. Anderson, *The Effective Pastor* (Chicago: Moody Press, 1985), 277.

Chapter 20

1. John C. Maxwell, *The 17 Essential Qualities of a Team Player* (Georgia: Maxwell Motivation Inc., 2000), 8.

2. Ken Blanchard, *The Heart of a Leader: Insight on the Art of Influence* (Tulsa, Oklahoma: Honor Books, 1999), 23.

Chapter 21

1. John C. Maxwell, *The 21 Most Powerful Minuites in a Leader's Day* (Nashville, Tennessee: Thomas Nelson, Inc., 2000), 58.

2. Allen Charles Kollar, *Solution Focused Pastoral Counselling* (Grand Rapids, Michigan: Zondervan Publishers, 1997), 165.

Chapter 22

1. Bob Briner and Ray Pritchard, *The Leadership Lessons of Jesus* (Nashville, Tennessee: Broadman & Holman Publishers, 1997), 12-17; John White, *Excellence in Leadership* (Leicester, England: InterVarsity Press, 2003), 115; Jay E. Adams, *Leaders after God's Heart* (Grand Rapids, Michigan: Zondervan Publishers, 1975), 453.

Chapter 23

1. Leith Anderson, *Leadership that Works* (Minneapolis, Minnesota: Bethany House Publishers, 1999), 154; James Berkly, *Leadership Handbook of Outreach and Care* (Grand Rapids, Michigan: Baker Books, 1994), 149.

2. Jay E. Adams, *Shepherding God's Flock* (Grand Rapids, Michigan: Zondervan Publishers, 1975), 453; David Pollock and Larry Burkett, *Business Management in the Local Church* (Chicago: Moody Press, 1995), 105.

Chapter 24

1. Gary D. Kinnaman and Alfred Ells, *Leaders that Last* (Grand Rapids, Michigan: Baker Books, 2003), 146.

Chapter 25

1. Oswald J. Sanders, *Dynamic Spiritual Leadership* (California: Discover House Publishers, 1999), 222.

Chapter 26

1. Genes Wilkes, *Jesus on Leadership* (Nashville, Tennessee: Lifeway Press, 2001), 5-57; Campbell McAlpine, *The Leadership of Jesus* (England: Clays Ltd., St. Ives Plc., n.d.), 14, 21; Paul Winslow and Dorman Filowwill, *Christ in Church Leadership* (Grand Rapids, Michigan: Discovery House Publications, 2001), 14-16; Tom Marshall, *Understanding Leadership* (England: Clays Ltd., St. Ives Plc, 1991), 66-81; John Adair, *Great Leaders* (Guildford, Surrey: The Talbot Adair Press, 1989), 39-56.

Chapter 27

1. Kenneth O. Gangel, *Leadership for Church Education* (Chicago: Moody Press, 1970), 183-184 and J. Oswald Sanders, *Spiritual Leadership* (Chicago: Moody Press, 1967), 65-66.

2. Kenneth O. Gangel, *Leadership for Church Education* (Chicago: Moody Press. 1970), 176; John C. Maxwell, *17 Essential Qualities of a Team Player* (Nashville, Tennessee: Thomas Nelson Inc., 2002), 107-109; Lee Ellis, *Leading Talents Leading Teams* (Chicago: Northfield Publishing, 2003), 210-212.

3. Campbell McAlpine, *The Leadership of Jesus* (England: Clays Ltd., St. Ives Plc., n.d .), 44-50 and Noel M. Tichy and Eli Cohen, *The Leadership Engine* (New York: Harper Business Essentials, 2002), 55.

4. Bob Gordon and David Fardouly, *Master Builders: Developing Life and Leadership in the Body of Christ Today* (Kent, England: Sovereign World, 1990), 48.

5. Tim Peters and Nancy Austin, *A Passion for Excellence: The Leadership Difference* (Glasgow: William Collins Sons and Company Ltd., 1985), 206 and Kenneth O. Gangel, *Coaching Ministry Teams* (Nashville, Tennessee: Word Publishing, 2000), 153.

6. Lawrence O. Richards and Clyde Hoeldtke, *Church Leadership* (Grand Rapids, Michigan: Zondervan Publishers, 1980)141-142.

Chapter 28

1. Campbell McAlpine, *The Leadership of Jesus* (England: Clays Ltd., St. Ives Plc., n.d.), 39-40

2. Tom Marshall, *Understanding Leadership* (England: Clays Ltd., St. Ives Plc., 1991), 9-19.

Chapter 29

1. Bob Gordon and David Fardouly, *Master Builders: Developing Life and Leadership in the Body of Christ Today* (Kent, England: Sovereign World, 1990), 45.

2. John MacArthrur, *The Master's Plan for the Church* (Chicago: Moody Press, 1991), 49-50.

Chapter 30

1. Michael Armstrong, *A Handbook of Human Resource Management Practice* (London: The Bath Press, 1999), 155.

2. Hans Finzel, *The Top Ten Mistakes Leaders Make* (Colorado Springs, Colorado: Cook Communications Ministries, 1994), 15.

3. Fremont E. Kast and James E. Rosenzweig, *Organization and Management* (Singapore: McGraw-Hill Book Company, 1985), 360 and Robert Salmon, *The Future of Management: All Roads Lead To Man* (Cambridge, Massachusetts: Blackwell Publishers Inc., 1994), 177.

Chapter 31

1. Rudolph W. Giuliani, *Leadership* (New York: Miramax Books, 2002), 354.

2. Leith Anderson, *Leadership that Works* (Grand Rapids, Michigan: Bethany House, 1999), 180; Kenneth Gangel, *Coaching Ministry Teams* (Nashville, Tennessee: Word Publishing, 2000), 169; Rudolph W. Giuliani, Leadership (New York: Miramax Books, 2002), 349.

3. John Adair, *Great Leaders* (Guildford, Surrey: The Talbot Adair Press, 1989), 13-28 and Oswald J. Sanders, *Dynamic Spiritual Leadership: Leading Like Paul* (Grand Rapids, Michigan: Discovery House Publishers, 1999), 70.

Chapter 32

1. John C. Maxwell, *The 21 Most Powerful Minutes in a Leader's Day* (Nashville, Tennessee: Thomas Nelson Publishers, 2000), 157.

2. Oswald J. Sanders, *Spiritual Leadership* (Chicago: Moody Press, 1967), 59-62.

Chapter 33

1. Oswald J. Sanders, *Dynamic Spiritual Leadership: Leading Like Paul* (Grand Rapids, Michigan: Discovery House Publishers, 1999), 170.

2. Oswald J. Sanders, *Dynamic Spiritual Leadership: Leading Like Paul* (Grand Rapids, Michigan: Discovery House Publishers, 1999), 105 and John C. Maxwell, *The 21 Most Powerful Minutes in a Leader's Day* (Nashville, Tennessee: Thomas Nelson Publishers, 2000), 229-301.

3. Hudson Armerding, *Leadership* (Wheaton, Illinois: Tyndale House Publishers, Inc., 1978), 141-153.

Chapter 34

1. LeRoy Eims, *Be a Motivational Leader* (Colorado Springs, Colorado: Cook Communication Ministries, 1996), 16-18.

2. Ibid., 66-74.

Chapter 35

1. John C. Maxwell, *The 17 Indisputable Laws of Teamwork* (Nashville, Tennessee: Thomas Nelson Publishers Inc., 2001), 93.

Chapter 36

1. Oswald J. Sanders, *Dynamic Spiritual Leadership: Leading Like Paul* (Grand Rapids, Michigan: Discovery House Publishers, 1999), 161; Kenneth O. Gangel, *Team Leadership in Christian Ministry* (Chicago: Moody Press, 1997), 47; Dale Launderville, *Piety and Politics* (Grand Rapids, Michigan: WM. B. Eerdmans Publishing Company, 2003), 43; Rudolph Guiliani, *Leadership* (New York: Miramax Books, 2002), 86; Win and Charles Arn, *The Master's Plan for Making Disciples* (Grand Rapids, Michigan: Baker Books, 1998), 91-92.

Chapter 37

1. Oswald J. Sanders, *Spiritual Leadership* (Chicago: Moody Press, 1967), 75-84, 101-110 and Dale Launderville, *Piety and Politics* (Grand Rapids, Michigan: WM. B. Eerdmans Publishing Company, 2003), 315-320.

2. Bob Gordon and David Fardouly, *Master Builders* (Kent, England: Sovereign World, 1990), 47.

Chapter 38

1. George Barna, ed., *Leaders on Leadership* (Ventura, California: Regal Books, 1997), 39-41.

2. Peter Wiwcharuk, *Building Effective Leadership* (Alberta, Canada: International Christian Leadership Development Foundation, 1987), 228-230.

3. Kenneth O. Gangel, *Team Leadership in Christian Ministry* (Chicago: Moody Press, 1997), 128-129.

4. George Barna, *The Power of Team Leadership* (Colorado Springs, Colorado: Waterbrook Press, 2001), 102.

5. Kenneth O. Gangel, *Team Leadership in Christian Ministry* (Chicago: Moody Press, 1997), 129.

6. Bob Briner and Richard Pritchard, *The Leadership Lessons of Jesus* (Nashville, Tennessee: Broadman & Holman Publishers, 1997), 121-123.

Chapter 39

1. Kenneth O. Gangel, *Team Leadership in Christian Ministry* (Chicago: Moody Press, 1997), 216 and James D. Berkley, *Leadership Handbook of Management and Administration* (Grand Rapids, Michigan: Baker Book House Co., 2003), 181.

2. John Hagee, *The Seven Secrets* (Lake Mary, Florida: Charisma House, 2004), 139.

3. Nii Boi E. Bennet, *Practical Leadership Skills for Christian Ministry* (Accra, Ghana: Challenge Enterprises of Ghana, 2004), 21-132 and James D. Berkley, ed., *Leadership Handbook of Management and Administration* (Grand Rapids, Michigan: Baker Book House Co., 2003), 28-29.

4. James D. Berkley, ed., *Leadership Handbook of Management and Administration* (Grand Rapids, Michigan: Baker Book House Co., 2003), 30-31.

5. J. Oswald Sanders, *Spiritual Leadership* (Chicago: Moody Press, 1994), 103-107.

6. Henry and Richard Blackaby, *Spiritual Leadership* (Nashville, Tennessee: Broadman & Holman Publishers, 2001), 212-214 and John Hagee, *The Seven Secrets* (Lake Mary, Florida: Charisma House, 2004), 183-204.

7. Henry and Richard Blackaby, *Spiritual Leadership* (Nashville, Tennessee: Broadman & Holman Publishers, 2001), 239-240.

8. Ibid., 214, 280 and John C. Maxwell, *Your Road Map for Success* (Nashville, Tennessee: Thomas Nelson Publishers, 2002), 179-181.

9. John C. Maxwell, *Your Road Map for Success* (Nashville, Tennessee: Thomas Nelson Publishers, 2002), 168-176.

10. Leith Anderson, *Leadership that Works* (Minneapolis, Minnesota: Bethany House Publishers, 1999), 76, 155 and John Hagee, *The Seven Secrets* (Lake Mary, Florida: Charisma House, 2004), 226.

11. John Hagee, *The Seven Secrets* (Lake Mary, Florida: Charisma House, 2004), 211-213.

12. Denny Gunderson, *Leadership Paradox* (Seattle, Washington: YWAM Publishing, 1997), 98.

13. Bob Briner and Ray Pritchard, *The Leadership Lessons of Jesus* (Nashville, Tennessee: Broadman &Holman Publishers, 1997), 29-32, 148.

14. Jeff C. Woods, *Better than Success: 8 Principles of Faithful Leadership* (Valley Forge, Pennsylvania: Judson Press, 2001), 109-120.

15. Paul J. Meyer, *Unlocking Your Legacy: 25 Keys for Success* (Chicago: Moody Press, 2002), 143.

Chapter 40

1. George Barna, Leaders on Leadership (Ventura, California: Regal Books, 1997), 70-72.

2. Ibid., 77.

Chapter 41

1. Henry and Richard Blackaby, *Spiritual Leadership* (Nashville, Tennessee: Broadman & Holman Publishers, 2001), 21.

2. Myles Munroe, *Maximising Your Potential* (Slippenburg, Pennsylvania: Destiny Image Publishers Inc., 2003), 132.

3. Henry and Richard Blackaby, *Spiritual Leadership* (Nashville, Tennessee: Broadman & Holman Publishers, 2001), 148-152; David Yonggi Cho and Harold Hostetler, *Successful Home Cell Groups* (Gainsville, Florida: Bridge Logos Publishers, 2001), 115-130.

4. Myles Munroe, *Maximising Your Potential* (Slippenburg, Pennsylvania: Destiny Image Publishers Inc., 2003), 129-130.

5. Bob Briner and Ray Pritchard, *The Leadership Lessons of Jesus* (Nashville, Tennessee: Broadman & Holman Publishers, 1997), 158-161.

6. John C. Maxwell, *Make Yours a Winning Team* (New York: Inspirational Press, 2000), 315.

Chapter 42

1. Michael Jinkins and Deborah Bradshaw, *The Character of Leadership* (San Francisco, California: Jossey-Bass Inc., Publishers, 1998), 126.

2. Bob Briner and Ray Pritchard, *The Leadership Lessons of Jesus* (Nashville, Tennessee: Broadman & Holman Publishers, 1997), 115-117.

3. Kenneth O. Gangel, *Team Leadership in Christian Ministry* (Chicago: Moody Press, 1997), 98, 111.

4. Willis Harman and John Hormon, *Creative Work* (Indianapolis, Indiana: Knowledge Systems, Inc., 1990), 177 and Anne Katherine, *Boundaries* (New York: MJF Books, 1991), 92.

Chapter 43

1. Bob Briner and Ray Pritchard, *The Leadership Lessons of Jesus* (Nashville, Tennessee: Broadman & Holman Publishers, 1997), 153-155.

2. Michael Jinkins and Deborah Bradshaw, *The Character of Leadership* (San Francisco, California: Jossey-Bass Inc., Publishers, 1998), 123-125.

3. Campbell McAlpine, *The Leadership of Jesus* (Kent, England: Sovereign World Ltd., n.d.), 46 and Tom McMahon, *Big Meetings Big Results* (Chicago, Illinois: NTC Business Books, 1990), 71.

Chapter 44

1. Kenneth O. Gangel, *Team Leadership in Christian Ministry* (Chicago: Moody Press, 1997), 115 and Paul J. Meyer, *Unlocking Your Legacy: 25 Keys for Success* (Chicago: Moody Press, 2002), 183-192.

2. Leith Anderson, *Leadership that Works* (Minneapolis, Minnesota: Bethany House Publishers, 1999), 156.

3. John C. Maxwell, *Developing the Leader Within You Workbook* (Nashville, Tennessee: Thomas Nelson Publishers, 2001), 23-25 and Jeff C. Woods, *Better than Success: 8 Principles of Faithful Leadership* (Valley Forge, Pennsylvania: Judson Press, 2001), 46-59.

Chapter 45

1. George Barna, *The Power of Team Leadership* (Colorado Springs, Colorado: Waterbrook Press, 2001), 26; Leith Anderson, *Leadership that Works* (Minneapolis, Minnesota: Bethany House Publishers, 1999), 191-202; Ken Blanchard and Robert Lorber, *Putting the One-Minute Manager to Work* (New York: William Morrow and Company Inc., 1985), 65.

2. Gary Heil, Tom Parker and Rick Tate, *Leadership and the Customer Revolution* (New York: Van Nostrand Reinhold, 1995), 64, 115-117 and George Barna, ed., *Leaders on Leadership* (Ventura, California: Regal Books, 1997), 54-60.

3. George Barna, *The Power of Team Leadership* (Colorado Springs, Colorado: Waterbrook Press, 2001), 127 and Kenneth O. Gangel, *Team Leadership in Christian Ministry* (Chicago: Moody Press, 1997), 214.

4. Bob Briner and Ray Pritchard, *The Leadership Lessons of Jesus* (Nashville, Tennessee: Broadman & Holman Publishers, 1997), 135-137 and George Barna, *The Power of Team Leadership* (Colorado Springs, Colorado: Waterbrook Press, 2001), 91.

5. Fred Smith, Sr., and David L. Goetz, eds., *Leading with Integrity* (Minneapolis, Minnesota: Bethany Press International, 1999), 153 and Ken Blanchard, Bill Hybels, Phil Hodges, *Leadership by the Book* (Colorado Springs, Colorado: Waterbrook Press, 1999), 154.

6. Annie Brooking, *Corporate Memory* (London: Thomson Business Press, 1999), 38.

7. George Barna, ed., *Leaders on Leadership* (Ventura, California: Regal Books, 1997), 138.

8. Denny Gunderson, *Leadership Paradox* (Seattle, Washington: YWAM Publishing, 1997), 86.

9. John C. Maxwell, *Developing the Leaders around You* (Nashville, Tennessee: Thomas Nelson Publishers, 1975), 184.

10. Ibid., 97.

11. Jack Orsburn et al., *Self-Directed Work Teams* (Homewood, Illinois: Business One Irwin, 1990), 112.

12. George Barna, *The Power of Team Leadership* (Colorado Springs, Colorado: Waterbrook Press, 2001), 25; Fred Smith, Sr., and David L. Goetz, eds., *Leading with Integrity* (Minneapolis, Minnesota: Bethany Press International, 1999), 113.

Chapter 46

1. Oswald J. Sanders, *Spiritual Leadership* (Chicago: Moody Press, 1994), 69.

2. Theodore Isaac Rubin, *The Angry Book* (New York: Collier Books, 1970), 21.

Chapter 47

1. Bob Briner and Ray Pritchard, *The Leadership Lessons of Jesus* (Nashville, Tennessee: Broadman & Holman Publishers, 1997), 24-26.

2. Ibid., 43-45 and Frank Damazio, *Effective Keys to Successful Leadership* (Portland, Oregon: City Bible Publishing, 1993), 65-70.

3. Frank Damazio, *Effective Keys to Successful Leadership* (Portland, Oregon: City Bible Publishing, 1993), 228-230, 248.

Chapter 48

1. John C. Maxwell, *Developing the Leader Within You Workbook* (Nashville, Tennessee: Thomas Nelson Publishers, 2001), 195-197.

2. John C. Maxwell, *Developing the Leaders Around You. (Nashville, Tennessee: Thomas Nelson Publishers,* 1975), 187.

Chapter 49

1. Bob Briner and Ray Pritchard, *The Leadership Lessons of Jesus* (Nashville, Tennessee: Broadman and Holman Publishers, 1997), 52.

2. David Cape and Tommy Tenny, *God's Secret to Greatness* (Ventura, California: Regal Books, 2000), 196.

3. Pat Williams, *The Paradox of Power* (U.S.A.: Warner Books, 2002), 150-152.

Chapter 50

1. Kenneth O. Gangel, *Team Leadership in Christian Ministry* (Chicago, Illinois: Moody Bible Institute, 1997), 98.

Chapter 51

1. Kenneth O. Gangel, *Team Leadership in Christian Ministry* (Chicago, Illinois: Moody Bible Institute, 1997), 251.

2. Myron Rush, *Management: A Biblical Approach* (Colorado Springs, Colorado: Cook Communications, 2002), 16-19.

Chapter 52

1. Gary D. Kinnaman and Alfred H. Ells, *Leaders that Last* (Grand Rapids, Michigan: Baker Books, 2003), 41.

Chapter 53

1. J. Oswald Sanders, *Spiritual Leadership* (Chicago, Illinois: Moody Bible Institute, 1967), 207.

2. Jay E. Adams, *Shepherding God's Flock* (Grand Rapids, Michigan: Zondervan Publishers, 1974), 339.

3. J. Oswald Sanders, *Dynamic Spiritual Leadership* (Grand Rapids, Michigan: Discovery House Publishers, 1999), 57.

Chapter 54

1. J. Oswald Sanders, *Spiritual Leadership* (Chicago, Illinois: Moody Bible Institute, 1967), 209.

2. Robert Lewis, *The Church of Irresistible Influence* (Grand Rapids, Michigan: Zondervan Publishing House, 2001), 57.

Chapter 57

1. Robert Lewis, *The Church of Irresistible Influence* (Grand Rapids, Michigan: Zondervan Publishing House, 2001), 65.

2. J. Oswald Sanders, *Spiritual Leadership* (Chicago, Illinois: Moody Bible Institute, 1967), 19.

Chapter 58

1. Leith Anderson, *Leadership that Works* (Minneapolis, Minnesota: Bethany House Publishers, 1999), 141 and John C. Maxwell, *The 17 Indisputable Laws of Teamwork* (Nashville, Tennessee: Thomas Nelson Publishers, 2001), 78-86.

2. John C. Maxwell, *The 17 Indisputable Laws of Teamwork* (Nashville, Tennessee: Thomas Nelson Publishers, 2001), 42.

Chapter 59

1. Destiny Law, *Interview with Art Linkletter* (Mouseplanet,com:electronically retrieved at http://www.mouseplanet.com/destiny/071700.htm.).

2. Kwame Nkrumah, *Dark Days in Ghana* (Herts, U.K.: Watford Printing Services, 1968), 75-96.

Chapter 60

1. John C. Maxwell, *Leadership 101* (Nashville, Tennessee: Thomas Nelson Publishers, 2002), 25-28.

Chapter 62

1. Bob Gordon, *The Leader's Motivation* (Tonbridge, Kent: Sovereign World Books, 1990), 94.

Chapter 66

1. Kenneth C. Gangel, *Leadership for Church Education* (Chicago: Moody Press, 1970), 26.

Chapter 67

1. Joseph M. Stowell, *Shepherding the Church* (Chicago: Moody Press, 1997), 152.

2. David G. Benner, *Strategic Pastoral Counselling* (Grand Rapids, Michigan: Baker Books, 2003), 26.

Chapter 68

1. Jim Van Yperen, *Making Peace: A Guide to Overcoming Church Conflict* (Chicago: Moody Press, 2002), 214.

2. Denny Gunderson, *Leadership Paradox* (Seattle, Washington: YWAM Publishing, 1997), 32.

3. George Barna, *How to Increase Giving in Your Church* (Ventura, California: Regal Books, 1997), 103.

4. David Hansen, *The Power of Loving Your Church* (Minneapolis, Minnesota: Bethany House Publishers, 1998), 157.

Chapter 69

1. Alexander Strauch, *Biblical Leadership* (Littleton, Colorado: Lewis and Roth Publishers, 1988), 105.

2. Leith Anderson, *Leadership that Works* (Minneapolis, Minnesota: Bethany House Publishers, 1999), 190.

3. Judson Cornwall, *Profiles of a Leader* (Gainsville, Florida: Bridge-Logos Publishers, 1980), 54.

4. John C. Maxwell, *Today Matters: 12 Daily Practices to Guarantee Tomorrow Success* (Nashville, Tennessee: Warner Faith, 1999), 49.

Chapter 70

1. Lawrence O. Richards and Clyde Hoelldtke, *Leadership Qualities* (Grand Rapids, Michigan: Zondervan Publishing House, 1980), 2.

2. Alexander Strauch, *Biblical Leadership* (Littleton, Colorado: Lewis and Roth Publishers, 1988), 105.

3. George Barna, *Leaders on Leadership* (Ventura, California: Regal Books, 1982), 50.

4. Gene A. Getz, *20 Attributes of a Godly Man* (Ventura, California: Regal Books, 1995), 210.

Chapter 71

1. Leroy Eims, *The Lost Art of Disciple-Making* (Grand Rapids, Michigan, Zondervan Publishing House, 1978), 186.

2. Alexander Strauch, *Minister of Mercy: The New Testament Deacon* (Littleton, Colorado: Lewis and Roth Publishers, 1992), 88.

3. John C. Maxwell, *Developng Leaders Around You* (Nashville, Tennessee: Thomas Nelson Publihsers, 1995), 68.

4. Bennet E. Nii Boi, *Practical Leadership Skills for Christian Ministry* (Challenge Enterprises of Ghana, 2004), 100 and John Glime, *Pastoral Ethics* (Grand Rapids, Michigan: Zondervan Publishing House, 2005), 88.

Chapter 72

1. Melvin J. Steinbron, *Can the Pastor Do it Alone?* (Ventura, California: Regal Books, 1992), 132.

Chapter 73

1. James Halcomb, David Hamilton and Howard Malmstadt, *Courageous Leaders: Transforming Their World* (Seattle, Washington: YWAM Publishing, 2000), 55.

Chapter 74

1. Myron Rush, *Management: A Biblical Approach* (Colorado Springs, Colorado: Cook Communications Ministries, 2002, 210 and John C. Maxwell, *Be a People Person* (Colorado Springs, Colorado: Nexgen, 2004), 25-31.

2. Leith Anderson, *Leadership that Works* (Grand Rapids, Michigan: Bethany House, 1999), 179.

3. Richard L. Daft, *Leadership: Theory and Practice* (Orlando, Florida: Harcourt College Publishers, 1999), 127-130; John C. Maxwell, *The 21 Irrefutable Laws of Leadership Workbook* (Nashville, Tennessee: Thomas Nelson Publishers, 2002, 13-18; Henry and Richard Blackaby, *Spiritual Leadership: Moving People on to God's Agenda* (Nashville, Tennessee: Broadman and Holman Publishers, 2001), 86-92.

4. John Adair, *Great Leaders* (Guildford, Surrey: The Talbot Adair Press, 1989), 57-72 and George Barna, *Growing True Disciples* (Colorado Springs, Colorado, 2004), 25-31.

Chapter 75

1. Tim Peters and Nancy Austin, *A Passion for Excellence: The Leadership Difference* (Glasgow, Great Britain: William Collins Sons and Company Ltd., 1985), 209.

2. Bob Gordon with David Fardouly, *Master Builders: Developing Life and Leadership in the Body of Christ Today* (Tonbridge, Kent: Sovereign World Books, 1990), 94.

Chapter 77

1. Kenneth O. Gangel, *Team Leadership in Christian Ministry* (Chicago: Moody Press, 1997), 257.

2. Leith Anderson, *Leadership that Works* (Grand Rapids, Michigan: Bethany House, 1999), 185.

3. Kenneth O. Gangel, *Team Leadership in Christian Ministry* (Chicago: Moody Press, 1997), 349.

4. Alan Barker, *How to Be Better at Managing People* (London, England: Kogan Page, 2000), 95 and Cy Charnes, *The Instant Manager* (London, U.K.: Kogan Page, 2001), 140.

Chapter 78

1. Michael Armstrong, *A Handbook of Human Resource Management Practice* (London: The Bath Press, 1999), 105-125.

2. Laurie J. Mullins, *Management and Organizational Behaviour* (Great Britain: Pitman Publishing, 1990), 27 and Bob Gordon, *The Leader's Motivation* (England: Clays Ltd., St. Ives Plc., 1991), 66-81.

3. DuBrin, *Leadership: Research Findings, Practice and Skills* (Boston, Massachusetts: Houghton Mission Company, 1995), 27.

Chapter 79

1. John C. Maxwell, *Be a People Person* (Colorado Springs, Colorado: NEXGEN, 2004), 61.

2. Oswald J. Sanders, *Dynamic Spiritual Leadership* (Grand Rapids, Michigan: Discovery House Publishers, 1999), 78.

3. F.A. Shull, A.L. Delbeckq and L.L. Cummings, *Organizational Decision-Making* (New York: McGraw-Hill Inc., 1970), 56.

4. LeRoy Eims, *Be a Motivational Leader* (Colorado Springs, Colorado: Cook Communication Ministries, 1996), 16-18.

5. Bob Gordon with David Fardouly, *Master Builders: Developing Life and Leadership in the Body of Christ Today* (Kent, England: Sovereign World, 1990), 49.

Chapter 80

1. Mohammed Zairi, *Best Practice Process Innovation Management* (London, England: Biddles Ltd., n.d.), 76.

2. John C. Maxwell, *Be All You Can Be* (Colorado Springs, Colorado: Victor Boks, 2003), 49.

Chapter 81

1. Bob Gordon with David Fardouly, *Master Builders: Developing Life and Leadership in the Body of Christ* (Tonbridge, Kent: Sovereign World Books, 1990), 235.

2. George Barna, *The Habits of Highly Effective Churches* (California, U.S.A.: Regal Books, 1999), 52.

3. Paul Birch, *Instant Leadership: Reach Your Full Potential Now!* (London, England: Kogan Page, 1999), 75.

4. Oswald J. Sanders, *Dynamic Spiritual Leadership* (Grand Rapids, Michigan: Discovery House Publishers, 1999), 57.

Chapter 82

1. Bob Gordon with David Fardouly, *Master Builders: Developing Life and Leadership in the Body of Christ Today* (Tonbridge, Kent: Sovereign World Books, 1990), 166-168.

2. John C. Maxwell, *Make Yours a Winning Team* (Colorado Springs, Colorado: Inspirational Press, 1989), 85-96.

3. Peter F. Haddon, *Mastering Personnel and Interpersonal Skills* (London, England: Thorogood, 1999), 236.

4. James Halcomb, David Hamilton and Malstadt Howard, *Courageous Leaders: Transforming Their World* (Seattle, Washington: YWAM Publishing, 2000), 80-86.

5. Paul Yonggi Cho, *Solving Life's Problems* (South Plainford, New Jersey: Bridge Publishing Inc., 1980), 53.

Chapter 83

1. Bob Gordon with David Fardouly, *Master Builders: Developing Life and Leadership in the Body of Christ Today* (Tonbridge, Kent: Sovereign World Books, 1990), 205.

Chapter 84

1. Wayne Cordeiro, *Doing Church as a Team* (Ventura, California: Regal Books, 2001), 32-36.

2. Selwyn Hughes, *The 7 Laws of Spiritual Success* (Finland: WS Bookwell, 2002), 53-63.

3. Ibid.

Chapter 85

1. Tim Peters and Nancy Austin, *A Passion for Excellence: The Leadership Difference* (Glasgow, Great Britain: William Collins Sons and Company Ltd., 1985), 284-286.

2. Tom Marshall, *Understanding Leadership* (England: Clays Ltd., St. Ives Plc., 1991), 35-41.

Chapter 86

1. Peter Wiwcharuk, *Building Effective Leadership* (Alberta, Canada: International Christian Leadership Development Foundation, 1987), 61.

2. Ken Blanchard, *The Heart of a Leader* (Guildford, Surrey: Eagle, 2001), 142.

3. Peter Wiwcharuk, *Building Effective Leadership* (Alberta, Canada: International Christian Leadership Development Foundation, 1987), 52-54 and George Barna, *The Power of Team Leadership* (Colorado Springs, Colorado: Waterbrook Press, 2001), 91.

Chapter 87

1. John C. Maxwell, *Make Yours a Winning Team* (New York: Inspirational Press, 2000), 207-217.

2. John C. Maxwell, *Your Road Map for Success* (Nashville, Tennessee: Thomas Nelson Publishers, 2002), 198.

3. David Gerwitz, *The Flexible Enterprise* (New York: John Wiley & Sons Inc., 1996), 236.

4. Ken Blanchard, Bill Hybels and Phil Hodges, *Leadership by the Book* (Colorado Springs, Colorado: Waterbrook Press, 1999), 130.

5. John C. Maxwell, *Thinking for a Change* (New York: Warner Books Inc., 2003), 233.

6. Kenneth O. Gangel, *Team Leadership in Christian Ministry* (Chicago: Moody Press, 1997), 86.

Chapter 88

1. Charles Garfield, *Second to None* (Homewood, Illinois: Business One Irwin, 1992), 257-263.

2. Peter Wiwcharuk, *Building Effective Leadership* (Alberta, Canada: International Christian Leadership Development Foundation, 1987), 19-23.

3. Brian Salter and Naomi Longford-Wood, *Successfully Dealing With Difficult People* (London: Hodder & Stoughton, 1998), 84.

4. George Barna, ed., *Leaders on Leadership* (Ventura, California: Regal Books, 1997), 113.

Chapter 89

1. Ian Britza, *The Absalom Spirit* (Tulsa, Oklahoma: Harrison House, 2004), 51.

2. George Barna, ed., *Leaders on Leadership* (Ventura, California: Regal Books, 1997), 112.

3. Myles Munroe, *Maximizing Your Potential* (Slippenburg, Pennsylvania: Destiny Image Publishers, Inc., 2003), 101-108.

4. John C. Maxwell, *Make Yours a Winning Team* (New York: Inspirational ress, 2000), 311.

5. Bob Briner and Ray Pritchard, *The Leadership Lessons of Jesus* (Nashville, Tennessee: Broadman & Holman Publishers, 1977), 52.

Chapter 90

1. Barbara Posthuma W., *Small Groups in Therapy Settings: Process and Leadership* (Boston, Massachusetts: College-Hill Press, 1989), 110.

2. Carol O'Connor, *Successful Leadership* (London: Hodder & Stoughton, 2002), 93.

3. Marlys Neis and Ruth T. Kingdon, *Leadership in Transition* (Schaumburg, Illinois: NOVA 1 Ltd., 1990), 106.

Chapter 91

1. Ian Britza, *The Absalom Spirit* (Tulsa, Oklahoma: Harrison House, 2004), 52.

2. Ibid., 53.

Chapter 92

1. It is important to recognize and deal effectively with employee defiance. See Farhard Analoui and Andrew Kakabadse, *Sabotage* (London: Mercury Books, 1991), 153.

2. James D. Berkley, ed., *Leadership Handbook on Management and Administration* (Grand Rapids, Michigan: Baker Book House Co., 2003), 33-35; Paul J. Meyer, *Unlocking Your Legacy. 25 Keys for Success* (Chicago: Moody Press, 2002), 121-128, 146-148;

Frank Damazio, *The Making of a Leader* (Portland, Oregon: City Bible Publishing, 1988), 220; Annie Brooking, *Corporate Memory* (London: Thomson Business Press, 1999), 55.

3. Ken Blanchard, *The Heart of a Leader* (Guildford, Surrey: Eagle, 2001), 152.

Chapter 93

1. Frank Damazio, *Effective Keys to Successful Leadership* (Portland, Oregon: City Bible Publishing, 1993), 27, 36.

2. John C. Maxwell, *Developing the Leader Within You. Workbook* (Nashville, Tennessee: Thomas Nelson Publishers, 2001), 142-145.

3. Ibid., 169-171 and Ken Blanchard, Bill Hybels and Phil Hodges, *Leadership by the Book* (Colorado Springs, Colorado: Waterbrook Press, 1999), 121.

4. John C. Maxwell, *Your Road Map for Success* (Nashville, Tennessee: Thomas Nelson Publishers, 2002), 12-16.

Chapter 94

1. Myles Munroe, *Maximising Your Potential* (Slippenburg, Pennsylvania: Destiny Image Publishers Inc., 2003), 83.

2. Bob Briner and Ray Pritchard, *The Leadership Lessons of Jesus* (Nashville, Tennessee: Broadman & Holman Publishers, 1997), 60-62.

3. John C. Maxwell, *Make Yours a Winning Team* (New York: Inspirational Press, 2000), 313-315.

4. Leadership is the ability to absorb pain/to handle rejection by people who do not love you. See James D. Berkley, ed., *Leadership Handbook of Management and Administration* (Grand Rapids, Michigan: Baker Book House Co., 2003) and Bob Briner and Ray Pritchard, *The Leadership Lessons of Jesus* (Nashville, Tennessee: Broadman & Holman Publishers, 1997), 92.

Chapter 95

1. Fred H. Maidment, ed., *Organizational Behaviour*, 1st Edition (Guildford, Connecticut: Dushkin/McGraw Hill Publishing Company, 2000), 114.

2. Mike Murdock, *The Leadership Secrets of Jesus* (Dallas, Texas: Wisdom International, 1996), 97.

3. George Barna, *The Power of Team Leadership* (Colorado Springs, Colorado: Waterbrook Press, 2001), 104.

Chapter 96

1. Bob Briner and Ray Pritchard, *The Leadership Lessons of Jesus* (Nashville, Tennessee: Broadman & Holman Publishers, 1997), 87.

2. John C. Maxwell, *Make Yours a Winning Team* (New York: Inspirational Press, 2000), 315.

Chapter 97

1. Peter Wiwcharuk, *Building Effective Leadership* (Alberta, Canada: International Christian Leadership Development Foundation, 1987), 296.

2. John C. Maxwell, *Developing the Leaders Around You* (Nashville, Tennessee: Thomas Nelson Publishers, 1975), 67.

Chapter 98

1. John C. Maxwell, *Developing Leaders Around You* (Nashvile, Tennessee: Thomas Nelson Publishers, 1975), 31.

2. ------, *Your Road Map for Success* (Nashville, Tennessee: Thomas Nelson Publishers, 2002), 192-199.

3. Leith Anderson, *Leadership that Works* (Minneapolis, Minnesota: Bethany House Publishers, 1999), 75.

Chapter 99

1. Lawrence O. Richards and Clyde Heoldtke, *A Theology of Church Leaders* (Grand Rapids, Michigan: Zondervan Publishing House, 1980), 106 and James Halcomb, David Hamilton and Howard Malmstadt, *Courageous Leaders: Transforming their World* (Seattle, Washington: YWAM Publishing, 2000), 57-61.

2. Pat Williams, *The Paradox of Power* (U.S.A.: AOL Time Warner Company, 2002), 187 and Win and Charles Arn, *The Master's Plan for Making Disciples* (Grand Rapids, Michigan: Baker Books, 2004), 139.

3. Denny Gunderson, *The Leadership Paradox* (Seattle, Washington: YWAM Publishing, 1997), 14-17, 75 and Lawrence O. Richards and Clyde Heoldtke, *Church Leadership* (Grand Rapids, Michigan: Zondervan Publishing House, 1980), 103.

4. Campbell McAlpine, *The Leadership of Jesus* (Kent, England: Clays Ltd., St. Ives Plc., n.d.), 57 and Alexander Strauch, *Biblical Eldership* (Littleton, Colorado: Lewis and Roth Publishers, 1986), 43.

5. J. Oswald Sanders, *Spiritual Leadership* (Chicago: Moody Press, 1979), 10.

Chapter 101

1. George Barna, *Leaders on Leadership* (Ventura, California: Regal Books, 1997), 32.

Chapter 102

1. Lee Ellis, *Leading Talents Leading Teams* (Chicago: Northfield Publishing, 2003), 211.

2. James D. Berkley, *Leadership Handbook of Outreach and Care* (Grand Rapids, Michigan: Baker Books, 1994), 241.

Chapter 103

1. Benny Hinn, *He Touched Me* (Nashville, Tennessee: Thomas Nelson Publishers, 1999), 52.

Chapter 104

1. Bob Gordon, *The Leader's Vision* (Kent, England: Clays Ltd., St. Ives Plc, 1990), 90.

2. James D. Berkley, *Leadership Handbook of Management and Administration* (Grand Rapids, Michigan: Baker Books, 2003), 79 and Henry and Richard Blackaby, *Spiritual Leadership* (Nashville, Tennessee: Broadman and Holman Publishers, 2001), 204.

3. Bob Gordon, *The Leader's Vision* (Kent, England: Clays Ltd., St. Ives Plc, 1990), 91; Kenneth O. Gangel, *Team Leadership in Christian Ministry* (Chicago: Moody Press, 1997), 115.

Chapter 105

1. Paul Winslow and Dorman Followwill, *Christ in Church Leadership* (Grand Rapids, Michigan: Discovery House Publishers, 2003), 146 and Alexander Strauch, *The New Testament Deacon* (Littlewood, Colorado: Lewis and Roth Publishers, 1992), 16.

2. Africans Ministry Resources, Kenya, *Church Leaders* (Accra, Ghana: Challenge Enterprises, 2004), 26.

Chapter 106

1. George Barna, *The Power of Team Leaders* (Colorado Springs, Colorado: WaterBrook Press, 2001), 37; John C. Maxwell, *Developing the Leader Within You* (Nashville, Tennessee: Thomas Nelson Publishers, 2001), 169; Roger Helland, *The Revived Church* (Kent, England: Clays Ltd., St. Ives Plc, 1998), 42.

2. Tom Marshall, *Understanding Leadership* (Kent, England: Clays Ltd., St. Ives Plc, 1991), 9; George Barna, *Leaders on Leadership* (Ventura, California: Regal Books, 1997), 47; George Barna, *The Habits of Highly Effective Churches* (Ventura, California: Regal Books, 1999), 4.

3. Bob Gordon, *The Leader's Vision* (Kent, England: Clays Ltd., St. Ives Plc, 1990), 7 ; Ken Blanchard, Bill Hybels and Phil Hodges, *Leadership by the Book* (New York: WaterBrook Press, 1999), 119-122; Wayne Cordeiro, *Doing Church as a Team* (Ventura, California: Regal Books, 1997), 122; John C. Maxwell, *Be All You Can Be* (Colorado Springs, Colorado: Victor Books, 1977), 50.

Chapter 107

1. Bob Gordon, *Master Builders* (Kent, England: Sovereign World, 1990), 286.

Chapter 109

1. John C. Maxwell, *Be a People's Person* (Colorado Springs, Colorado: NEXGEN, 2004), 131; George Barna, *How to Increase Giving in Your Church* (Ventura, California: Regal Books, 1997), 59.

2. David Pollock, *Business Management in the Local Church* (Chicago: Moody Press, 1996), 60.

3. James D. Berkley, *Leadership Handbook of Management and Administration* (Grand Rapids, Michigan: Baker Books, 1994), 429.

4. John C. Maxwell, *The 21 Irrefutable Laws of Leadership Workbook* (Nashville, Tennessee: Thomas Nelson Publishers, 2002), 63.

Chapter 110

1. Leith Anderson, *A Church for the 21st Century* (Minneapolis, Minnesota: Bethany House Publishers, 1992), 201 and David Fisher, *The 21st Century Pastor* (Grand Rapids, Michigan: Zondervan Publishing House, 1996), 163.

2. Joseph M. Stowell, *Shepherding the Church* (Chicago: Moody Press, 1994), 179.

3. Kenneth Gangel, *Coaching Ministry Teams* (Nashville, Tennessee: Thomas Nelson Publishers, 2000), 156.

4. Ian M. Duguide, *Hero of Heroes* (Phillipsburg, New Jersey: P&R Publishing Company, 2001), 61.

5. Alexander Strauch, *The New Testament Deacon* (Littleton, Colorado: Lewis and Roth Publishers, 1992), 154.

Chapter 111

1. Peter Wiwcharuk, *Building Effective Leadership* (Alberta, Canada: International Christian Leadership Development Foundation, Inc., 1987), 296 and Gary D. Kinnaman and Alfred H, Ells, *Leaders that Last* (Grand Rapids, Michigan: Baker Books, 2003), 109.

2. Fred Smith, Sr., *Leading with Integrity* (Minneapolis, Minnesota: Bethany House Publishers, 1999), 34.

Chapter 112

1. Hans Finzel, *The Top Ten Mistakes Leaders Make* (Colorado Springs, Colorado: Cook Communications Ministries, 2000), 29-31.

2. Jay E. Adams, *Shepherding God's Flock* (Grand Rapids, Michigan: Baker Books, 1979), 322.

3. Henry and Richard Blackaby, *Spiritual Leadership* (Nashville, Tennessee: Broadman and Holman Publishers, 2001), 153.

4. John MacArthur, *The Master's Plan for the Church* (Chicago: Moody Press, 1999), 157.

Chapter 117

1. Jay E. Adams, *Shepherding God's Flock* (Grand Rapids, Michigan: Zondervan Publishing House, 1975), 339.

2. Frank Damazio, *Effective Keys to Successful Leadership* (Portland, Oregon: City Bible Publishing, 1993), 35.

3. John C. Maxwell, *Developing the Leaders Around You* (Nashville, Tennessee: Thomas Nelson Publishers, 1995), 10-11.

Chapter 122

1. Alan E. Nelson, *Spirituality and Leadership* (Colorado Springs, Colorado: Nav Press, 2002), 140 and David Yonggi Cho, *Successful Home Cell Groups* (Gainsville, Florida: Bridge Logos Publishers, 2001), 136.

2. Alan E. Nelson, *Spirituality and Leadership* (Colorado Springs, Colorado: Nav Press, 2002), 141.

Chapter 123

1. Henry and Richard Blackaby, *Spiritual Leadership* (Nashville, Tennessee: Broadman and Holman Publishers, 2001), 188.

2. Herschel W. Ford, *Simple Sermons on Conversion and Commitment* (Grand Rapids, Michigan: Zondervan Publishing House, 1977), 19.

Bibliography

Adair, John. *Great Leaders*. Guildford, Surrey: The Talbot Adair Press, 1989.

Adams, Jay E. *Shepherding God's Flock*. Grand Rapids, Michigan: Zondervan Publishers, 1974.

-----. *Leaders after God's Heart*. Grand Rapids, Michigan: Zondervan Publishers, 1975.

*Africans Ministry Resources, Kenya, Church Leaders Accra, Ghana: Challenge Enterprises, 2004

Analoui, Farhard and Andrew Kakabadse. *Sabotage*. London: Mercury Books, 1991.

Anderson, Leith. *A Church for the 21st Century*. Minneapolis, Minnesota: Bethany House Publishers, 1992.

----- *Leadership that Works*. Minneapolis, Minnesota: Bethany House Publishers, 1999.

Anderson, Robert C. *The Effective Pastor. Chicago*: Moody Press, 1985.

Ansah, Emmanuel Kwabena. *Keys to Successful Succession*. Accra, Ghana: Scrolls Publishing House Ltd., 2002.

Armerding, Hudson. *Leadership*. Wheaton, Illinois: Tyndale House Publishers Inc., 1978.

Armstrong, Michael. *A Handbook of Human Resource Management* Practice. London: The Bath Press, 1999.

Arn, Win and Charles. *The Master's Plan for Making Disciples*. Grand Rapids, Michigan: Baker Books, 2004.

Barker, Alan. *How to Be Better at Managing People*. London, England: Kogan Page, 2000.

Barna, George ed. *Leaders on Leadership*. Ventura, California: Regal Books, 1997.

-----*Growing True Disciples*. Colorado Springs, Colorado, 2004.

-----*How to Increase Giving in Your Church*. Ventura, California: Regal Books, 1997.

-----*The Habits of Highly Effective Churches*. California, U.S.A.: Regal Books, 1999.

-----*The Power of Team Leadership*. Colorado Springs, Colorado: Waterbrook Press, 2001.

Benner, David G. *Strategic Pastoral Counselling*. Grand Rapids, Michigan: Baker Books, 2003.

Bennet, Nii Boi E. *Practical Leadership Skills for Christian Ministry*. Accra, Ghana: Challenge Enterprises of Ghana, 2004.

Berkley, James D. ed. *Leadership Handbook of Management and Administration*. Grand Rapids, Michigan: Baker Book House Co., 2003.

-----. *Leadership Handbook of Outreach and Care*. Grand Rapids, Michigan: Baker Books, 1994.

Birch, Paul. *Instant Leadership:* Reach Your Full Potential Now. London, England: Kogan Page, 1999.

Blackaby, Henry and Richard. *Spiritual Leadership*. Nashville, Tennessee: Broadman & Holman Publishers, 2001.

Blanchard, Ken, Bill Hybels and Phil Hodges. *Leadership by the Book*. Colorado Springs, Colorado: Waterbrook Press, 1999.

Blanchard, Ken and Robert Lorber. *Putting the One-Minute Manager to Work.* New York: William Morrow and Company Inc., 1985.

Blanchard, Ken. *The Heart of a Leader*. Guildford, Surrey: Eagle, 2001.

Boi, Bennet E. Nii. *Practical Leadership Skills for Christian Ministry*. Accra, Ghana: Challenge Enterprises of Ghana, 2004.

Briner, Bob and Ray Pritchard. *The Leadership Lessons of Jesus.* Nashville, Tennessee: Broadman & Holman Publishers, 1997.

Britza, Ian. *The Absalom Spirit*. Tulsa, Oklahoma: Harrison House, 2004.

Brooking, Annie. *Corporate Memory*. London: Thomson Business Press, 1999.

Cape, David and Tommy Tenny. *God's Secret to Greatness*. Ventura, California: Regal Books, 2000.

Charnes, Cy. *The Instant Manager.* London, U.K.: Kogan Page, 2001.

Cho, David Yonggi and Harold Hostetler. *Successful Home Cell Groups*. Gainsville, Florida: Bridge Logos Publishers, 2001.

Cho, Paul Yonggi. *Solving Life's Problems*. South Plainford, New Jersey: Bridge Publishing Inc., 1980.

Cordeiro, Wayne. *Doing Church as a Team*. Ventura, California: Regal Books, 1997.

Cornwall, Judson. *Profiles of a Leader*. Gainsville, Florida: Bridge-Logos Publishers, 1980.

D'Souza, Anthony. *Being a Leader.* Accra, Ghana: Africa Christian Press, 1990.

Daft, Richard L. *Leadership: Theory and Practice.* Orlando, Florida: Harcourt College Publishers, 1999.

Dake, Jennings F. *The Dake's Annotated Bible*. Lawrenceville, Georgia: Dake Bible Sales Inc., 1997.

Damazio, Frank. *Effective Keys to Successful Leadership*. Portland, Oregon: City Bible Publishing, 1993.

----- *The Making of a Leader.* Portland, Oregon: City Bible Publishing, 1988.

Depree, Max. *Leadership Is an Art*. New York: Dell Publishers, 1989.

DuBrin, *Leadership*: Research Findings, Practice and Skills. Boston, Massachusetts: Houghton Mission Company, 1995.

Duguide, Ian M. *Hero of Heroes* . Phillipsburg, New Jersey: P&R Publishing Company, 2001.

Eims, LeRoy. *Be a Motivational Leader.* Colorado Springs, Colorado: Cook Communications, 1996.

----- *The Lost Art of Disciple-Making* .Grand Rapids, Michigan, Zondervan Publishing House, 1978.

Ellis, Lee. *Leading Talents Leading Teams.* Chicago, Illinois: Northfield Publishing, 2003.

Finzel, Hans. *The Top Ten Mistakes Leaders Make* .Colorado Springs, Colorado: Cook Communications Ministries, 1994.

Fisher, David. *The 21st Century Pastor.* Grand Rapids, Michigan: Zondervan Publishing House, 1996.

Ford, Herschel W., Simple. *Sermons on Conversion and Commitment* Grand Rapids, Michigan: Zondervan Publishing House, 1977.

Foxe, John. *Foxe's Book of Martyrs.* Grand Rapids, Michigan, 1967.

Gangel, Kenneth C. Leadership for Church Education. Chicago: Moody Press, 1970.

----- *Team Leadership in Christian Ministry.* Chicago, Illinois: Moody Bible Institute, 1997.

----- *Coaching Ministry Teams.* Nashville, Tennessee: Word Publishing, 2000.

-----.*Team Leadership in Christian Ministry* . Chicago, Illinois: Moody Bible Institute, 1997.

Garfield, Charles. *Second to None.* Homewood, Illinois: Business One Irwin, 1992.

Gerwitz, David. *The Flexible Enterprise*. New York: John Wiley & Sons Inc., 1996.

Getz, Gene A. *20 Attributes of a Godly Man.* Ventura, California: Regal Books, 1995.

Glime, John. *Pastoral Ethics.* Grand Rapids, Michigan: Zondervan Publishing House, 2005.

Giuliani, Rudolph W. *Leadership.* New York: Miramax Books, 2002.

Gordon, Bob with David Fardouly. *Master Builders. Developing Life and Leadership in the Body of Christ Today.* Tonbridge, Kent: Sovereign World Books, 1990.

Gordon, Bob. *The Leader's Motivation.* England: Clays Ltd., St. Ives Plc., 1991.

----- *The Leader's Vision.* Kent, England: Clays Ltd., St. Ives Plc, 1990.

Gunderson, Denny. *Leadership Paradox*. Seattle, Washington: YWAM Publishing, 1997.

Haddon, Peter F. *Mastering Personnel and Interpersonal Skill*s. London, England: Thorogood, 1999.

Hagee, John. *The Seven Secrets.* Lake Mary, Florida: Charisma House, 2004.

Haggard, Ted. *The Life Giving Church*. Ventura, California: Regal Books, 2002.

Halcomb, James David Hamilton and Howard Malmstadt. *Courageous Leaders: Transforming Their World*. Seattle, Washington: YWAM Publishing, 2000.

Hansen, David. *The Power of Loving Your Church*. Minneapolis, Minnesota: Bethany House Publishers, 1998.

Harman, Willis and John Hormon. *Creative Work*. Indianapolis, Indiana: Knowledge Systems, Inc., 1990.

Heil, Gary, Tom Parker and Rick Tate. *Leadership and the Customer* Revolution. New York: Van Nostrand Reinhold, 1995.

Helland, Roger. *The Revived Church*. Kent, England: Clays Ltd., St. Ives Plc, 1998.

Hinn, Benny. *He Touched Me*. Nashville, Tennessee: Thomas Nelson Publishers, 1999.

Hughes, Selwyn. *The 7 Laws of Spiritual Success*. Finland: WS Bookwell, 2002.

James D. ed. *Leadership Handbook of Management and Administration*. Grand Rapids, Berkley, Michigan: Baker Book House Co., 2003.

Jinkins, Michael and Deborah Bradshaw. *The Character of Leadership*. San Francisco, California: Jossey-Bass Inc., Publishers, 1998.

Kast, Fremont E. and James E. Rosenzweig. *Organization and Management*. Singapore: McGraw-Hill Book Company, 1985.

Katherine, Anne. *Boundaries*. New York: MJF Books, 1991.

Kinnaman, Gary D. and Alfred Ells. *Leaders that Last*. Grand Rapids, Michigan: Baker Books, 2003.

Kollar, Allen Charles. *Solution Focused Pastoral Counselling*. Grand Rapids, Michigan: Zondervan Publishers, 1997.

Launderville, Dale. **Piety and Politics**. Grand Rapids, Michigan: W.M.B. Eerdmans Publishing Company, 2003.*Law, Destiny.Interview with Art Linkletter Mouseplanet,com:electronically retrieved at http://www.mouseplanet.com/destiny/071700.htm.).

Lawrence, Richard O. and Hoeldtke Clyde. *Church Leadership Following the Example of Jesus Christ*. Grand Rapids, Michigan: Zondervan Publishers, 1996.

Leith, Anderson. *Leadership that Works*. Grand Rapids, Michigan: Bethany House, 1999

Lewis, Robert. *The Church of Irresistible Influence*. Grand Rapids, Michigan: Zondervan Publishing House, 2001.

MacArthur, John. *The Master's Plan for the Church*. Chicago: Moody Press, 1991.

Maidment, Fred H. ed. *Organizational Behaviour, 1st Edition.* Guildford, Connecticut: Dushkin/McGraw Hill Publishing Company, 2000.

Malphurs, Aubrey and Will Mancini. *Building Leaders.* Grand Rapids, Michigan: Baker Books, 2004.

Marshall, Tom. *Understanding Leadership.* England: Clays Ltd., St. Ives Plc, 1991.

Maxwell, John C. and Jim Dornan. *Becoming a Person of Influence.* California: Maxwell Motivation Inc., 1997.

----- *Be a People Person.* Colorado Springs, Colorado: Nexgen, 2004.

-----*17 Essential Qualities of a Team Player.* Nashville, Tennessee: Thomas Nelson Inc., 2002.

-----.*Be All You Can Be.* Colorado Springs, Colorado: Cook Communication Ministries, 2003.

----- *Developing the Leader Within You. Workbook.* Nashville, Tennessee: Thomas Nelson Publishers, 2001.

-----.*Developing the Leaders Around You.* Nashville, Tennessee: Thomas Nelson Publishers, 1975.

-----. *Leadership 101.* Nashville, Tennessee: Thomas Nelson Publishers, 2002.

----- *Make Yours a Winning Team.* Colorado Springs, Colorado: Inspirational Press, 1989..

----- *The 21 Most Powerful Minutes in a Leader's Day.* Nashville, Tennessee: Thomas Nelson, Inc., 2000.

-----. *Thinking for a Change.* New York: Warner Books Inc., 2003.

-----. *Today Matters: 12 Daily Practices to Guarantee Tomorrow Success.* Nashville, Tennessee: Warner Faith, 1999.

-----. *Your Road Map for Success.* Nashville, Tennessee: Thomas Nelson Publishers, 2002.

-----. *The 17 Indisputable Laws of Teamwork.* Nashville, Tennessee: Thomas Nelson Publishers Inc., 2001.

McAlpine, Campbell. *The Leadership of Jesus.* England: Clays Ltd., St. Ives Plc., n.d..

McMahon, Tom. *Big Meetings Big Results.* Chicago, Illinois: NTC Business Books, 1990.

Meyer, Paul J. *Unlocking Your Legacy. 25 Keys for Success.* Chicago: Moody Press, 2002.

Mullins, Laurie J. *Management and Organizational Behaviour.* Great Britain: Pitman Publishing, 1990.

Munroe Myles. *Maximising Your Potential.* Slippenburg, Pennsylvania: Destiny Image Publishers Inc., 2003.

Murdock, Mike. *The Leadership Secrets of Jesus.* Dallas, Texas: Wisdom International, 1996.

Neis, Marlys and Ruth T. Kingdon. *Leadership in Transition.* Schaumburg, Illinois: NOVA 1 Ltd., 1990.

Nelson, Alan E. *Spirituality and Leadership.* Colorado Springs, Colorado: Nav Press, 2002.

Nkrumah, Kwame. *Dark Days in Ghana.* Herts, U.K.: Watford Printing Services, 1968.

O'Connor, Carol. *Successful Leadership.* London: Hodder & Stoughton, 2002.

Orsburn, Jack et al. *Self-Directed Work Teams.* Homewood, Illinois: Business One Irwin, 1990.

Perkins, Bill. *Awaken the Leader Within.* Grand Rapids, Michigan: Zondervan Publishers, 2000.

Anderson, Leith. *Leadership that Works.* Minneapolis, Minnesota: Bethany House Publishers, 1999

Peters ,Tim and Nancy Austin. *A Passion for Excellence: The Leadership Difference.* Glasgow, Great Britain: William Collins Sons and Company Ltd., 1985.

Pollock, David and Larry Burkett. *Business Management in the Local Church.* Chicago: Moody Press, 1995.

Pollock, David. *Business Management in the Local Church.* Chicago: Moody Press, 1996.

Posthuma, Barbara W. *Small Groups in Therapy Settings: Process and Leadership.* Boston, Massachusetts: College-Hill Press, 1989.

Powers, Bruce P. *Church Administration Handbook.* Nashville, Tennessee: Broadman and Holman Publishers, 1997.

Richards, Lawrence O. and Clyde Heoldtke. *Church Leadership.* Grand Rapids, Michigan: Zondervan Publishing House, 1980.

Rubin, Theodore Isaac. *The Angry Book.* New York: Collier Books, 1970.

Rush, Myron. *Management: A Biblical Approach.* Colorado Springs, Colorado: Cook Communications, 2002.

Salmon, Robert. *The Future of Management: All Roads Lead To Man.* Cambridge, Massachusetts: Blackwell Publishers Inc., 1994.

Salter, Brian and Naomi Longford-Wood. *Successfully Dealing With Difficult People.* London: Hodder & Stoughton, 1998.

Sanders, J. Oswald. *Dynamic Spiritual Leadership.* Grand Rapids, Michigan, 1999.

----- *Spiritual Leadership.* Chicago: Moody Press, 1967.

Shull, F.A. A.L. Delbeckq and L.L. Cummings. *Organizational Decision-Making.* New York: McGraw-Hill Inc., 1970.

Smith Fred, Sr. *Leading with Integrity.* Minneapolis, Minnesota: Bethany House Publishers, 1999.

Smith, Fred Sr. and David L. Goetz, eds. *Leading with Integrity*. (Minneapolis, Minnesota: Bethany Press International, 1999.

Steinbron, Melvin J. *Can the Pastor Do It Alone?* Ventura, California: Regal Books, 1992.

Stowell, Joseph M. *Shepherding the Church*. Chicago, Illinois: Moody Press, 1997.

Strauch, Alexander. *Biblical Eldership*. Littleton, Colorado: Lewis and Roth Publishers, 1986.

----- *Minister of Mercy. The New Testament Deacon* Littleton, Colorado: Lewis and Roth Publishers, 1992.

----- *The New Testament Deacon*. Littleton, Colorado: Lewis and Roth Publishers, 1992.

----- *Biblical Leadership*. Littleton, Colorado: Lewis and Roth Publishers, 1988.

----- *The New Testament Deacon*. Littlewood, Colorado: Lewis and Roth Publishers, 1992.

Tichy, Noel M. and Eli Cohen. *The Leadership Engine*. New York: Harper Business Essentials, 2002.

White, John. *Excellence in Leadership*. Leicester, England: InterVarsity Press, 2003.

White, Jerry Honesty. *Morality and Conscience*. Colorado Springs, Colorado: Navpress, 1978.

Wilkes, Genes. *Jesus on Leadership*. Nashville, Tennessee: Lifeway Press, 2001.

Williams, Pat. *The Paradox of Power*. U.S.A.: AOL Time Warner Company, 2002.

Winslow, Paul and Dorman Filowwill. *Christ in Church Leadership*. Grand Rapids, Michigan: Discovery House Publications, 2001.

Wiwcharuk, Peter. *Building Effective Leadership*. Alberta, Canada: International Christian Leadership Development Foundation, 1987.

Woods, Jeff C. *Better than Success: 8 Principles of Faithful Leadership*. Valley Forge, Pennsylvania: Judson Press, 2001

Yperen, Jim Van. *Making Peace: A Guide to Overcoming Church Conflict*. Chicago: Moody Press, 2002.

Zairi, Mohammed. *Best Practice Process Innovation Management*. London, England: Biddles Ltd., n.d.

Other Books by Dag Heward-Mills

7 Great Principles
100% Answered Prayer
Aids to Leadership
*All about Fornication
Allos: Another of the Same Kind
*Anagkazo: Compelling Power
Backsliding: Develop Your Staying Power
*Bearing Fruit after Your Own Kind
*Beauty
*Born Again
Catch the Anointing
Church Administration
Church Planting
Demons and How to Deal with Them
*Duality
Essentials of Leadership
Excellence in Leadership
*Forgiveness Made Easy
Gethsemane Devotional
Horeb Devotional
How to Become a Leader
How to Overcome Barrenness in Ministry
*Lay People and the Ministry
Leaders and Loyalty
Leadership Made Easy
Leading Difficult People
Lecture Notes on Leadership
*Loyalty and Disloyalty
*Ministerial Ethics
Model Marriage
My Father, My Father
Name it! Claim it! Take it!
Olives Devotional
Opportunities

*Poison
Preaching, Teaching and Healing
Principles of Leadership
Principles of Success
Proton: First Things First
Quiet Time
Secrets of Success
Sinai Devotional
Success and Wealth
Strategies for Prayer
Supernatural Power
Take up Your Cross
The Art of Hearing
The Beast of Prodigality
The Megachurch
The Minister's Handbook
*The Strange Woman
The Successful Leader
The Words of Jesus
*They Went to Hell
Transform Your Pastoral Ministry
Unbeatable Prosperity
Win the Lost at Any Cost
Wisdom for Leaders

Mini Books
How to Recognize Demons at Work
How to Start a Church
Key Facts for New Christians
Sacrifice versus Obedience
The Secret
The Tent Ministry

*These titles are also available in Spanish and French. Information about other foreign translations of some of the titles above may be obtained by writing to our address below.

For additional information on Dag Heward-Mills' books, tapes and videos write to these addresses:

In Africa:
Parchment House
P.O. Box DC 1034
Dansoman, Accra
Ghana-West Africa

Rest of the world:
Lighthouse Chapel International
P.O. Box 39394
London SE13 5WN

Website:
www.daghewardmills.org